Sugar Heritage and Tourism in Transition

MIX
Paper from
responsible sources
FSC® C014540
FSC
www.fsc.org

TOURISM AND CULTURAL CHANGE

Series Editors: Professor Mike Robinson, *Institute of Archaeology and Antiquity, University of Birmingham, UK* and Dr Alison Phipps, *University of Glasgow, Scotland, UK*

Understanding tourism's relationships with culture(s) and vice versa, is of ever-increasing significance in a globalising world. This series will critically examine the dynamic inter-relationships between tourism and culture(s). Theoretical explorations, research-informed analyses and detailed historical reviews from a variety of disciplinary perspectives are invited to consider such relationships.

Full details of all the books in this series and of all our other publications can be found on http://www.channelviewpublications.com, or by writing to Channel View Publications, St Nicholas House, 31–34 High Street, Bristol BS1 2AW, UK.

Sugar Heritage and Tourism in Transition

Edited by
Lee Jolliffe

CHANNEL VIEW PUBLICATIONS
Bristol • Buffalo • Toronto

Library of Congress Cataloging in Publication Data
A catalog record for this book is available from the Library of Congress.
Sugar Heritage and Tourism in Transition/Edited by Lee Jolliffe. — 1st ed.
Tourism and Cultural Change: 32
Includes bibliographical references and index.
1. Heritage tourism. 2. Sugar—Social aspects. 3. Sugar industry—History. I. Jolliffe, Lee.
G156.5.H47S84 2013
338.1'73609–dc23 2012036511

British Library Cataloguing in Publication Data
A catalogue entry for this book is available from the British Library.

ISBN-13: 978-1-84541-387-3 (hbk)
ISBN-13: 978-1-84541-386-6 (pbk)

Channel View Publications
UK: St Nicholas House, 31–34 High Street, Bristol BS1 2AW, UK.
USA: UTP, 2250 Military Road, Tonawanda, NY 14150, USA.
Canada: UTP, 5201 Dufferin Street, North York, Ontario M3H 5T8, Canada.

The policy of Multilingual Matters/Channel View Publications is to use papers that are natural, renewable and recyclable products, made from wood grown in sustainable forests. In the manufacturing process of our books, and to further support our policy, preference is given to printers that have FSC and PEFC Chain of Custody certification. The FSC and/or PEFC logos will appear on those books where full certification has been granted to the printer concerned.

Typeset by Techset Composition Ltd., Salisbury, UK.
Printed and bound in Great Britain by Short Run Press Ltd.

Contents

Acknowledgements

This book builds upon my previous studies of the connections between tea and tourism, *Tea and Tourism, Tourists, Traditions and Transformations* (2007) and coffee culture and tourism, *Coffee Culture, Destinations and Tourism* (2010), considering the evolving relationship between the heritage of sugar and tourism. As an editor for this book I drew on my background in sociology, museum studies, heritage management and tourism development, developing an interdisciplinary perspective of the transition of many destinations from sugar based economies to tourism focused economies. As in the case of the previous volumes, I cannot take complete credit for the work and I am grateful to my team of colleagues around the world who have contributed.

As ever, I must thank my family for their continued support of my academic and scholarly endeavors. I also deeply appreciate the opportunity afforded by the University of the West Indies, Cave Hill, Barbados, during my one-year tenure there in 2010–2011, as it was there that the book proposal was conceived. This also provided the opportunity to participate in events that would influence my viewpoint, including the book launch for Alvyn Thompson's 2010 book *Confronting Slavery: Breaking Through the Corridors of Silence* (Thompson Business Services Inc., 2010); a pilot tour for the new product Freedom Footprints, a product designed by the Barbados Museum; and the UNESCO SIDS World Heritage Meeting. Living and working in Barbados also afforded the opportunity to personally experience the sites and attractions associated with the history of sugar, and especially the remains of plantation heritage on the island and in the region through visits to Martinique, St Vincent, St Lucia, Trinidad and Tobago.

I am grateful to colleagues who provided support and encouragement during the process of developing the book, including Justin Robinson, Sherma Roberts and Tara A. Inniss in Barbados, Jenny Cave in New Zealand and Dallen Timothy in the United States. I appreciate interactions on topics related to the book with Larry Warren at St Nicholas Abby, Karl Watson at the Barbados National Trust, Kevin Horsfield at Rawlins Plantation Inn in St Kitts, David Rollinson, Steve Hites at the St Kitts Scenic Railway Inc., Neil Singh at the Sugar Heritage Museum and Village project in Trinidad and Allisandra Cummins of ICOM and the Barbados Museum.

As ever was the case with my previous books, the continued support of Channel View Publications is sincerely appreciated, especially of Sarah Williams and Elinor Robertson, and series editors Mike Robinson and Alison Phipps.

I take responsibility for any errors and omissions that may be found within. I do hope that the book will open up the subject of sugar heritage in relation to tourism and may act as a springboard for further research on this sweet yet dark topic.

Contributors

Mechelle N. Best, California State University Northridge, United States

Paul Cleave, University of Exeter, UK

Rachel Dodds, Ryerson University, Canada

Angela Cabral Flecha, Federal University of Ouro Preto, Brazil

Linda Joyce Forristal, Drexel University, United States

Peter D. Griggs, James Cook University, Australia

Tara A. Inniss, University of the West Indies, Barbados

Lee Jolliffe, University of New Brunswick, Canada

Jane Legget, Auckland University of Technology, New Zealand

Winston F. Phulgence, Sir Arthur Lewis Community College, Saint Lucia

Leanne White, Victoria University, Australia

Part 1
Introduction

1 Connecting Sugar Heritage and Tourism

Lee Jolliffe

Sugar is an integral part of our everyday lives, as we add it to our coffee or tea and consume sugar based treats. As indicated by Galloway (1989), sugar seems to have been with us in all parts of the world at all times, valued for its ability to bring out flavours and colours in food, but also as a preservative and fermenting agent. But sugar is much more than just part of global and local cuisines and food-ways. Sugar is a global commodity and the history of its cultivation and production has formed our world today, from impacting the nature of cultures to influencing what we eat (Abbott, 2008; Menard, 2006). There are many roles and facets to the story of sugar, including the shaping of cultures and identities though the history of colonization and enslavement-related migration, as well as the ongoing transitions of this global commodity from planting to processing, and from refining to consumption. The use of sugar in contemporary society is also related to the global food industries, as well as to associated health impacts related to sugar consumption (Menard, 2006) and environmental consequences connected to its growth.

With a complex and evolving relationship there are many questions about the realities of sugar history and heritage. How has sugar influenced cultures and societies? What happens when production at particular locations declines? What are the consequences when countries completely exit from being sugar producers and transition towards tourism? How is sugar ingrained as part of national identities, what does this mean to so many countries and how is this reflected in the tourism product? In what ways can the dark history of sugar production be interpreted and understood in relation to our contemporary world? These are only some of the key questions related to the heritage and the global and local legacies of sugar cultivation and production.

The aim of this first chapter then is to provide a background to the subject of sugar heritage in relation to tourism, defining and discussing key concepts and then outlining a research framework for the rest of the volume. The chapter also discusses the rationale for the book and outlines how it is organized.

Definitions

What do we mean by *sugar*? According to the *Oxford Dictionary* it is a sweet crystalline substance derived from various plants, mainly sugarcane and sugar beet, consisting essentially of sucrose, and used as a sweetener in food and drink. When discussing sugar in this book the scope has been limited to sugar from sugarcane, which accounts for about 80% of world production, while not discounting the subjects of sugar in relation to sugar beets, honey and maple syrup as worth consideration for other studies.

Today sugarcane is in cultivation around the world, with the top producers (as of 2010) including Brazil, India and the People's Republic of China (Anon., 2012). However, sugar is produced in many more countries, in fact a total of 90 as reported by the Food and Agriculture Organization of the United Nations (Anon., 2012). Issues with contemporary sugarcane cultivation include competitiveness in terms of production and with other sources, especially sugar beet. Molasses derived from sugarcane is also used for the production of rum. In addition, new uses for sugarcane, such as the production of biofuels (ethanol) from cane, are now propelling the industry.

With many small countries, formerly kingpins in the global sugar business, having declining or no sugarcane harvests (such as Trinidad which closed their nationalized sugar industry in 2003), sugar for domestic use and rum production must be imported. Due to declining sugar production, Barbados also now has to import molasses, which is a byproduct of sugar production, for the manufacture of rum.

Sugar heritage can be broadly defined as the heritage related to the history and culture, cultivation, production and consumption of sugar derived from sugarcane. This is a rich and varied heritage that derives from a long and contested history, not often discussed and recognized, as the colonial quest for sugar propelled the transatlantic slave trade leaving a legacy of disputed heritage that is only now beginning to be rediscovered by the descendants of both the colonizers and the enslaved. Discussing the dark legacies of the story of sugar is not easy, this is what Timothy and Boyd (2003) refer to as an excluded past, but open discussions can lead to insights as to the origins of cultures and cultural change, and to the loss of civil liberties due to the domination of sugar in the face of colonial expansion and capitalism. Such tough discussions can be initiated by the publication of books with their associated book launches, such as that for *Confronting Slavery: Breaking the*

Corridors of Silence (Thompson, 2010), and museum exhibitions, as evidenced at the Kura Hulanda Museum in Curacao (Scott, 2010).

Today, as locales formerly dominated by king sugar recreate themselves, often without sugar, investigations into the past legacies of sugar and the plantation system under which it was produced can shed new light not only on the past, but on the future. Tourism, despite its negative aspects discussed in this chapter, can potentially provide both locals and guests with opportunities to learn about and gain insights into sugar heritage, through visitation to related sites and attractions, and can do some good in contributing to personal reflections and perspectives related to the legacies and heritage of the global production of sugar.

Sugar heritage tourism is gradually emerging. This can be defined as tourism related to the heritage of sugar, utilizing sugar heritage resources to develop products and experiences for tourists to consume. In global locations where traditional sugar cultivation and production are in decline the vestiges of the former industries (landscapes shaped by the growth of cane, former plantations and estates and the heritage structures associated with them, such as plantation houses, factories and their components, windmills, etc.) may now be valued as heritage tourism resources. Since the history of forced labour in the form of both enslavement and indentureship was often connected to sugar plantations and production there is a contested heritage to be interpreted (Thompson, 2010). In cases where island economies once depended on sugarcane as the primary basis for their economic activity there may have been a complete transition to a reliance on tourism, reflected by the associated cultural change.

The heritage of sugar then is multifaceted, and like any heritage resource is represented in both the tangible and intangible cultural heritage resources of a destination. In terms of tourism planning and development, heritage, such as that of sugar, is a resource that can be commodified and packaged for tourism (Timothy & Boyd, 2003). At locations where sugar still dominates as an industry there may be a lack of interest or recognition of the potential that sugar heritage holds for developing new forms of tourism. When sugar industries are no longer operating then sugar is valued more for its heritage aspects, which may have been imbedded in local cultures and traditions, as in the case of Cuba (Barnet & Lindstrom, 1980).

Examples of the sugar heritage and tourism nexus are found in the Caribbean, formerly a key sugar-producing region. Here, the UNESCO Slavery Heritage Projects (including the Slave Route and the Places of Memory for the route in the Caribbean) influenced the heritage tourism product, i.e. in Barbados the Footprints to Freedom tour product. Individual entrepreneurs (such as Larry Warren at Saint Nicholas Abbey in Barbados) across the region are contributing to developing sugar heritage related tourism, especially in situations in the region where the government and public bodies do not have the resources for such development. The role of the universities in the region should also be noted, on the Mona campus of the University of the West Indies in Jamaica, a former sugar plantation, the university has developed a heritage tour as a product. Here vestiges of the former plantation structures form an enduring part of the landscape of the university, such as the aqueduct that carried water for the plantation.

In relation to tourism, using sugar heritage as a lens thus gives a distinctive way of tracing the movements of people, products and experiences in relation to a global commodity that has shaped our modern world. This gives a unique perspective on the changes that migration, both forced and voluntary, has brought in the past and is bringing today to global culture.

Sugar contributes to the production of souvenirs, playing a key role in the production of popular sugar based confectionaries sold as mementos of a place, so there are in addition culinary and experiential aspects to interpreting the heritage of sugar to be considered. Sugar is inherent in hospitality and food service experiences as it is a key ingredient in both beverages and desserts, and with dining being a popular tourist activity, memories and mementos of this experience can be tied back to sugar. Traditions such as afternoon tea, sought out as souvenirs of destination experiences, are also dependent on sugar (Jolliffe, 2007).

So sugar, once produced and refined, becomes a key ingredient in the sweet products associated with tourism, ranging from special cakes that are distinctive of particular destinations (such as the Eccles cake or the Bakewell tart, both named after the UK towns where they originated) to souvenir candies (such as the rock candy sold in England's seaside resorts such as Blackpool) that are distinctive of place.

Specialty sugars are also produced as souvenirs, as with the classic tin of Barbados Plantation Reserve Sugar, where a joint equity company between the government and small producers (designed to counter the decline in traditional sugar processing) is producing a high quality cane sugar marketed throughout the Caribbean as well as through UK supermarkets and higher end food outlets such as Harrods and Fortnum and Mason.

Research Framework

The research framework discussed below is delineated along the themes of:

- Contexts – historical; economic; cultural change; cultural heritage management.

- Points of view – postcolonialism; commodification; sustainability.
- Issues – politics; globalization; tourism development.

Contexts

Historical

Historically, sugar provided one of the original motivations for European expansion, colonization and authority in the New World, precipitating events that would change the course of history in the western hemisphere. The migration of people caused by the development of colonial sugar industries, in the form of plantation owners from Europe and the forced labour provided by the transatlantic slave trade, precipitated the development of new cultures in new lands, as people came together in plantation settings creating new cultures (Barnet & Lindstrom, 1980).

The history of sugar, dating back to the ancient world and continuing to the present day, is considered in detail in Chapter 2. Briefly stated, the cultivation, production and use of sugar has evolved over time, being a key motivation for the process of colonization, wars between one country and another, enslavement and apprenticeship of large populations to provide labour, influencing the creolization of societies as people from all over the world came together on sugar estates and plantations in the 'New World'. A chronology of sugar begins with its discovery and use in ancient times, and is still ongoing, with locales where sugar is no longer produced beginning to recognize the residual heritage values that can be employed for the benefit of local populations, economies and visitors.

The history of sugar is thus global, beginning with its origins as a grass in New Guinea (8000 bc) and the crushing of sugarcane and extraction of crystals in India (1st century ad) (Ferdinand & Williams, 2012). In the New World sugar history begins with Columbus introducing sugarcane on his second voyage to the Caribbean (from the Canary Islands to Hispaniola; ad 1493), and within the next decade the first enslaved Africans were brought to the Caribbean to work on sugar plantations (1510). The transnational slave trade provided the workers for the labour-intensive sugar production using the plantation model, until slavery was ended by England in 1834 and by France in 1848; although slavery was to end later in other jurisdictions, such as Puerto Rico (1876) and Cuba (1884). After the demise of slavery, in some cases, such as in British colonies, indentured labourers from India were brought to the Caribbean to replace the slave labour.

After the abolition of slavery there was still migration to the sugar-producing West Indies, but now from different parts of the world in the form of indentured labourers from Asia. This has brought a multicultural dimension to many islands, such as Trinidad and Togabo (TT) where today Carnival, a celebration occurring after Lent, originating in plantation times, is still a highlight of the annual calendar, as well as a major draw for cultural tourism (Nurse, 2008). The plantation-related origins of this event are evident 'Carnival celebrations in TT originated from French immigrant planters and their slaves who came to the island due to liberal immigration policies introduced by Spanish colonisers' (Ferdinand & Williams, 2012).

Economic

An economic perspective is also important, as both sugar and tourism are linked to forms of economic exploitation in both colonial and contemporary times (Chambers, 1997). Aspects of this link persist, as noted by a number of researchers (Patullo, 1996), in the case of contemporary tourism utilizing sugar heritage resources, as attractions on former plantations use local employees as hosts (some descended from the enslaved plantation workers) and to serve guests (some descended from the former plantation owners and with ties to the former colonial countries).

The economics of heritage is also relevant. Heritage attractions receive some direct operational and project funding from government, but heritage facilities are increasingly required to generate their own revenues, through user fees, special events, retailing, grants and donations (Timothy & Boyd, 2003). International tourism thus produces pressures for sites, including those related to sugar heritage, to develop facilities and interpretation that caters to the needs of tourists and to undertake marketing to attract visitors (Law, 2001).

Cultural change

Sugar culture for the sugar-producing locales became a part of the very being of sugar-producing places; for example, in the West Indies where the year became characterized by the cycle of the sugar harvest. Beyond the West Indies sugar influenced the development of ports, such as Bristol and Liverpool, which depended upon the sugar industry as refining and packaging factories were set up. Sugar fed the industrial revolution in England, as workers were able to gain sustenance from tea and sugar to sustain the long hours working in factories. In other parts of the world refining facilities were similarly established; for example, sugar refineries were set up in the Canadian port cities of Montreal, Quebec (1888); Vancouver, British Columbia (1890s); Saint John, New Brunswick (1912) and Toronto, Ontario (1950s). The reach of sugar in terms of its influence on local cultures was therefore well beyond the producing locales.

Cultural heritage management

The management of culture also provides useful perspectives for the study of sugar heritage tourism. For example, the historical trajectory of tourism replacing sugar, especially in the Caribbean, as several islands abandoned sugar, 'leaving behind only the decaying remnants of former plantations' (Found, 2004: 141). A bias in the protection of sugar heritage resources, towards the great plantation houses of the former plantation owners, is noted in the Caribbean: 'Preserving the housing of the elite from colonial times has been a priority throughout the region' (Found, 2004: 145). Other authors have found that in the interpretation of slavery it has been common for plantations and plantation houses to be rearticulated as heritage products (Buzinde & Santos, 2008). There are also marketing and interpretive challenges at sensitive historic sites, such as former sugar plantation settings (Austin, 2002), as well as particular issues that relate to the interpretation of slavery (Buzinde & Santos, 2009).

Developing sustainable sugar-related heritage tourism sites that provide a quality visitor experience can contribute to the tourism development objectives of destinations (Drummond & Yeoman, 2001) as well as to the desired national heritage discourses and identities (Frew & White, 2011). A variety of types of sugar-related heritage attractions and experiences are part of contemporary tourism, and given the depth and breadth of the heritage of sugar many more could be developed. Attractions related to sugar run the gambit from traditional museums and heritage sites, to sugar-related tourist railways and theme parks. These attractions use sugar heritage in theming exhibits and activities that educate and inform, or just provide for a nostalgic experience. Due to the contested heritage of sugar, related to the associated enslavement and indentureship in a colonial context, the more serious of these attractions can provide a space and a place for contemplation and the rediscovery of lost heritages and traditions.

A few indicative examples of sugar-related attractions are listed here:

- Sugar Train, Wushulin Recreation Park, Taiwan (sugar-related transportation attraction). Here former sugarcane trains carry tourists for a nostalgic journey in this Taiwan Sugar Corporation operated park, where a plant processed sugar from 1910–1983 (Her, 2010).
- Redpath Sugar Museum, Toronto, Canada is located on the Toronto waterfront adjacent to a historic and still operating sugar refinery.
- Lower Estate Sugar Works Museum, Tortolla, British Virgin Islands, West Indies (sugar-related architectural site). Here local history exhibits and contemporary art exhibitions can be found in the setting of a historic sugar works.

The first two examples above illustrate the involvement of former sugar industry companies in developing attractions. They are using their sugar-related assets to develop attractions for the public that illustrate aspects of the industry. In the third example, the architectural remnants of a former sugar plantation have been repurposed as a cultural centre, not interpreting the sugar story per se, but still serving as a powerful reminder of the former colonial sugarcane plantation system. These examples also highlight the potential for community benefits from sugar-related tourism.

Points of view

Postcolonial

Looking at current trends in how sugar heritage relates to contemporary tourism it is necessary to look back at historical contexts in order to understand today's postcolonial realities. Contemporary tourism, in the view of Jamaica Kincaid (in her book, *A Small Place, a Satire on Tourism in Antigua* (1988)), is an extension of colonial opportunity and authority. Scholars examining postcolonial developments have examined the politics of sugar in such settings (Sandiford, 2000). The granting of independence to many former sugar-producing locations has had an impact on the directions taken by sugar industries, as well as on the development of forms of postcolonial tourism; as sugar declines it seems to be accompanied over time by a nostalgia for the former sugar industries, which has currency as a heritage resource for tourism.

Commodification

The commodification of sugar heritage for the purposes of tourism can threaten the authenticity of local cultures, which have been shaped to a large extent by sugar. The role of heritage and tourism in reconstructing communities (Patullo, 1996) is relevant to the issue of the sugar heritage/tourism nexus. However, there may be negative consequences of this commodification of culture: as heritage is commodified, culture is potentially altered for tourism. For example, the authenticity of local sugar heritages can be threatened by 'staged authenticity', in which local regions go through a process of being staged for tourism consumption (MacCannell, 1976).

There is another side of the argument regarding commodification, which is that the assembling of heritage resources into products and the so-called 'heritagisation' of the past has in fact led to an increased interest in the consumption of heritage tourism products and the inclusion of formerly marginalized groups in the development of tourism (Smith, 2003).

Tourism as development

Viewing sugar heritage as a resource for tourism is useful but does have limitations, as while there are benefits to be accrued from developing sugar-related tourism there are also drawbacks, as noted above. However, a potential benefit to local communities and visitors of linking sugar heritage and tourism is the opportunity to use sugar heritage tourism attractions as spaces and places for reflecting on the past and educating about the future (including recognition by UNESCO as World Heritage Sites). The recent growth and interest in heritage tourism has also provided prospects for developing new products that will improve the sustainability of tourism at locations with sugar heritage. The transition from sugar as industry to sugar as tourism is an important perspective that can be viewed within the context of international migration and the movement of products, both tangible (sugar) and intangible (tourism experiences).

Tourism scholars have only peripherally addressed the heritage associated with sugar; for example, in terms of discussions and debates related to the interpretation of enslavement and the industrial heritage of the commodity (Buzinde & Santos, 2009; Found, 2004; Patullo, 1996).

Sustainability

There is, in addition, more awareness of the environmental consequences of monocultures, such as sugar, and a trend towards more sustainable means of producing. However, the refining of sugar from sugarcane is in some aspects a sustainable process. After harvesting, the sugarcane must immediately be transferred to the factory. During processing there are several byproducts: bagasse, the fibrous material from the cane stalks, can be used as a fuel for the process, and molasses is used as a food and in the production of rum.

Processes have changed little over the years since the sugarcane was refined on site at plantations or estates to today when cane is transported (by cart, truck or cane train) to central factories. Transitioning from the plantation to the factory model of production, with the establishment of railways leading to central factories, was part of the industrialization of the industry at different points around the world. In developed countries there are also sugar refineries that import raw sugar from producing countries and further refine it for domestic markets.

Since sugar forms a significant part of the global diet, with significant health consequences, its relationship to health and wellness is also relevant to the sustainability of both the sugar industries and the global population.

Issues

Politics

Culture is recognized as dynamic rather than static and cultural change is thus part of all societies. Smith (2003) notes that culture and commerce are entwined, as culture has become a commodity to be packaged and sold. The concept of culture has been politicized and employed by countries to either create or enhance national identities (Frew & White, 2011). In the case of the many decolonized locales where sugar industries dominate, sugar heritages linked to the former processes of colonization may be recreated as new national identities; for example, the sugar heritage of the now independent Barbados, linked historically as a centre of the transatlantic slave trade and with a plantation economy of a British colony, is now being interpreted as 'The Story of Sugar'. A tentative World Heritage Site nomination and a tourism product, Freedom Footprints, has been created, focusing on the path to freedom through emancipation rather than the former story of enslavement.

Only a few former sugar-related industrial sites have been protected, some receiving UNESCO World Heritage Site status. Since designation is a political process this is somewhat reflective of the politics of cultural heritage (Ashworth, 2006), for sites must be put forward for the tentative list of sites to be nominated by state parties. There is also a fine line here between balancing conservation and tourism objectives.

Globalization

To some extent global culture is becoming more standardized and homogenized, in part, according to Smith (2003), as a result of decolonization, mass immigration and international tourism. However, these phenomena have also contributed to enriching cultures, nurturing multiculturalism. Juxtaposed against global culture is local culture and heritage, which is valued for a sense of identity and differentiation.

The globalization of tourism has however, to some extent, highlighted the inequalities inherent in the guest–host relationship. Concepts from tourism studies of the host–guest relationship are not only historical in terms of the plantation model for producing sugar, but as reconstructed in the modern tourism industry relations at locations formerly plantation based, with tourism being referred to as a 'new slavery' (Kincaid, 1988).

Tourism development

Tourism development, if managed properly, offers the potential for communities to benefit in terms of economic development (Smith, 2003). However, especially in the case of developing countries, if tourism is viewed as a quick solution to economic woes it needs to be managed with local input and consideration of potential sociocultural and environmental perspectives.

From a destination perspective it is important to understand the juxtaposition of the development of sugar-related tourism where sugar is produced, as well as the transition of destinations once based on sugar economies into tourism economies with cultural change accompanied by the commodification of sugar cultures. At locations where sugar is still produced (such as India, Brazil, etc.) sugar production facilities can contribute to industrial tourism experiences, and the heritage aspects can still be promoted; for example, through tourist rides on the former sugarcane trains (as in both Australia and Cuba). However, where sugar still has a predominately industrial focus, sugar-related tourism will most likely take a back seat to tourism, in fact sugar heritage may be employed by the sugar companies in part as a public relations exercise, as is the case with the Australian Sugar Industry Museum. However, in transitions where sugar is no longer produced what is the role of the former sugar companies, how can both the employers and their employees participate in transitioning their assets from sugar production into the creation of tourism products? This process is just beginning in Trinidad (2012) where the central site of the former nationalized sugar industry is being transformed into a Sugar Heritage Village and Museum. A member of the committee overseeing the project commented on the significance of sugar to Trinidad and Tobago:

> This industry started in slavery. It moved into indentureship when East Indians and Chinese came for labour and the country's economic and social development took place from then until now. In earlier times it [the sugar industry] was named 'King Sugar' because it was very profitable to work in the sugar industry. In that lies a great part of our history. (Ragoonath, 2012)

Rationale for the Book

Existing studies of sugar have taken for the most part a historical perspective of sugar, some with a global perspective (Galloway, 1989; Abbott, 2008). There have also been historical studies of individual locales where sugar has shaped cultures and destinies, for example in Cuba (Barnet & Lindstrom, 1980) and Barbados (Menard, 2006). The cultural politics of sugar in terms of slavery and colonization have also been examined (Sandiford, 2000). However, since there is depth in the history and heritage of sugar and the current transitions of sugar from industry to heritage, as noted by Found (2004), there is still a need for investigating sugar and its transition from commodity to heritage and tourism. The importance of sugar heritage to contemporary culture, societies and nations thus warrants the necessity for a volume such as this. This provides the opportunity to examine key issues in the transition of sugar, from production industries to service based tourism industries.

Researching sugar and its transition towards tourism requires both an interdisciplinary approach and the use of mixed research methods. The contributors to the book include researchers with specialties in the history of sugar; the history of slavery; cultural heritage tourism development, management and marketing; culinary tourism and food-ways; island tourism; contested tourism; and museum studies. The various perspectives of the authors bring an interdisciplinary view of the subject of sugar in relation to tourism. The research methods used by the authors have been varied. Many chapters draw from historical research on sugar, while others are based on fieldwork at sugar-related sites and destinations, employing surveys and interviews as well as participant observation research techniques. Some chapters use the case study method (Yin, 2009). Other authors draw from both their practical experiences of the development of sugar-related historic sites (both small museums and UNESCO World Heritage Sites) and their personal and participatory experiences of visiting such sites. In addition, some chapters draw from the analysis of secondary documentation on sugar heritage sites and attractions.

A limitation is that the book is a compilation of various views, based on focused research enquiries, on emerging sugar-related tourism as a reflection of cultural change, especially in cases where sugar dominates industrial production in a country, is transitioning towards tourism or has moved from industry to heritage. As an initial enquiry in relation to tourism the book then does not claim to be comprehensive, but is the beginning of enquiry into the relationship of sugar heritage to contemporary tourism.

Organization of the Book

Sugar history and heritage are a common thread spun throughout the book as the development of related aspects of tourism and cultural change are documented. The first part of the book, the Introduction, contains Chapter 1, 'Connecting Sugar Heritage and Tourism' and is written by the editor, Lee Jolliffe. This introductory chapter sets out the research framework for themes to be pursued throughout the volume, outlining the rationale for the book and the organization of the chapters. The three threads discussed in this initial chapter of *contexts* (historical; economic; cultural change; cultural heritage management), *points of view* (postcolonialism; commodification; sustainability) and *issues* (politics; globalization; tourism development) set the scene for the chapters that follow.

The second section of the book takes both a historical and geographical view, 'Perspectives from Sugar-Producing Countries' presents both historical and contemporary perspectives of sugar culture from three of the world's major sugar producing countries: India, Australia and Brazil. In Chapter 2, 'Tourism Potential at the Origins of Sugar Production', culinary tourism specialist Linda Joyce Forristal traces the history of sugar from its origins in India, providing a foundation for subsequent chapters. She also relates this heritage to contemporary tourism experiences, where dedicated sugar tourism is not developed but instead is experienced as part of agri-tourism and culinary tourism. In Chapter 3, 'Sugar-Related Tourism in Australia: A Historical Perspective', noted sugar historian Peter D. Griggs traces not only the origin and rich history of the Australian sugar industry, but also discusses the tourism products currently based on the rich sugar history there. These products and experiences notably include the Australian Sugar Industry Museum and a sugarcane steam train attraction, the Bally Hooley (analyzed as a tourism product in Chapter 10). Griggs notes that a number of Australian destinations have missed opportunities for interpreting the Australian tourism industry to visitors. In Chapter 4, 'Brazil's Sugar Heritage and Tourism – From Engenhos to Cachaça', tourism specialist Angela Cabral Flecha, along with culinary tourism researcher Linda Joyce Forristal, uses archival and present-day sources to provide an original investigation into the various threads of Brazilian sugar history and heritage that have potential for tourism. This chapter on Brazil includes a study of the sugar based national drink Cachaça that has developed into an attraction in terms of related festivals and routes, highlighting the potential for developing the culinary based aspects of sugar-related tourism. There is also evidence here that the history of sugar is also reflective of the story of slavery, in the form of the remaining *engenhos* or plantation houses that are now open to tourists, a theme that will be further developed in subsequent chapters (Chapters 4 and 5).

The third part of the book, 'Perspectives from Countries Transitioning from Sugar to Tourism', focuses on the fact that many countries around the world are transitioning from sugar production as industry to utilizing sugar heritage for tourism. Three chapters are from the Caribbean, an area that was traditionally focused on intensive sugar production, for the most part on islands, where in some cases an exit from production as well as a need for the diversification of tourism products has heightened the interest in developing tourism related to the heritage of the former sugar industries. An additional chapter is from Taiwan, where the national sugar industry is phasing out and its assets used to develop leisure and tourism facilities. In Chapter 5, 'The Industrial Heritage of Sugar at World Heritage Sites in the Caribbean', slavery historian Tara A. Inniss and editor Lee Jolliffe examine the representation of sugar heritage by UNESCO World Heritage Sites in the Caribbean. This chapter includes considerations of the nature of sugar heritage in the Caribbean, the process of designating and then listing sugar-related properties, reflecting on lessons from sites in Cuba, the Dominican Republic and Barbados. The authors contend that using the lens of labour history to view the region's sugar heritage would do much to further the development of insightful interpretations of the remaining material and intangible culture, as well as the recognition of sugar heritage as having outstanding universal value embodied in recognition of more World Heritage Sites. In Chapter 6, 'Developing Sugar Heritage Tourism in St Kitts', sustainable tourism researcher Rachel Dodds and editor Lee Jolliffe document the emergence of sugar-related heritage tourism in this small island country in the wake of the closure of the formerly nationalized sugar industry. A notable aspect of this case is the involvement of entrepreneurs, who are utilizing the remains of the industry in the form of both the rail line and plantation properties to develop products that cater for the most part to cruise visitor excursions for passengers arriving on the increasing number of cruise ships visiting Port Zante, the port for the capital city Basseterre. In Chapter 7, 'The Contested Heritage of Sugar and Slavery at Tourism Attractions in Barbados and St Lucia', tourism scholars Mechelle N. Best and Winston F. Phulgence examine the interpretive experience at plantation house attractions in both locations, finding that the history of slavery at these sites is not part of the discourse, which instead favours the plantation lifestyles of the former owners. As previously noted by Found (2004), this preservation of elite housing from the colonial period seems to have been a priority throughout the Caribbean region. This is a significant chapter, calling for a balance of interpretation of sugar history, in particular that relating to the slavery heritage of enslavement at both locations. It best captures the links between labour and sugar production. In Chapter 8, 'Transforming Taiwan's Sugar Refineries for Leisure and Tourism', tourism academic Abby Liu traces the history of sugar in Taiwan, highlighting the various approaches taken by the contemporary Taiwan Sugar Corporation (TSC) to utilize their considerable assets not only for sugar processing, but also for the development of a variety of leisure and tourism facilities. Sugar-related tourism in Taiwan therefore spans a broad spectrum of products and experiences, from riding a former sugarcane train, to visiting the remains of sugar refineries, to experiencing sugar-related treats. However, not all developments of the former TSC industrial properties have a direct relation to the former sugar production, as is evidenced by the Taiwan Sugar – Pastoral Farm Resort. In addition, the earlier, more contested, dark history of the sugar industry under Japanese occupation does not seem to be interpreted.

In the fourth part of the book, 'Consuming Sugar and its Heritage', four chapters consider the consumer experience of and the issues associated with both tangible and intangible sugar-related tourism products. This part of the book has a more global focus, first focusing on souvenirs produced with sugar as a primary ingredient in the UK, then profiling sugar-related sites (representing production, processing and refinement of cane sugar) in both Australia and New Zealand, concluding with an overview of how the heritage of sugar is exhibited and interpreted in museums and related sites around the world. In Chapter 9, 'Sugar in Tourism: "Wrapped in Devonshire Sunshine"', scholar Paul Cleave, who studies the evolving relationship between food and tourism, traces how sugar is the foundation of a popular holiday treat and souvenir in the south of England, Devon fudge. As a product, Devon fudge has a history that is closely linked with the evolution of holidays in Devon and the author demonstrates yet another role for sugar in relation to tourism, that of the primary ingredient in a confectionary that is closely linked with memories of the visit and the place. This links back to Chapter 6 and the use of the local sugar cake as a souvenir of the ride on the former sugarcane train line, now the St Kitts Scenic Railway. In Chapter 10, 'Sugarcane and the Sugar Train: Linking Tradition, Trade and Tourism in Tropical North Queensland', tourism scholar Leanne White examines the heritage-tourism-trade linkages between sugarcane and sugarcane trains in a producing region of Australia, North Queensland. This chapter links to Chapter 3 on sugar history in Australia while taking a more product and marketing orientated view of Australia's sugar heritage resources, tracing the ways in which the relationships of sugar heritage to tourism are communicated in a prominent sugar-producing region of Australia. Heritage tourism scholar Jane Legget in Chapter 11, 'From Sugar as Industry to Sugar as Heritage: Changing Perceptions of the Chelsea Sugar Works', traces the evolution of New Zealand's Chelsea Sugar Works from an industrial to a leisure focus. A particular highlight here is the involvement of the community in shaping the future of the land based assets of this sugar production facility. In Chapter 12, 'Exhibiting and Interpreting Sugar Heritage in the World's Museums', editor and museologist Lee Jolliffe considers how sugar heritage is reflected by museums around the world. A variety of sugar-focused museums exist, coming into existence in some cases from the refining or processing aspects of sugar production. Other museums related to the story of sugar include those interpreting the history of slavery, and the life of the gentry on sugar plantations through plantation houses acting as heritage house museums. This chapter has linkages back to earlier chapters in the book that highlight various instances of sugar heritage being on exhibition (including Chapters 5, 6 and 7 on sites in the Caribbean). There is still considerable scope for the development of sugar-related exhibitions as a way to educate the public regarding the industry and heritage, and as places for reflecting on what Abbott (2008) referred to as a bittersweet history.

The last section of the book, the Conclusion, Chapter 13, 'Issues and Trends in Sugar Heritage Tourism', provides a summary and critical analysis of the complex set of issues associated with the sugar-related aspects of contemporary tourism while highlighting current trends in such tourism.

References

Abbott, E. (2008) *Sugar: A Bittersweet History*. Toronto: Penguin Canada.
Anon. (2012) *FAOSTAT*. Rome: Food and Agricultural Organization of the UN, accessed 18 June 2012. http://faostat.fao.org.
Ashworth, G. (2006) The politics of world heritage: Negotiating tourism and conservation. *Annals of Tourism Research* 33 (1), 273–275.
Austin, N.K. (2002) Managing heritage attractions: Marketing challenges at sensitive historical sites. *International Journal of Tourism Research* 4 (6), 447–457.
Barnet, M. and Lindstrom, N. (1980) The culture that sugar created. *Latin American Literary Review* 8 (16), 38–46.
Buzinde, C.N. and Santos, C.A. (2008) Representations of slavery. *Annals of Tourism Research* 35 (2), 469–488.
Buzinde, C.N. and Santos, C.A. (2009) Interpreting slavery tourism. *Annals of Tourism Research* 36 (3), 439–458.
Chambers, E. (1997) *Tourism and Culture: An Applied Perspective*. State University of New York Press, Albany.
Drummond, S. and Yeoman, I. (2001) *Quality Issues in Heritage Visitor Attractions*. Oxford: Butterworth-Heinemann.
Ferdinand, N. and Williams, N.L. (2012) International festivals as experience production systems. *Tourism Management*. http://dx.doi.org/10.1016/j.tourman.2012.05.001
Found, W. (2004) Historic sites, material culture and tourism in the Caribbean islands. In *Tourism in the Caribbean: Trends, Developments, Prospects* (pp. 136–151). London: Routledge.
Frew, E. and White, L. (eds) (2011) *Tourism and National Identities: An International Perspective*. London; New York: Routledge.
Galloway, J.H. (1989) *The Sugar Cane Industry*. Cambridge: Cambridge University Press.
Her, K. (2010) A Sweet Journey. *Taiwan Review* 60 (2), accessed 1 February 2012. http://taiwanreview.nat.gov.tw/ct.asp?xItem=92072&CtNode=1361.
Jolliffe, L. (2007) *Tea and Tourism: Tourists, Traditions and Transformations*. Clevedon, UK: Channel View Publications.
Kincaid, J. (1988) *A Small Place*. London: Farrar, Straus and Giroux.
Law, E. (2001) Management of cultural and heritage destinations. In I. Yeoman and S. Drummond (eds) *Quality Issues in Heritage Visitor Attractions* (pp. 78–96). Oxford: Butterworth-Heinemann.
MacCannell, D. (1976) *The Tourist*. New York: Schocken Books.

Menard, R.R. (2006) *Sweet Negotiations: Sugar, Slavery, and Plantation Agriculture in Early Barbados.* Charlottesville, VA: Virginia University Press.

Nurse, K. (2008) *Development of a Strategic Business Management Model for the Sustainable Development of Heritage Tourism Products in the Caribbean.* Barbados: The Caribbean Tourism Organization.

Oxford University Press (1989) *The Oxford English Dictionary.* Oxford: Oxford University Press.

Patullo, P. (1996) *Last Resorts.* Kingston, Jamaica: Ian Randle Publishers.

Ragoonath, R. (2012) Facelift for Caroni's Sevilla House, accessed 12 July 2012. http://www.guardian.co.tt/news/2012-04-12/facelift-caroni%E2%80%99s-sevilla-house.

Sandiford, K.A. (2000) *Cultural Politics of Sugar: Caribbean Slavery & Narratives of Colonialism.* Port Chester, NY: Cambridge University Press.

Scott, A. (2010) The Kura Hulanda Museum in Curacao – looking back on a dark history of slave trade. *Gadling*, accessed 13 July 2012. http://www.gadling.com/2010/10/08/the-kura-hulanda-museum-in-curacao-looking-back-on-a-dark-hist/.

Smith, M. (2003) *Issues in Cultural Tourism Studies.* London: Routledge.

Thompson, A.O. (2010) *Confronting Slavery: Breaking Through the Corridors of Silence.* Barbados: Thompson Business Services Inc.

Timothy, D.J. and Boyd, S.W. (2003) *Heritage Tourism.* Harlow: Pearson Education Limited.

Yin, R.K. (2009) *Case Study Research: Design and Methods.* Thousand Oaks, CA: Sage Publications.

Part 2

Perspectives from Sugar-Producing Countries

2 Tourism Potential at the Origins of Sugar Production

Linda Joyce Forristal

The history of sugar has moved from east to west. The native distributions of the six species of sugarcane lie in South and Southeast Asia, with some scholars believing that the home of sugarcane is somewhere in the south Pacific (Deerr, 1949: 13; Mintz, 1985), most probably New Guinea. In the past some Indian scholars have claimed sugarcane as indigenous to the subcontinent (Gopal, 1964) from 'time immemorial' (Pandey, 2007) or that it is 'evident from *Atharvaveda* and *Charaka Samhita* that India was the home of sugarcane since ancient times' (Pandey, 2007). But, according to Mintz (1985), sugarcane was first domesticated in New Guinea around 8000 bc and was carried to India about 2000 years later. The art of making crystalline sugar from sugarcane commenced in, and is credited to, India around the time of Siddhartha Gautama, the Buddha, about 500 bc (Daniels, 1996: 405; Galloway, 1989: 22). Ancient India later introduced the techniques for making clarified, drained and beaten sugars to the Chinese in the mid-17th century (Daniels, 1996: 406).

Scholars believe the landing place for sugarcane on the Indian subcontinent was the kingdom of Magadha, one of the 16 kingdoms of ancient India, which roughly corresponds with modern-day southern Bihar and parts of Bengal to the east (see Figure 2.1). In ancient times, the sugar production belt stretched across subtropical northern India, just south of the Himalayas, from Bengal expanding west into Uttar Pradesh.

Because sugarcane is climate-dependent, demanding an 'abundance of heat and water the year round for the best results' (Galloway, 1989: 14), India's subtropical and tropical climates make it well suited for sugarcane production. It is the second largest global producer after Brazil, and the world's largest sugar consumer. This means that there is a lot of sugar production and consumption in India. Currently, there are approximately 670 working sugar mills in India (see Figure 2.2).

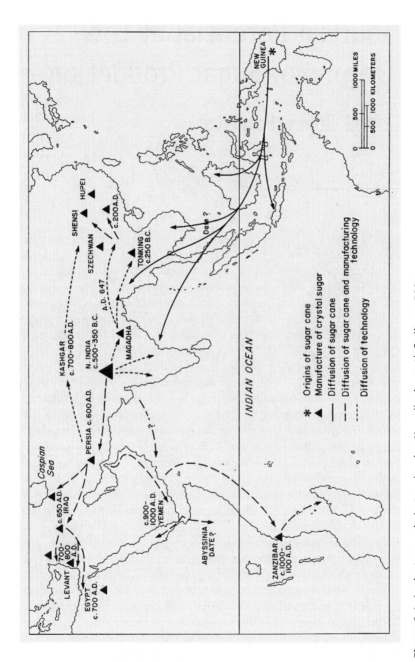

Figure 2.1 Ancient sugar industry showing Magadha in north Indian, c.500 BC

Source: Courtesy Cambridge University Press from J.M. Galloway (1989) The Sugar Cane Industry: An Historical Geography from its origin to 1914.

Figure 2.2 Indian sugar map, 2010
Source: Courtesy Indian Sugar Mills Association (2011)

Ancient to Modern-Day Sugar Production

One of the most important aspects of material culture tied to ancient sugar production in India is the device or implement used for crushing the sugarcane. The *ghani*, a crushing device for high oil content seeds, such as sesame, was an animal-driven mortar and pestle in use for at least 2500 years (Achaya, 1992; Van Bergen, 2007). The *ghani*, sometimes referred to as a *kolhu*, was adopted and adapted for crushing sugarcane (Daniels, 1996: 288–292). The mortar was generally made of stone, but sometimes of hollowed wood (Sangwan, 2007). Two men were required to run the device, one to feed the mortar with freshly cut cane and the other to balance the system

Chinapatam Sugar-mill

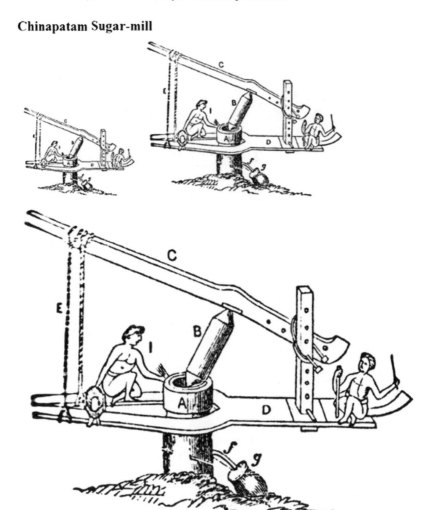

Figure 2.3 Ghani-type sugar mill
Source: Chambers, W. and Chambers, R. (1881) *Encyclopedia – A Dictionary of Universal Knowledge for the People*. Philadelphia: J.B. Lippincott & Co.

and drive the oxen (see Figure 2.3). According to Daniels (1996: 289), the first known illustration of the *kolhu*, or indeed a sugarcane mill anywhere in the world, can be found in a Jain manuscript called the *Mahapurana*, dated 1540. The lower right-hand panel pictures a sugarcane field and a *kolhu* powered by two oxen (see Figure 2.4).

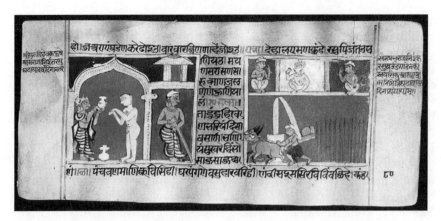

Figure 2.4 Ancient Jain text with sugarcane and *ghani* panel in lower right-hand corner
Source: Color image received by Linda Joyce Forristal from William D. van Bergen, who personally received it from Christian Daniels

British interest in Indian sugar production and trading between India and Britain was formalized some time after a royal charter was granted by Queen Elizabeth I on 31 December 1600 to the East India Company. The rich history of Indian-British relations is too varied and complex to adequately explore here, but by the late 1700s the East India Company concentrated its efforts on Bengal hoping to revive the production and export of sugar to markets in Europe. However, Indian sugar production remained 'technologically stagnant' (Galloway, 1989: 198; Kumar, 1983: 15–16) and substantial investment in sugarcane production on the subcontinent of India did not take place until the passage of the Sugar Protection Act of 1832 that placed a tariff on imported sugar, which served to protect this important agro-industry from outside competitors such as Japan (Agrawal, 2010). Another key impetus for the British was the emancipation of slaves in the West Indies in 1834 (Deerr, 1949: 56), which led to some of the former West Indian sugar plantation owners migrating their investments to the north Indian provinces of Bengal and Behar. Although slavery could no longer be the chief means of labour for production, as it had been in the Caribbean, individuals from the lower castes in India were often engaged as labourers in the growing and production of sugarcane. Two crucial improvements in Indian sugar production introduced by the British were the steam-powered stationary mill engines to run the equipment to replace outdated manual methods of sugarcane juice extraction (Hill, n.d.), such as the *ghani*, and the direct vacuum-pan method of boiling sugarcane juice in a closed vessel under partial vacuum to more efficiently evaporate enough water to induce crystallization. Railroads were also built to move sugarcane from field to factory and sugar from factory to end markets.

From the Indian side, a strong impetus for investment in the domestic sugar industry was a rapidly growing population (which has quadrupled since its independence from Britain in 1947) with a sweet tooth. After 1932, sugar production expanded south into the states of Gujarat, Maharashtra, Karnataka, Andra Pardesh and Tamil Nadu. Fast forward 80 years, and the two powerhouses of modern-day sugar production are the states of Uttar Pradesh, with 30.1% of India's production, and Maharashtra, with 27.1% (Agrawal, 2010: 35) (Figure 2.5). Despite high domestic demand, India is a major exporter of sugar, often ranking fourth in world exports of sugar behind Brazil, Thailand and Australia, respectively (OECD/FAO, 2012). The latest available export statistics (October 2010–March 2011) indicate

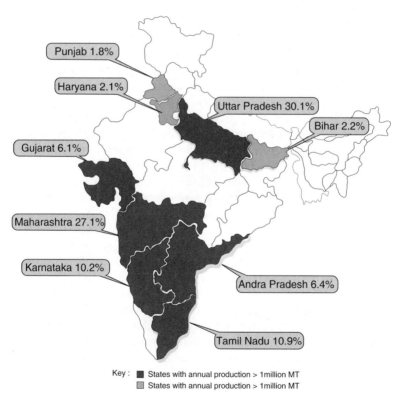

Key : ■ States with annual production > 1million MT
       ▨ States with annual production > 1million MT

Figure 2.5 Sugar production statistics by state
Source: Courtesy Agrawal (2010)

that India exported over 2.7 million tonnes of sugar, mostly to Thailand, UAE, Singapore, Malaysia, Iran, Yemen, Kenya, Djibouti, Bangladesh, and other neighbouring countries such as Sri Lanka and Pakistan, and extended duty-free imports of raw and white sugar through 30 November 2011 (GAIN, 2011).

Indian Sugar Types

According to Galloway (1989), the earliest forms of Sanskrit literature contain references to the cultivation of sugarcane, but not the manufacture of sugar. Scholars have tried to date the beginning of sugar production in India from the etymology of two Sanskrit words for sugar: *sarkara* and *guda* (or *gula*). The Sanskrit word *sarkara* originally meant 'granular particles or gravel' and has come to mean crystalline sugar. *Guda*, with Indo-European roots, has the meaning 'to make into a ball', and in Sanskrit came to mean a sugary coagulate produced by boiling sugar, or *gur*. In modern terms, *gur* is an 'unrefined brown lump sugar made from sugarcane by farmers and unregulated, small-scale enterprises' (Landes, 2010: 3). This low-tech sugar is sometimes also referred to as *jaggery*, but *jaggery* can also refer to Indian palm-sugar. *Gur* or *jaggery* is a 'pure, wholesome, traditional, unrefined, whole sugar' (Agrawal, 2010), containing the minerals and vitamins inherently present in sugarcane juice before molasses is removed, and as such is very similar to brown-coloured Mexican *panela* or *piloncillo*. Another early Sanskrit word describing a type of sugar was *khanda*, a word that has come in English to mean candy (Galloway, 1989: 20). Khandsari sugar or *khandsari* has smaller crystals (soft-grained) and was historically produced by beating a supersaturated solution of sugar with a paddle, a technique that was discovered in India 'in the first centuries of our era' (Daniels, 1996: 405). Modern-day *khandsari* is 'centrifugal sugar' produced by small-scale, unregulated firms (Landes, 2010). There is no beet sugar production in India (GAIN, 2011).

The distinction between these three Indian sugar types is important because white sugar or 'refined centrifugal sugar' (Landes, 2010) is produced industrially. The earlier figure of approximately 670 Indian sugar mills refers solely to industrial sugar mills that produce white sugar, while *gur* and *khandsari* sugar-producing units in India, which are small-scale and unregulated, are estimated at 5694 by Agrawal (2010). Despite the high numbers, *gur* only accounts for 25% of the market share and *khandsari* 3% (Landes, 2010).

Sugar mills in India can be categorized into three different sectors: public (i.e. owned by the Indian government), private and cooperative. According to Agrawal (2010), the state of Uttar Pradesh has the highest number of privately owned sugar mills, which collect sugarcane from thousands of smaller cane growers and transport it to central mills, much like some wineries procure grapes from small vineyards. However, in recent years some ailing private mills have been taken over by the state government, and vice versa some government-owned ailing mills have been auctioned off to the private sector (personal communication with Sagar Singh, Centre for Tourism Research and Development, Lucknow, 10 December 2011).

Sweet Potential for Tourism

Despite a vast landscape of 5 million hectares devoted to sugarcane cultivation and multiple sites of sugar production throughout a large swath of the country, sugar tourism is not officially developed or promoted on the Indian subcontinent. According to government tourism officials contacted for this research, tourism related to sugar is 'not a concept they are familiar with' (personal communication with P. Rangarajan, 28 October 2010).

Nor is Indian sugar tourism promoted in travel guidebooks. The narrative, images and photographs and the mix of selected sites in guidebooks, which can be accessed by entries in the index, can be seen as a key promotional tool as well as a gauge of the level of awareness about a specific destination or amenity by the presence or absence of information. At their core, guidebooks function as a 'surrogate tourism guide' (Bhattacharyya, 1997: 373), acting as a middleman between hosts and guests. That tourism in relation to sugar is off the tourism radar is enforced by the fact that neither Fodor's *India* (2008) nor Lonely Planet's *India* (Singh, 2011) lists sugarcane, sugar, sweets or candy in their indexes. In short, the absence of sugar-themed index entries in these popular Indian guidebooks is a confirmation of a low level of awareness about the history and heritage of sugarcane and sugar in India.

To date, sugar tourism can be categorized as organic, rather than induced in nature, yet unrecognized as a potential type of niche tourism. Thus, for the purposes of exploring the potential of sugar tourism in India, we will first look at the resources in Uttar Pradesh and Maharashtra, the aforementioned two biggest sugar-producing states, including some anecdotal evidence that supports its potential. We will also explore the potential of agri-tourism and culinary tourism related to sugar.

A spontaneous and informal example of sugar tourism is expressed in the following anecdote:

Sugar tourism is not developed in India at all, although it exists. Most of the tourism to sugar mills consists of Visiting Friends and Relatives

Tourism. As a child, I remember I went twice with one of my parents and my brother to a sugar mill in Baheri (west Uttar Pradesh state in India) because my mother's female friend's husband used to be the General Manager of that mill. The characteristic narrow gauge railway lines and the experience of riding the steam engine (thanks to the General Manager) that led the wagons carrying sugar to connect with the broad gauge railway line for transportation to cities and towns, was exhilarating and eating fresh sugar balls were some of the charms associated with it. (Personal communication with Sagar Singh, Centre for Tourism Research and Development, Lucknow, 5 December 2011)

This experience occurred in Uttar Pradesh, one of the ancient and now the largest sugar-producing states, and refers to a sugar mill in Baheri that opened in 1931 (Sajnani, 2001: 388). The above reflection also hints at another potential for tourism related to sugar production, namely the historic railway lines and trains associated with transporting sugarcane to the factories and sugar to the consumer and industrial end-users, which may have potential as tourism attractions.

In the state of Maharashtra, inland from the capital city of Mumbai, lie thousands of acres of fertile agricultural land. The strong agriculture sector in the state has made a significant contribution to the economic development of the region and sugar has been one of the key economic engines. Fresh-squeezed sugarcane juice served with a dash of lemon and black pepper is a regional offering most of the year in and around Mumbai, the capital city (personal communication with Rohan Tikekar, 14 December 2011).

The regional tourism policy includes an agri-tourism component (Raghunandan et al., 2010), but does not specifically mention sugar heritage tourism. Despite the lack of formalization and official promotion of sugar tourism, early agri-tourism adopters near Baramati are using social media such as Facebook to promote tourism offerings that include a stop at a 'sugar factory and jaggery making units'.

Agri Tourism offer edutainment farm tours in Malegaon Village, where guests would be given information about cultivation of grapes, sugarcane, pomegranate, guava, mango, chikkoo, custard apple, coconut, lime, banana, alma, jackfruit, anjeer and many more fruits plantation. There will be visit[s] to [a] dairy farm, milk collection centers, [a] goat farm, emu farm, or get an insight of sericulture (silk producing) [and the] production of jaggery and sugar. (Taware, 2006)

Malegaon Village in Baramati is described as Maharashtra's 'first agricultural tourism village' and described amenities include the Malegaon sugar factory (Taware, 2006). This indicates that elements of sugar-related heritage tourism are being informally added to existing agri-tourism itineraries to some degree. However, neither the main Indian tourism website *Incredible India* (2011) nor any of its new microsites, promotes agri-tourism as a specialized or developed form of tourism.

The potential of agri-tourism is perhaps strongest and most easily adopted by small entrepreneurial producers of *gur* and *khandsari* rather than huge industrial sugar producers. For example, tours of the Domino sugar factory in Baltimore, Maryland, one of the only remaining industrial sugar factories in the United States, can be arranged for alumni or professional food-related groups on a limited basis, but the facility is not open for general tourism, stating concern over guest safety and security. The same issues may come up for Indian industrial sugar producers, which could provide a window of opportunity for small-scale *gur* and *khandsari* producers to develop, market and execute sugar tourism. This could be a strategy to help relieve poverty in rural India. Pandurang Taware, ADTC and Malegaon Village founder, is an agri-tourism advocate, stating the 'agriculture is the backbone of the Indian economy' and that since 50% of the population still lives in villages 'only if villages become self-sufficient, will the nation develop' (Raghunandan *et al.*, 2010).

Culinary or food based tourism can play a major role in sustaining regional identity (Everett & Aitchison, 2008) because there is a 'strong relationship between food and identity' and between 'certain localities and certain types of foods' (Richards, 2002: 5). Local food and drink can also help differentiate destinations (Haven-Tang & Jones, 2005). But, when one thinks of Indian food and food identity spices are often the first association, not sugar. Indeed, Columbus was looking for a route to India for its spices when he 'discovered' the New World, so the importance of Keralite black pepper, coriander, cumin, turmeric, cardamom and cinnamon has been well-known and appreciated for centuries. Thus, culinary or gastronomic tourism in relation to sugar heritage and culinary expressions should be considered for further development in India, as they have been in Canada.

For example, the Canadian province of Quebec is the world's largest producer of maple syrup, an alternative natural sweetener often used in place of white sugar and one with a long culinary tradition. Tourism in relation to the processing and products of maple syrup (and crystallized maple sugar) is very popular. During the 'sugaring off' season that runs from March to early April, approximately 400 maple syrup operations called *cabanes à sucre* are open for visitors to watch the boiling down of the syrup, to sample such sweet desserts as hot maple taffy served on snow (Hashimoto & Telfer,

2006) and to buy a bottle of maple syrup to take home as a souvenir or a gift. This type of tourism, along with maple syrup festivals, is also popular in New England in the USA. Most maple syrup operations are family owned and intrinsically rural by nature. Thus, maple syrup or maple sugar tourism could serve as a good model for *gur* or *khandsari* sugar makers to consider.

Sugar based gastronomic, culinary or food tourism based on a strong food identity could be developed more in relation to the vast numbers of Indian sweets and candies, some having a more free-standing identity than others. For example, in northeast India, Bengal was one of the ancient sites of sugar production in India. Its main coastal city of Kolkata (formerly Calcutta before the official name change in 2001) was the official capital of British India. Thus, it has been a key trading port city for centuries and not just for the British, but also the Dutch and the Portuguese. The state of West Bengal is famous for its Bengali sweets, and in Kolkata there is a sweet shop or *moira* on almost every corner (Krondl, 2010; Sen, 1996). The two most popular Bengali sweets are *sandesh* and *rosogulla* (multiple spellings), milk based sweets made from *chhana*, a ricotta-like soft cheese. One theory is that this process was perfected after the Portuguese introduced the process of how to intentionally curdle milk in the 1860s (Sen, 1996), but others believe that milk based sweets have been made in Bengal since the 1600s or as early as the Middle Ages (Krondl, 2010). No matter their provenance, these colourful, soft candies are sold at shops all over Kolkata, but because they are very perishable one really must travel there to experience the real thing, as is the case with Devon fudge discussed in Chapter 9. However, to their credit, the *DK Eyewitness Travel India* guidebook, includes images of Bengali sweets (2011: 264–265) and recommends KC Das & Sons as the best purveyors of *sandesh* and *rosogulla* in Kolkata (2011: 292). Krondl (2010) recommends both KC Das and Nakur.

In addition to confections, Bengal is also famous for another 'sweet' called *mishti doi*, a yogurt based dessert made with *gur* and topped with a burnt sugar coating much like crème brûlée. And, in the West Bengal Hills north of Kolkata lies Darjeeling (Dorje Ling), one of the most prized sites for tea production and a tourist destination in its own right. Thus, a Kolkata tourist can experience *in situ* Indian tea (chai) sweetened with spoonsful of local sugar, along with their choice of a vast array of colourful and fresh Bengali sweets.

Conclusion

With the right planning and marketing strategies, sugar heritage tourism could become an element of heritage tourism, cultural tourism, agri-tourism, rural tourism and/or culinary tourism throughout a large swath of India. For example, Uttar Pradesh is not only the largest sugar-producing state in India and the most populous Indian state, but it is also home to the Taj Mahal, one of the most visited iconic tourism structures in the world. Undoubtedly, unsuspecting tourists are catapulted by field after field of sugarcane and sugar mills on their way to visit this New Seventh Wonder of the World. There seems to be an opportunity to create sugar routes in partnership with both low and high-tech sugar producers or at least to post adequate signage or create literature to educate tourists of the state's long and rich sugar history.

The state of Maharashtra has hundreds of sugarcane fields and small producers of *gur* and *khandsari* as well as large producers of industrial white sugar within a day trip from its capital Mumbai, a thriving metropolis and tourism destination with an international airport. Future research could investigate the interest and feasibility of tourism in other sugar-producing Indian states, such as Karnataka. For example, the city of Mandya is the site of one of the biggest and oldest sugar factories in the country (Sajnani, 2001) and under the right circumstances could be developed as a day trip from Bangalore.

A network of self-guided tours with website support or professional guided tours could introduce tourists to sugarcane production, depending on the season, as well as the products of sugar production, from the sweets of Bengal to a refreshing sugarcane drink or sweet lassi on the streets of Mumbai. In addition to visits to sweetshops or confectioners, visits to hard candy factories and candy shops, such as those to Hershey's chocolate factory in Hershey, Pennsylvania, could also be developed. Another way to raise the awareness of the country's rich sugar heritage and the wide variety of sugar resources both for residents and guests would be to implement a national sugar festival or several regional ones, which do not exist at this time. Tourism officials and providers could also partner with international travel guidebook publishers to include or update their information on sugar history and sugar-related tourism resources.

Ironically, the place where sugar production got its start is behind the curve when it comes to capitalizing on its sweet heritage for tourism, but its potential is rich. Sugar-related tourism experiences in India can be built upon both ancient and modern-day sugar processing practices in several Indian states as well as on varied culinary traditions.

References

Achaya, K.T. (1992) Indian oilpress (ghani). *Indian Journal of History of Science* 27 (1), 5–13.
Agrawal, N. (2010) *Sugar Industry in India.* Bhilai, India: Chhattisgarh Swami Vivikanand Technical University, accessed 9 December 2011. http://www.scribd.com/doc/49764898/38460451-Sugar-Industry-Report.

Bhattacharyya, D.A. (1997) Mediating India: An analysis of a guidebook. *Annals of Tourism Research* 24 (2), 371–389.

Daniels, C. (1996) Science and civilisation in China. In J. Needham (ed.) *Volume 6: Biology and Biological Technology: Part III Agro-Industries: Sugarcane Technology.* Cambridge, UK: Cambridge University Press.

Deerr, N. (1949) *The History of Sugar.* London: Chapman and Hall.

DK Publishing (2011) *DK Eyewitness Travel India.* New York: DK Publishing.

Everett, S. and Aitchison, C. (2008) The role of food tourism in sustaining regional identity: A case study of Cornwall, South West England. *Journal of Sustainable Tourism* 16 (2), 150–167.

Fodor's (2008) *India.* New York: Fodor's.

Galloway, J.H. (1989) *The Sugar Cane Industry: An Historical Geography from its Origin to 1914.* New York; London: Cambridge University Press.

Global Agricultural Information Network (GAIN) (2011) *India Sugar Semi-Annual* (No. IN1199). Washington, DC: USDA Foreign Agricultural Service.

Gopal, L. (1964) Sugar-making in ancient India. *Journal of the Economic and Social History of the Orient* 7 (1), 57–72.

Hashimoto, A. and Telfer, D.J. (2006) Selling Canadian culinary tourism: Branding the global and the regional product. *Tourism Geographies* 8 (1), 31–55.

Haven-Tang, C. and Jones, E. (2005) Using local food and drink to differentiate tourism destinations through a sense of place: A story from Wales – dining at Monmouthshire's great table. *Journal of Culinary Science & Technology* 4 (4), 69–86.

Hill, G. (n.d.) *Steam Engines in the Indian Sugar Industry,* accessed 5 December 2010. http://www.internationalsteam.co.uk/mills/indiamill03.htm.

Incredible India (2011) Accessed 5 January 2012. http://www.incredibleindia.org and http://www.incredibleindia.org/newsite/incredible_microsite.htm.

Indian Sugar Mills Association (2011) Sugar map of India, accessed 10 November 2011. http://www.indiansugar.com/Transaction/map.aspx.

Krondl, M. (2010) The sweetshops of Kolkata. *Gastronomica* 10 (3), 58–65.

Kumar, D.D.M. (1983) *The Cambridge Economic History of India. Vol.2, c.1757–c.1970.* Cambridge: Cambridge University Press.

Landes, M.R. (2010) *Indian Sugar Sector Cycles Down, Poised to Rebound* (No. SSS-M-260-01). Washington, DC: USDA Economic Research Service.

Mintz, S.W. (1985) *Sweetness and Power: The Place of Sugar in Modern History.* New York: Viking.

OECD/FAO (2012). *OECD-FAO Agricultural Outlook 2012-2021* (pp. 145–161), OECD Publishing and FAO. Retrieved August 19, 2012 from http://dx.doi.org/10.1787/agr_outlook-2012-en

Pandey, A.P. (2007) *Indian Sugar Industry: A Strong Industrial Base For Rural India.* Banaras Hindu University, accessed 1 October 2010. http://mpra.ub.uni-muenchen.de/6065/1/MPRA_paper_6065.pdf.

Raghunandan, A., Horner, S. and Schuepbach, E. (2010) Agritourism in India: the potential for sustainable development and growth. Paper presented at the Passion for Hospitality Excellence conference, sponsored by EuroCHRIE, 25–28 October, Amsterdam.

Richards, G. (2002) Gastronomy: An essential ingredient in tourism production and consumption? In A.M. Hjalager and G. Richards (eds) *Tourism and Gastronomy* (pp. 3–20). London: Routledge.

Sajnani, M. (2001) *Encyclopedia of Tourism Resources in India* (Vol. 1). New Delhi: Kalpaz Publishers.

Sangwan, S. (2007) Level of agricultural technology in India (1757–1857). *Asian Agri-History* 11 (1), 5–25.

Sen, C.T. (1996) The Portuguese influence on Bengali cuisine. Presented at Food on the Move: Proceedings of the Oxford Symposium on Food and Cookery, Summer, St Katherine's College, Oxford.

Singh, S. (2011) *India*. London: Lonely Planet.

Taware, P. (2006) Baramati Agri Tourism. Retrieved August 19, 2012 from http://www.scribd.com/doc/109326/Baramati-Agri-Tourism

van Bergen, W.D. (2007) Sugarcane milling throughout the centuries. Paper presented at the 12th International Molinological Society (TIMS) Symposium, 2–10 June, the Netherlands.

3 Sugar-Related Tourism in Australia: A Historical Perspective

Peter D. Griggs

There's a soughing like the sea, though we're twenty miles inland, 'Tis the wind in the canefields! – Oh the scent! – the song! the chime! The laden trucks come lumbering in to the sugar mills at Ingham. All the air is sugar-sweet through the North at crushing time.
Clement Christensen, 1937

The above quote from Clement Christensen's 1937 book *Queensland Journey* was accompanied by a colour painting of what one assumes to be Victoria Sugar Mill, near Ingham, although there is no caption to indicate the name of the sugar mill. In front of the sugar mill was a locomotive pulling cane trucks loaded with harvested cane. The quote and painting occupy an entire page that starts the section in the book which deals with information for tourists travelling to North Queensland. This text is loaded with imagery associated with the production of sugar: 'the pennon of smoke' from the Victoria crushing mill at Ingham; 'a million acres of verdant plantations'; 'green fields of sugar cane spread over hills and dales like a shoreless sea'; and 'in the crushing season the mills pulsate with life, and by night the flares of burning trash illuminate a landscape which has all the appearances of a foreign country' (Christensen, 1937: 36, 83 and 105). Moreover, this book is just one of many pre-World War II publications that were produced for the tourists visiting tropical Queensland, especially during the winter months.

Such promotional material comes from a bygone era when the activities associated with the production of sugar were actually considered a major tourist drawcard in coastal Queensland and northern New South Wales. With the passage of time, however, the presence of a sugar industry has dwindled in importance as an attraction in the marketing of Queensland to international and domestic tourists. Presently, Queensland is marketed as a destination that has '300 warm and sunny days'. Outdoor adventures, wildlife tours, sandy beaches, Aboriginal culture, food and wine and theme parks are promoted heavily as the state's main attractions (Queensland Holidays, 2011). Nevertheless, today tourists can still visit several different attractions associated with the production of sugar in Queensland and northern New South Wales, although the visitors may find it difficult to locate information on the presence of these attractions. Moreover, currently the Australian sugar industry displays little interest in promoting its rich heritage, missing the opportunity to tap into the mass tourism market which has grown substantially in Queensland since the 1970s.

The purpose of this chapter is to examine the history of sugar-related tourism in the sugar-producing lands of eastern Australia. It commences with a brief overview of the development of the Australian sugar industry. The emergence of northern New South Wales and coastal Queensland as tourist destinations is outlined in the second section. Next, the growth of sugar tourism in eastern Australia is considered in some depth. The chapter concludes with a discussion about how Australian sugar industry organisations and other bodies that promote tourism in Queensland and northern New South Wales are currently not effectively promoting sugar production and its heritage as potential tourist attractions. The narrative is informed by the literature on the history of the Australian sugar industry (such as Griggs, 2011) and also draws heavily upon historical descriptions of visits to Australian sugar-producing districts, handbooks and brochures produced by the Queensland Government Tourist Bureau (and successor organisations) and an analysis of current brochures and web-based information on specific sugar-related visitor attractions (e.g. Fairymead House Sugar Museum) and the promotion of particular regions in Queensland and northern New South Wales to international and domestic visitors.

The Australian Cane Sugar Industry

Australia's sugar industry was established between 1864 and 1884, and over the following 40 years the area under sugarcane in Australia rose rapidly, reaching almost 103,000 ha in 1924 (Griggs, 2011). This period was also a time of experimentation, when the different coastal districts in northern New South Wales and Queensland were tested to see if the cultivation of sugarcane was suitable in particular districts. By 1920 the Ipswich and Rockhampton districts had been abandoned as sugar-producing districts, and sugarcane cultivation had become concentrated along the deltaic and levee soils of the main rivers and creeks in 16 discrete areas over almost 2500 km of eastern Australia's coastline, separated by areas of unreliable rainfall and/ or unsuitable soils (see Figure 3.1). Almost 95% of the Australian sugar output, however, came from Queensland, with northern New South Wales being only a minor sugar-producing region.

Initially, the sugar industry in Queensland mirrored the established global production model, being based on plantations, although the field workers were indentured South Sea Islanders, Chinese, Japanese or Malays, not slaves. In contrast, few plantations were established in New South Wales, with the dominant production model being European farmers on small farms supplying proprietary central mills staffed with Europeans. However, opposition to the employment of non-European workers in the Queensland sugar industry and the implementation of the White Australia Policy after 1900 led to a transformation in the production structure of Australia's sugar industry during the 1890s and 1900s. European-owned small family farms supplying sugarcane to cooperative or proprietary sugar mills took the place of plantations. Moreover, most of the indentured Pacific Islanders were repatriated to their home islands after 1906 and in 1913 legislation was introduced in Queensland prohibiting non-Europeans from leasing or owning sugarcane farms. Europeans replaced indentured workers in the field and sugar mills. Some of these Europeans were British-Australians, often ex-miners looking for employment following the decline in output from the gold and copper mines in North Queensland; others were southern Europeans, especially Italians, Greeks and Yugoslavs, who came to North Queensland and worked as canecutters (Griggs, 2011). Moreover, this production system became particularly enduring. In 2007–2008, the number of Australian sugar producers stood at slightly more than 4100. They grew between 40 and 120 ha of cane and on average harvested 8249 tonnes of cane, which was crushed at 27 sugar mills (Australian Bureau of Agricultural and Resource Economics, 2008).

Concerns about sugar over-production in Australia arose during the 1910s, as output rapidly approached the country's demand for sugar. Eventually, the Australian cane sugar industry in 1924 was forced to export for the first time nearly 20% of the country's total sugar output, at unremunerative prices. Consequently, measures were introduced to restrict production in order to avoid over-production and its consequences. These measures included limitations on the tonnage of sugarcane produced on a cane farm (i.e. farm peak), the allocation of production quotas to each sugar mill (i.e. mill peaks), and restrictions on the amount of land cultivated with sugarcane (Griggs, 2011). Thereafter, expansions in the Australian sugar industry were tightly regulated by the Queensland government, until deregulation in the

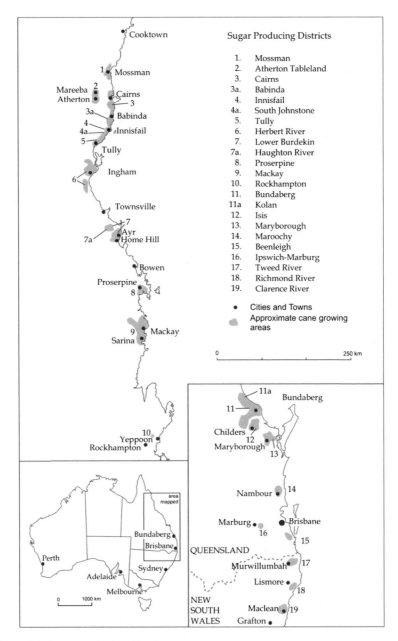

Figure 3.1 Sugar-producing districts
Source: Map by Peter Griggs, first published by Peter Lang AG in 2011, reprinted by permission.

late 1980s and early 1990s (Robinson, 1995). These regulations ensured that the supply of raw sugar matched the overseas demand for the product. Continued strong demand for Australian sugar, however, led to a further expansion in the area under cane in Australia, with nearly 450,000 ha being under the crop in 2003. Since then, the loss of cane-growing lands to urban expansion and competition from other crops (e.g. bananas, agro-forestry, vegetables) has seen the area under sugarcane in Australia drop back to around 360,000 ha in 2008 (*Australian Sugarcane Annual*, 2009: 33). Despite this decline, Australia during the 2000s had become one of largest exporters of raw sugar after Brazil and one of the world's top five sugar exporters.

Australian Sugar-Producing Regions as Tourist Destinations

During the 1880s and 1890s, the sugar-producing regions to the north and south of Brisbane, the state's capital, were attracting visitors who were drawn to the beach resorts, such as Southport, Coolangatta and Tweed Heads (near Nerang, in the Beenleigh sugar-producing district) and Teewantin, Maroochydore and Caloundra (near Nambour in the Maroochy sugar-producing district). By 1910, the Queensland government was promoting its southern Queensland beach resorts in Melbourne and Sydney. Consequently, a growing number of wealthy southern visitors were journeying north. Upon their return home, they spread the word about the wonderful winter climate they had experienced in Queensland (Russell, 1995: 76–80; Richardson, 1999: 70; Osborne, 2010: 46–55). A small number of these southern visitors ventured further north. By the early 1900s, the Cairns district was one of the coastal sugar-producing regions where a nascent tourism industry was developing (Berry, 2000: 174).

During the period 1915–1945, there was probably a substantial increase in the number of tourists visiting the coastal sugar-producing regions of Queensland and northern New South Wales. By the late 1930s, one tourist-related publication for the Cairns district claimed that 'during the winter months thousands of visitors take the opportunity of visiting the "sunny North" in order to escape the rigours of the southern winter' (Anon., 1938: 39). Part of this upsurge can be attributed to the completion of the Brisbane to Cairns rail link in 1924, thereby ensuring that Queensland was connected to all the Australian mainland capital cities. Subsequently, rail journeys along the coast of Queensland were then heavily promoted by the Queensland Government Tourist Bureau. In addition, visitors could still reach coastal destinations by passenger ships that travelled along the eastern seaboard of

Australia – at each major port half-day or day trips could be arranged. The Cairns district remained a favourite tourist destination, while Mackay emerged as another popular place for visiting tourists, even if some were en route to the Whitsunday Islands, approximately 100 km north of Mackay (Berry, 2000: 178–183; Barr, 1990: 1–19).

Since World War II there has been a substantial expansion in tourism in Queensland – the state became a global destination after 1980. International visitors who spent at least one night in Queensland rose rapidly from 52,000 in 1974, to 164,000 in 1985, to 1,969,800 in 2009–2010 (Queensland Tourist and Travel Corporation and Boeing Commercial Airplane Company, 1981: 24; Queensland Office of Economic and Statistical Research, 2010). The seaside resorts to the south of Brisbane became the city of the Gold Coast, and one of Queensland's major tourist drawcards (Richardson, 1999: 156–158; Davidson & Spearritt, 2000: 141–143). Sugar production, which had once been important in this region, however, had contracted to a small area supplying only the Rocky Point Mill, near Beenleigh. To the north of Brisbane, the coastal resorts became collectively known as the Sunshine Coast, and began offering rival attractions to the Gold Coast (Davidson & Spearritt, 2000: 144). Despite the loss of land to residential and tourist-related development, sugar production continued in the Maroochy district, until the closure of the Moreton Sugar Mill at Nambour in 2003. The Cairns-Atherton Tableland district emerged as another important destination for international visitors in Queensland during the 1980s, following Japanese investment in a range of tourist-related infra-structure. However, as the city of Cairns grew, fuelled by the influx of foreign visitors, cane growing land was lost to residential development, leading to the closure of Hambledon Sugar Mill in 1991 (Stimson *et al.*, 1998; Davidson & Spearritt, 2000: 340–343). Elsewhere, the sugar-producing districts along the Queensland coast and northern New South Wales are not as prominent des-tinations for international tourists, but have been visited by growing numbers of domestic tourists, especially grey nomads who reach these destinations by road (Cridland, 2008).

Sugar-Related Tourism in Northern New South Wales and Coastal Queensland

Between 1900 and 1939 the first publications were produced for the growing number of tourists visiting coastal destinations in northern New South Wales and Queensland. Some of these brochures and booklets pro-moted the presence of sugar mills and fields of sugarcane as tourist attrac-tions. Visitors to the Innisfail district in 1905, for example, were urged to complete a half-hour run up the Johnstone River for they would encounter 'the fields of sugar-cane and bananas' and a run inland on the Johnstone Shire Tramway would show 'toiling Kanakas and Hindoos' clearing fresh fields for the cultivation of sugarcane and bananas (Queensland Department of Lands and Queensland Department of Agriculture and Stock, 1905: 16 and 17). Tourists to the Maroochy district were advised in 1910 that a ride on one of the tramways up the range 'through the heart of the canefields is a delightful experience' (Anon., 1910: 14). By the early 1910s (and beyond), the town of Mackay marketed itself as 'the Sugaropolis of Queensland', where visitors could view the cultivation of sugarcane, the 'aristocracy of agriculture', and six sugar mills (Queensland Railways, c.1913; Anon., c.1925; Queensland Tourist Bureau, 1936: 11; Anon., 1937; Anon., 1962b). In 1924, a 40-page booklet covering the Townsville and Ayr district mentioned that 'the tourist with plenty of time at his disposal can visit the sugar-cane growing areas at Giru and Ayr' (Queensland Government Intelligence and Tourist Bureau, 1924: 9). A book focusing upon the mountain and seaside resorts of southern Queensland advised visitors to Brisbane in 1927 that they could 'view the whole process of raw sugar manufacture' by taking a trip to the Moreton Sugar Mill at Nambour during the crushing season (Queensland Government Intelligence and Tourist Bureau, 1927: 30).

The Cairns district, of all the Australian sugar-producing districts, however, was marketed the most heavily to tourists during the 1920s and 1930s. Activities involving aspects of the local sugar industry were considered an essential part of the tourist experience. By 1929 the Cairns Tableland Publicity Association was issuing 'a neat, artistic little folder for the guidance of tourism in the Cairns district'. The folder contained an eight-page pamphlet which conveyed valuable information to travellers, including advertisements for 'the sugar mills and short rail trips', and a colourful map in which the areas cultivated with sugarcane for Hambledon, Mulgrave and Babinda Mills were shown in pink, green and yellow, respectively (*Cairns Post*, 7 March 1929: 4). In 1932 and 1933 this organisation issued small booklets which contained information on the tours available in the Cairns region. Tourists were advised that a 'profitable time' could be spent inspecting Mulgrave, Hambledon or Babinda Sugar Mills. Opportunities to watch the field work associated with growing sugarcane were also available (Tablelands Publicity Association, 1932: 16; Kennedy, 1933: 105). Two year later, the Queensland Government Tourist Bureau issued a smaller folded sheet promoting the Cairns district. This document used vivid imagery, including the presence of sugarcane, to sell the region to tourists. Readers of this literature were told that 'seemingly interminable canefields spread to the distant foothills and enclose the silver thread of the Barron River in a beautiful emerald setting. For miles to the south there is a succession of canefields, sugar mills and jungle'. Moreover, it was possible to organise 'a trip by rail or road motor car through typical sugar lands, including an inspection of the Mulgrave Central Sugar Mill' (Queensland Government Tourist Bureau, c.1935). The region's appeal had even been promoted by the new medium of cinematography. A black and white film, issued c.1923 was titled *Cairns, Centre of Australia's Sugar Industry*. Three years later the production company Cinema Branch produced another black and white film with the title *Sugar Industry in Cairns and a Trip to the Great Barrier Reef*. Viewers of this documentary were shown raw sugar being loaded by a mechanical conveyor belt at the Cairns Harbour and scenes associated with the cultivation of sugarcane (Anon., c.1923; Cinema Branch, c.1926).

Assessing if any of this promotional material encouraged tourists to visit the sugar-producing regions of Queensland or northern New South Wales or their sugar mills is difficult. The fragmentary historical evidence, however, suggests that some of the Queensland sugar mills had become regular places visited by tourists throughout the 1920s and 1930s, not only because of the interest in the industrial process, but because several of the mill managers' gardens were very attractive (e.g. Mulgrave; Victoria). 'All tourists sooner or later visit one of the district's sugar mills', writes Victor Kennedy in his book on winter tours in the Cairns region (Kennedy, 1933: 105). Motor coach day and half-day tours in the Cairns region often included visits to either Hambledon or Mulgrave Sugar Mills (see for example *Cairns Post*, 16 July 1923: 4; 5 June 1924: 8; 8 October 1925: 4; and 13 August 1930: 5). Indeed, a journalist observed in 1924 that Hambledon Mill's spraypond with its 'delicate fountains of ten reflecting miniature rainbows' proved an 'irresistible attraction, providing excellent snapshots for the amateur photographer' (*Cairns Post*, 24 July 1924: 4), while nearby Mulgrave Mill was also a favourite destination as 'the vast amount of machinery and the novelty of the sugar factory' attracted the interest of tourists (*Cairns Post*, 3 June 1929: 11). By 1940 the Mulgrave Central Mill Co. Ltd had even produced a small 16-page booklet for visitors on the growing and harvest of sugarcane and the milling process (Mulgrave Central Mill Co. Ltd, 1940). Other contemporary published accounts of visits to the districts of coastal Queensland mention tourists visiting Babinda, Mourilyan, Moreton, Millaquin and Bingera Sugar Mills (see for example *Brisbane Courier*, 28 June 1923: 4; 22 June 1928: 20; 25 August 1928: 23; Stephens, 1936: 20; Nixon, 1941: 121). The Moreton Central Sugar Mill Company Limited even deliberately used its local tramway network to attract the profitable tourist traffic and installed rows of back-to-back seating on cane wagons. Visitors could travel from Maroochydore throughout the district on these tourist trains (Gregory, 1991: 89).

Following the interruptions caused by World War II, the promotion of Queensland as a tourist destination resumed, and the presence of a sugar industry continued being used in the marketing material issued by the Queensland Government Tourist Bureau during the 1950s and 1960s. A *c.*1950 brochure outlining activities along the 'Sunshine Route', for instance, advised tourists that it took less than 48 hours for the traveller to be transported from Brisbane to the 'fecund beauty of Tropical Australia, with its jungle and sugar cane plantations', while those who broke their journey at Mackay could visit the 'picturesque Pioneer valley choked with waving acres of sugar cane' (Queensland Government Tourist Bureau, *c.*1950, no pagination). In 1959, a small booklet listed a number of possible tours that could be taken in Queensland. Tour No. 9 covered the Cairns district and advised visitors that they could travel south from Cairns to Innisfail which was 'surrounded by vast sugarcane fields' and it was possible to inspect a sugar mill in operation during the crushing season (Queensland Government Tourist Bureau, 1959: 18). A year later a more comprehensive 264-page book was produced on Queensland's attractions by the Queensland Government Tourist Bureau. It contained an advertisement advising travellers that the state's sugar mills could be visited (see Figure 3.2), the Mackay district was famous for its 'waving sugar cane fields' and mentioned for the first time that the newly constructed bulk sugar terminals at Lucinda and Mourilyan could be inspected by visitors (Queensland Government Tourist Bureau, 1960: 194, 195 and 213–214).

After World War II, non-government organisations also commenced producing publicity material for tourists intending to visit districts along the North Queensland coastline. Again, aspects of sugar production were used to sell particular districts. A visitors' directory published for Cairns in 1949 contained the advice that 'sugar mills in action', were of interest to visitors (Anon., 1949: 10). Twenty years later, another visitors' guidebook for Cairns advised tourists that every week night between June and November there was a coach tour that included a visit to Hambledon Sugar Mill. Nightly 'sugar cane burn offs' were also 'within easy motoring distance by car or taxi'. By 1962, Innisfail's Sugar Festival, the newly erected figure of a canecutter in white marble sculptured in Carrara, Italy, and 'the sweep of sugar lands, with their patchwork of greens and reds' were promoted as attractions for tourists visiting Innisfail (Anon., 1962a: 22 and 31; Hamilton-Wilkes, 1969: 52, 58 and 111). The 'wonders of the sugar industry', 'the largest sugar bulk storage in the World' and the 'Rosewyn' Sugar Farm Tour (see Figure 3.3) were listed as points of interest for the Mackay district in a 1969 tourist guidebook for Queensland (Anon., 1969a: Section 10, pp. 1 and 15). Bundaberg was being promoted as one of only two places in the world where a visitor

SUGAR MILLS MAY BE INSPECTED

Mills like the one illustrated below for processing the sugar cane into raw sugar are dotted at frequent intervals along the eastern coast of Queensland. Tourists who are passing through the cane lands will find a visit of inspection to a mill during the crushing season (in the latter half of the year) quite an interesting experience.

Figure 3.2 An advertisement highlighting that sugar mills could be visited in Queensland
Source: Queensland Government Tourist Bureau (1960) *Guide to Queensland. The Sunshine State of Australia*. Brisbane: Queensland Government Tourist Bureau, p. 260.

could 'see the sugar industry from the first green cane shoot to the sugar in your tea, the syrup on your pancakes, the icing on your cake and the rum in your coffee' and as the world's largest centre for the manufacture of cane harvesting equipment (Anon., c.1960; Bundaberg Chamber of Commerce and Promotion Bureau, 1967).

Promotional material reached a new zenith in the late 1960s when G.K. ('Bob') Bolton, a Cairns-based printer, published an annual magazine for tourists between 1966 and 1972. Titled *The North Queensland Annual*, this non-paginated publication contained numerous glossy photographs, including scenes associated with the production and transport of sugar in North Queensland, and many references to sugar-related tourist activities. In two of the publications, the 'brilliant green of the sugar cane' or 'green lakes of sugar cane' were emphasised as sites to see. Travellers were also urged to watch the 'burning-off of the cane before harvesting' as it was 'a magnificent sight' (*The North Queensland Annual*, 1966, 1967). Visitors to the Innisfail district were advised to view the marble monument to the Italian canecutter

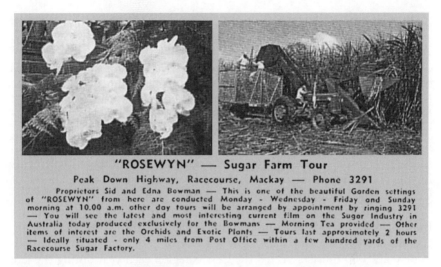

"ROSEWYN" — Sugar Farm Tour

Peak Down Highway, Racecourse, Mackay — Phone 3291

Proprietors Sid and Edna Bowman — This is one of the beautiful Garden settings of "ROSEWYN" from here are conducted Monday - Wednesday - Friday and Sunday morning at 10.00 a.m. other day tours will be arranged by appointment by ringing 3291 — You will see the latest and most interesting current film on the Sugar Industry in Australia today produced exclusively for the Bowmans — Morning Tea provided — Other items of interest are the Orchids and Exotic Plants — Tours last approximately 2 hours — Ideally situated - only 4 miles from Post Office within a few hundred yards of the Racecourse Sugar Factory.

Figure 3.3 A 1969 advertisement for a sugar farm tour in the Mackay district
Source: Anon. (1969a) *ADA: Queensland Tourist Guide: Directory of Accommodation, Resorts, Essential Services and Attractions*. Brisbane: P.McNiven, Section 10, p. 15.

and that guided tours were conducted through the Mourilyan Bulk Sugar Terminal and the local sugar mills. If present around the end of September they could witness the Sugar Festival. Moreover, visitors were informed that they viewed a unique production system, as nowhere else in the world was sugarcane cultivated by 'white' labour (*The North Queensland Annual*, 1968). A large photograph of the Mackay Bulk Sugar Terminal appeared in the 1970 issue of *The North Queensland Annual*. The accompanying text advised intending visitors that this complex was one of the largest bulk sugar storage sheds in the world (in fact today it is the largest bulk sugar storage complex in the world). The final issue of *The North Queensland Annual* in 1972 emphasised that visitors could now see a new sight – mechanical cane harvesters were 'crawling through sugar fields at the sides of most roads'.

Just what sugar industry facilities in Queensland were being visited between 1945 and 1975 is not easy to reconstruct, given the paucity and fragmentary nature of tourism-related information from this period. Brochures for tourists visiting Townsville during the 1960s contain advertisements for regular daily tours from Townsville either to the Ingham or the Lower Burdekin districts, where a visit to a sugar mill was part of the itinerary (see for example Anon., 1960; Anon., 1964; Anon., 1969b). Tourists visiting the Cairns region could avail themselves of tours of Mossman Mill or regular half-day tours to the bulk sugar terminal (after 1964) and evening tours of Hambledon Sugar Mill during the crushing season (see, for example, *Cairns Post*, 30 October 1945: 7; *Townsville Daily Bulletin*, 8 August 1947: 2; *Tropics* 7 (3), March 1972: 6; and *Tropics* 9 (1), January 1974: 3). In the Ingham district, the visit to Victoria Mill was accompanied by a bus tour of the farms so that the tourists could see the cultivation and harvesting of the sugarcane (see, for example, Rotary Club of Ingham, 1948; *Townsville Daily Bulletin*, 4 November 1953: 5). Travellers visiting Bundaberg during the 1960s were able to visit the sugar mills and were also welcome to inspect the manufacture of mechanical cane harvesters at the premises of Toft Brothers Pty Ltd and Massey Ferguson's Cane Equipment division or the building of implements for the cultivation of sugarcane at Bonel Brothers (Bundaberg Chamber of Commerce and Promotion Bureau, 1967: 50).

Numbers availing themselves of these tours are hard to judge, except for the Cairns district where visitation numbers appear to have become substantial. An entry in the *Australian Sugar Yearbook* of 1970 claimed that approximately 200,000 tourists visited the Cairns region each year during the late 1960s, and that 'sugar mills in the area welcome visitors, and thousands of people go through the mills each year' (*Australian Sugar Year Book*, 1963: 211). By the early 1960s, visits to the Proserpine Sugar Mill had also been restricted to a Tuesday, suggesting that visitation had become more regulated, possibly because too many tourists were trying to see the factory (*Australian Sugar Year Book*, 1963: 311). However, at least one visitor to a sugar mill during this period was not impressed with the experience, writing a letter to the *Cairns Post* claiming that the noise of the machinery was so much that it drowned out the voice of their guide and that visitors needed to be supplied with information sheets (*Cairns Post*, 29 August 1947: 7).

As tourism in Queensland became a more important industry, the Australian National Travel Association completed the first comprehensive survey of tourist attractions in North Queensland in 1971 and Central Queensland in 1972. The two surveys identified the sugar-related features visited by tourists. Visitors to the sugar-producing regions, if they so desired, could visit working sugar mills during the crushing season (e.g. Hambledon, Victoria and Proserpine Sugar Mills), the power alcohol plant at Sarina and some of the newly constructed bulk sugar terminals. Tourists could also visit a working sugarcane farm in the Mackay district (i.e. Rosewyn Cane Farm). Interestingly, the Australian National Travel Association suggested that there was considerable scope for the development of sugar-related tourism, particularly in the Herbert River district. The consultant who prepared the report observed that there were several steam locomotives still being used on the extensive network of narrow gauge railways throughout the Herbert River district. It was suggested that 'a ride on a cane train would be a major tourist attraction'. In addition, the consultant recommended that the history of the sugar industry in the Ingham district could be better presented to the tourists through use of some of the interesting relics of the past still present in the local area – a set of canecutters' quarters dating back to when Pacific Islanders were used as field labourers was mentioned as a potential tourist attraction (Australian National Travel Association, 1971: v, 6–7; and 1972: vi, 14–15).

The growing number of tourists visiting North Queensland, particularly during the winter months, undoubtedly influenced the Johnstone Shire Council and a group of Innisfail district canegrowers who decided they needed to 'preserve the heritage of the Australian Sugar Industry' (Australian Sugar Industry Museum, 1977: 5). After raising the necessary funds and gathering display material, they established the Australian Sugar Industry Museum. The initial exhibits, which opened in July 1977, were located at Mourilyan, about 70 minutes' drive south of Cairns, and were housed in the town's former Sugarama Theatre (Anon., 1978: 204). Following receipt of Australian Bicentennial funding, the original complex was expanded in 1988 to include additional display space and a modern theatrette (Anon., 1988a; Anon., 1988c). During the late 1970s and 1980s, tourists visiting the Australian Sugar Museum could see implements used in the cultivation of sugarcane, early mechanical cane harvesters and historical photographs. They were able to purchase small booklets that provided a brief history of the Australian sugar industry and details about the growing and harvesting of sugarcane and the production and bulk handling of sugar in Australia (Australian Sugar Industry Museum, 1977; Australian Sugar Industry Museum, 1985). Its tourism potential, however, was not recognised by the Pacific Area Travel Association Development Authority which concluded in 1981 that the displays needed more explanation about the tools and machinery and that it was 'not worth making a special trip from Cairns for' (Pacific Area Travel Association Development Authority, 1981: V-12).

During the 1980s several new sugar-related tourism ventures were initiated in Queensland. In 1986 the Bundaberg Distilling Company commenced guided tours through the Bundaberg Rum Distillery. Five years later the experience for visitors was enhanced following the transportation of Spring Hill House – the former sugar planter's residence at Spring Hill plantation – to the Bundaberg Rum Distillery site, where it was restored and transformed into a museum and souvenir store, complete with a bar, enabling visitors to taste Bundaberg Rum (Bundaberg Rum, 2011). From 1987 onwards, visitors to North Queensland interested in the farming of sugarcane were able to join Polstone's Sugar Farm tours at Homebush, near Mackay (Cecmar Enterprises, 2009). A display on the sugar industry's heritage in southern Queensland received a boost in 1981 when the Moran family, the new owners of the Beenleigh Rum Distillery, created a small museum containing displays on the history of sugar and rum production in the Beenleigh district (Beenleigh Rum Distillery, 1982; Environmental Protection Agency, 2009). By 1999 this tourism venture had become associated with Rum Runner Tours and included a distillery and museum tour and boat cruise on nearby Moreton Bay. However, the museum had closed by c.2005, and the stills, vats and photographs were transferred to the Beenleigh Historical Village (Trimarchi, 1999: Appendix A; Beenleigh Historical Village, 2011). In 1988 a group of railway enthusiasts at Bundaberg commenced running a steam-powered tourist train over 1 km of narrow gauge track erected through the Bundaberg Botanic Gardens. The locomotives had been acquired from the Bundaberg Sugar Company and restored by the Bundaberg Steam Tramway Preservation Society. This tourist venture was renamed the Australian Sugar Cane Railway in late 2003 (Australian Sugar Cane Railway, 2010).

Elsewhere in Queensland falling international sugar prices and declining profits during the 1980s prompted three sugar milling companies to diversify into tourism-related activities (Griggs, 2011). The first to take advantage of the growing number of visitors was the Mossman Central Mill Company Ltd. The firm built a tourist centre in 1980, complete with the Bally Hooley Steam Express – a refurbished steam locomotive that pulled four brightly painted carriages running on a line from the Mossman Sugar Mill to Port Douglas. Tourists had the choice of a half-day tour to Mossman Sugar Mill or a longer day tour that incorporated a run to the Newell Beach turnoff and return (Kerr, 1995: 162–164). Paying tourists were also welcomed at Tully Mill from the start of the 1986 crushing season. Trevor Fuelling, the technical development officer with the Tully Cooperative Sugar Milling Association Ltd, observed that 'the tourists themselves were valuable as they often departed as ambassadors for sugar and sugar milling itself' (Hudson, 2000: 281). At Gordonvale, the Mulgrave Central Mill Company Ltd developed a tourist venture in 1989. In addition to guided mill tours, visitors could join the Mulgrave Rambler, a narrow gauge steam-powered tourist train that ran several kilometres through the canefields of the Mulgrave River valley (Morton, 1995: 170, 179 and 222). However, a proposal in 1988 by a consortium of Gold Coast businessmen to erect a $14 million theme park, based on sugarcane, next to Condong Sugar Mill in northern New South Wales never eventuated (Anon., 1988b; Briody, 2003: 60).

As a result of these new developments, tourists visiting Queensland during the late 1980s could undertake many different sugar-related activities (see Table 3.1). Cane fire viewing was popular, as cane fires were still frequent in the evening. Indeed a travel guide for Far North Queensland in 1982

Table 3.1 A non-exhaustive listing of sugar-related tourist attractions in eastern Australia in 1988, 1999 and 2010

District	1988	1999	2010
Mossman	Mossman Sugar Mill tour Bally Hooley Steam Train	Bally Hooley Steam Train	Mossman Sugar Mill tour (closed after 2009) Bally Hooley Steam Train
Cairns/Atherton Tableland	Bulk Sugar Terminal tour	Arriga Park Farm Stay Bulk Sugar Terminal tour	Cairns Museum (sugar industry display)
Innisfail	Australian Sugar Museum Marble canecutter monument	Australian Sugar Museum Marble canecutter monument	Australian Sugar Museum The Canecutter Way Marble canecutter monument
Tully	Tully Sugar Mill tour	Tully Sugar Mill tour	Tully Sugar Mill tour
Herbert River	Victoria Sugar Mill tour		
Proserpine		Historical Proserpine Museum (sugar industry display)	Historical Proserpine Museum (sugar industry display)
Mackay/Sarina	Racecourse Sugar Mill tour Polstone Sugar Farm Tours	Farleigh Sugar Mill tour Polstone Sugar Farm Tours	Sarina Sugar Shed Farleigh Sugar Mill tour Polstone Sugar Farm Tours
Rockhampton			Joskeleigh South Sea Islander Museum
Bundaberg-Isis	Australian Sugar Cane Railway South Sea Islander-built stone walls and swimming enclosure Bundaberg Rum Distillery tours Isis Central Sugar Mill tours Bundaberg Bulk Sugar Terminal	Fairymead House Sugar Museum Australian Sugar Cane Railway South Sea Islander-built stone walls and swimming enclosure Isis Central Mill tours Bundaberg Rum Distillery tours	Fairymead House Sugar Museum Australian Sugar Cane Railway South Sea Islander-built stone walls and swimming enclosure Bundaberg Rum Distillery tours

(continued)

Table 3.1 (*Continued*)

District	1988	1999	2010
Maryborough-Hervey Bay	South Sea Islander Memorial and Cemetery, Polson Cemetery	South Sea Islander Memorial and Cemetery, Polson Cemetery	South Sea Islander Memorial and Cemetery, Polson Cemetery
Brisbane-Beenleigh	Sugar mill ruins, St Helena Island Beenleigh Rum Distillery Museum	Sugar mill ruins, St Helena Island Beenleigh Rum Distillery Museum	Sugar mill ruins, St Helena Island 'Commentary in the Canefields' tour Beenleigh Historical Village (Beenleigh Rum distillery display)
Northern New South Wales		Maclean District Historical Society Museum (sugar industry display) Tweed Regional Museum, Murwillumbah (sugar industry display)	Reeves Family Sugar Farm Tour (near Maclean) The Shed Gallery Sugar Industry Museum (near Maclean) Maclean District Historical Society Museum (sugar industry display) Tweed Regional Museum, Murwillumbah (sugar industry display) Sugar Cane Tourist Drive (Tweed River district)

Sources: Based upon the following: Queensland Tourist and Travel Corporation (1988: 9, 19, 21, 23); Trimarchi (1999); and http://www.queenslandholidays.com.au (search using the keyword 'sugar'), accessed 11–12 May 2011.

noted that 'burning of the cane in the late afternoon provides a spectacular attraction for the camera enthusiast' (Anon., 1982: 15).

Tourists travelling by road could stop and see from a distance the operation of mechanical harvesters or the jetty at Lucinda (near Ingham), which, at 5.76 km long, is the longest offshore bulk sugar loading facility anywhere in the world. Travellers had the choice of joining at least five sugar mill tours and they could inspect the interior of the Bundaberg and Mackay Bulk Sugar Terminals (Queensland Tourist and Travel Corporation, 1983:4; Queensland Tourist and Travel Corporation, 1988: 23). Visitors interested in the Australian sugar industry's heritage could view the ruins of the late-19th-century sugar mill that operated on St Helena Island or visit the Australian Sugar Museum and Beenleigh Rum Distillery Museum. Rum drinking travellers could see the production of their tipple at the Bundaberg Rum Distillery from 1986 onwards.

Sugar-related tourism in Queensland was characterised by several changes during the 1990s. The nightly cane fires which had enthralled so many visitors to North Queensland began to be phased out due to the switch to green cane harvesting which relied on no pre-harvest burning of the crops of cane. Visitors were now most likely to only see cane fires in the Lower Burdekin district, where green cane harvesting was least advanced (Griggs, 2011). In the Cairns district, Hambledon Sugar Mill – the focus of so much mill tourism in Far North Queensland before 1975 – closed at the end of the 1991 crushing season. Nevertheless, visitors to Cairns, if they were interested in the production of sugar, could still take guided tours through the Mulgrave Sugar Mill, although the associated Mulgrave Rambler steam train had ceased after 1996 (McKillop, 1997). Alternatively, they could travel north to join a tour through Mossman Sugar Mill, although the Mossman Central Mill Company Ltd decided in 1995 to cease operating the Bally Hooley Steam Express (Kerr, 1995: 164). Other tourists travelling north from Brisbane by road along the coast of Queensland could still join mill tours at Mourilyan, Victoria and Isis Sugar Mills (Anon., 1990a: 7; Rutledge, 1993: 48 and 66).

Several new sugar-related tourism ventures emerged during the 1990s. Travellers could stop over at Girraween Host Farm, near Home Hill. Here visitors were promised 'spectacular cane fires' and tours of either a local sugar mill or the rice mill (Anon., 1990b; Anon., 1995). Visitors to Cairns or the Atherton Tableland could also stay overnight on a sugarcane farm if they selected the Arriga Park Farm Stay, which commenced operations in 1995. The farm stay experience comprised guided tours of the fully operational cane farm and picking and tasting of exotic tropical fruit which was also grown on the property (Trimarchi, 1999). At Bundaberg, the historic Fairymead House – once owned by the pioneering Young family of Fairymead Sugar Plantation – was donated to the Bundaberg City Council by the Bundaberg Sugar

Company. The building was relocated to the Bundaberg City Botanic Gardens, restored and opened in 1994 as a museum dedicated to the region's sugar industry (Anon., 1994). A year later, the Proserpine Historical Museum was opened in temporary premises. The displays included implements, machinery and photographs associated with the district's sugar industry. Eventually this museum moved into a permanent facility in 2001 (Proserpine Historical Museum, 2011).

Some marketing of Queensland destinations during the 1980s and early 1990s continued promoting the presence of a sugar industry. The Burnett Regional Tourism Board, for example, marketed the Bundaberg-Maryborough districts by adopting the slogan 'The Sugar Coast', urging tourists that it was the 'sweetest holiday spot' (Burnett Regional Tourism Board?, 1988: 4). During the 1980s the monthly publication *About Cairns* regularly contained advertisements for the Bally Hooley Steam Express and mentioned that during the crushing season visitors may take a tour throughout Mossman Sugar Mill (see, for example, *About Cairns*, January/February 1986: 40). Early 1980s travel guides for Far North Queensland listed the presence of the canecutter monument at Innisfail, sugar mill tours and mechanical cane harvesters as local attractions (Anon., 1982: 9, 11, 10 and 15; Anon., 1983: 8 and Appendix: Attractions Section). *Up North: The North Queensland Magazine*, which was produced for visitors to North Queensland during the mid-1980s, contained entries promoting Mackay as the unofficial 'Sugar Capital of Australia' (see, for example, *Up North*, 1984: 98). Most of this literature, however, had ceased to use the presence of endless kilometres of canefields and their associated colours as a marketing ploy, unlike the pre-1950 tourist literature. Yet a survey of 300 visitors to Far North Queensland in 1996 found that one aspect they liked about the region was the 'sugar cane fields and scenery' (Brian Sweeney & Associates, 1996: 34).

During the early 2000s, tourists visiting the coastal districts of Queensland and northern New South Wales could continue to visit sugar mills, the Bundaberg Rum Distillery or a sugarcane farm (see Table 3.1). However, the number of sugar mills which could be visited by tourists in 2010 had dwindled to two – Tully and Farleigh (see Figure 3.4). Tourism operators and mill owners had withdrawn from this activity due to rising public liability insurance expenses and concerns about the safety of the visitors. On the other hand, some new sugar-related tourism ventures became available during the 2000s. The Joskeleigh South Sea Islander Museum, 5 km south of Emu Park, near Rockhampton, opened in 2001 (Mullins & Gistitin, 2006: 188–189). The displays celebrate the South Sea Islanders' contribution to Queensland, especially the sugar industry, and their role in developing the sugar plantation at Farnborough, near Rockhampton (Joskeleigh South Sea

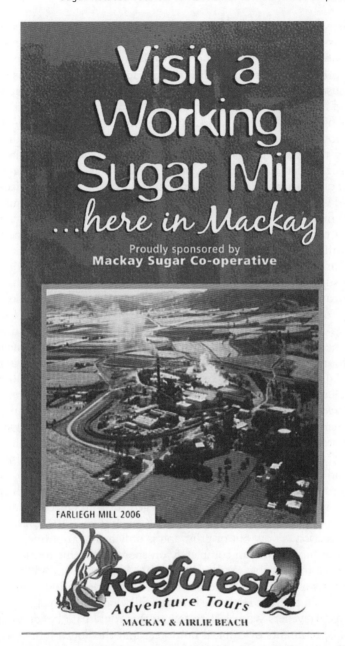

Figure 3.4 A brochure advertising a sugar mill tour in the Mackay district, Australia, 2010
Source: Reproduced with permission of Mr Col Adamson, owner of Reeforest Adventure Tours.

Islander Museum, 2004). Photographs, a range of cane knives and other objects associated with the growing and harvesting of sugarcane form the nucleus of The Shed Gallery at Goodwood Island, near Harwood in northern New South Wales. Opened in 2003, this attraction markets itself as the 'only sugar museum in NSW' (The Shed Gallery, 2011). A different approach is to be found in the Sarina Sugar Shed, which commenced operations in 2006. Consisting of a miniature working sugar mill and distillery, visitors are shown how the 'sugar cane is transformed into the granules we pour into our morning tea' (Sarina Sugar Shed, 2011). The most recent addition to the state's sugar-related tourism is 'Commentary in the Canefields', a day-long bus tour of the sugar-producing district near Beenleigh between Brisbane and the Gold Coast. This venture, which commenced in 2010, is unique in that it caters mainly for groups of senior citizens or social clubs. Participants on this tour through the canefields are shown the location of the Rocky Point Sugar Mill (Australia's only privately owned sugar mill), Cogeneration Plant and Ethanol Plant, and provided with information on the history of the region's sugar industry, the cycle associated with the growing and harvesting of sugarcane and the production of sugar (personal communication, James Herbst, Tour Owner, 27 May 2011; see also Day Away Tours, 2011).

Sugar-related tourism in Australia also expanded in new directions during the 2000s. For the first time visitors were provided with some possible 'drive' tourism trails that incorporated features associated with sugar production in Australia. The earliest to be developed was produced in 2001 as part of the Queensland Heritage Trails Network. The publication *Heritage Trails of the Tropical North* was a detailed and informative guide that contained maps and numerous historical photographs. Some of most significant sugar-related places listed included the following: Mossman Sugar Mill, which retained many interesting buildings such as the original 19th-century administration office and laboratory, workers' barracks, staff houses and steam locomotive and steam shed; the historic Cairns based White's Sugar Shed, which is the only surviving shed for the storage of bagged sugar in Queensland; and the Italian canecutters' memorial at Innisfail (Cohen *et al.*, 2001). Unfortunately this publication is now out of print and is only available online, but as neither of the trails is shown completely on the website this tourism product has become inaccessible (Wills, 2010: 171). A more recent addition to the 'drive' tourism trail is the Canecutter Way. Developed in 2005, this trail follows the original Bruce Highway between Silkwood and Innisfail, just south of Cairns. Travellers who elect to follow this route pass beside undulating canefields, remnants of tropical rainforest and the South Johnstone Sugar Mill (The Canecutter Way, 2011). However, as heritage and museum professional Joanna Wills notes, the trail, although scenic, falls short of 'providing any real historical information or context' and 'represents a missed opportunity as a vehicle to effectively remember the sugar history of the district' (Wills, 2010: 170–171). Moreover, the Australian Sugar Museum at Mourilyan is not even listed as a feature on the trail. Further south, tourists in northern New South Wales can follow the Sugar Cane Tourist Drive, which commences in Murwillumbah and winds along the Tweed River through the canefields past the 120-year-old Condong Sugar Mill, although they are not provided with much information on the significance of the sites or the history of the district (Sugar Cane Tourist Drive, 2011).

Sightseers visiting the sugar-producing districts of eastern Australia today can purchase a variety of sugar-related souvenirs or memorabilia. Postcards, teaspoons and tea towels showing sugar mills, cane fires or mechanical harvesters are available. Far North Plantations, a small company based in Cairns, sells 150-gram bottles of raw sugar that are often packaged together with Daintree Tea, which comes from a small tea plantation in Far North Queensland. However, this product is only sold as far south as Innisfail (personal communication, Ms Julie McGregor, owner Far North Plantations, 23 May 2011). Visitors to the Australian Sugar Museum can also obtain copies of its publications (Neville, 1999; Berry, M., 2000), while a small book that details the architectural character and usage of cane barracks from the 1890s to the present can be purchased at a variety of outlets in North Queensland (see Navarre, 2007). Tourists who like kitsch or the bizarre can even acquire cane toad products (e.g. stuffed toads, toad purses, toad novelty key rings) as a reminder of these ugly alien invaders which were brought to Queensland in 1935 in an attempt to control the crop depredations of the cane beetles and cane grubs. These amphibians may have been seen at night by the tourists on their journeys throughout North Queensland.

Conclusions and Recommendations

Currently, international and domestic visitors to Queensland who may be interested in sugar and its production are presented with major challenges when trying to find information about possible attractions. A search of the website 'Queensland Holidays – Queensland Tourism and Travel' using the keyword 'sugar' or 'sugar industry' does reveal some of the attractions listed in Table 3.1. However, attractions such as the ruins of the 19th-century sugar mill on St Helena Island and the Joskeleigh South Sea Islander Museum are not listed on that website. In addition, the stone walls and sheltered swimming area built by the indentured South Sea Islander workers in the Bundaberg district are not picked up by searching using the word 'sugar' or 'sugar industry'.

Instead, the search term 'kanaka' has to be used. Accessing information about sugar industry attractions in northern New South Wales is also a difficult task. A search of Tourism New South Wales' website using the keywords 'sugar' or 'sugar industry' does produce some links to the Tweed district or Maclean, but the tourist attractions in these areas related to sugar production are not obvious or well highlighted. Tourists achieve better results searching the websites for particular sugar-producing regions in northern New South Wales (see, for example, http://www. tweedtourism.com.au). However, international visitors may not be familiar with the geographical names for these regions. It is reasonable to assume that many international and domestic visitors to Queensland and northern New South Wales discover attractions about the sugar industry from road signage or the local visitor information centres.

Aspects of Australia's sugar industry are also not well presented to tourists. None of the state's bulk sugar terminals provide tourists with organised tours through their facilities, although a persistent visitor may be able to arrange an ad hoc tour if staff are available for such a task. The substantial contribution made by southern Europeans, especially Italians, Greeks and Yugoslavs, and German immigrants to the pre-1950 development of the Australian sugar industry is not highlighted, even in the Ingham district, which was the centre of the immigrant Italian community in North Queensland. Decaying canecutters' barracks are still visible throughout the sugar-producing districts, but the significance of these structures and their potential as tourist attractions have been really overlooked. Moreover, according to Joanna Wills, the outputs and prominence of the then Australian Sugar Museum, the premier organisation for presenting the industry's heritage, had diminished during the 2000s. In her opinion (and it is a view shared by this author), the museum fell short of conveying the 'drama, heritage and innovations of the sugar industry'. Its inability to remain viable and to creatively explore the substantial legacy of the sugar industry in Far North Queensland in a material culture context is a 'major failing' (Wills, 2010: 172). However, very recently the Australian Sugar Museum has been re-named the Australian Sugar Heritage Centre, and the new manager has embarked upon an upgrade of the displays, including the development of a new interactive display which will focus on how sugarcane is grown and how crystal sugar is formed (personal communication, Wayne Thomas, Australian Sugar Heritage Centre, 4 October 2011; see also http:www.sugarmsuem.com.au).

Clearly, better marketing of the range of sugar-related tourist activities in Queensland is needed. The Australian Sugar Museum's idea in 1999 of a sugar trail needs to be revived and updated (Trimarchi, 1999). Details about the trail could be published on a website dedicated to sugar-related tourism in Australia or as a brochure distributed to each of the regional tourist and visitor information centres located in most centres in northern New South Wales and along the coast of Queensland. Instead of just one sugar trail it may be possible to design several trails that focus on different aspects of the Australian sugar industry. A dedicated South Sea Islander trail, for example, could be developed to highlight the contribution of indentured labour to the industry's history and incorporate attractions such as the Joskeleigh South Sea Islander Museum, the South Sea Islander Memorial and Cemetery at Hervey Bay and the display of historical photographs of South Sea Islander workers that make up the *Refined White* exhibition at the Australian Sugar Museum. Another trail could centre on the architecture of the Australian sugar industry, highlighting either Spring Hill House or Fairymead House (examples of a Queensland sugar planter's residence), cane barracks and some of the historic administration buildings at the state's sugar mills (e.g. 19th-century office building at Mossman Mill). Railway enthusiasts could be catered for by the development of a sugar transport trail that would include the Australian Sugar Cane Railway at Bundaberg, the transport display at the Australian Sugar Museum and the Bally Hooley Steam Train at Port Douglas.

Therefore, current destination management organisations in Queensland and northern New South Wales (e.g. Queensland Tourist and Travel Corporation) need to be made more aware that sugar has been and can be used as an instrument for tourism development. Moreover, culinary and heritage tourism are growing fields, and some international visitors may be interested in experiencing Australia's historical and contemporary sugar-related attractions. Individual operators of sugar-related attractions can be involved in promoting the development of sugar tourism in Australia, but the different Australian sugar industry organisations need to be more engaged in this process. Currently, several organisations are associated with the production of sugar in Australia. The Australian Sugar Milling Council represents Australian raw sugar mill owners, two associations represent the interest of Australian cane-growers – the Australian Cane Farmers Association and CANEGROWERS – and Queensland Sugar Limited is responsible for marketing much of Queensland's raw sugar. In New South Wales, the New South Wales Sugar Milling Association, a canegrowers' cooperative, is responsible for the production, refining and marketing of sugar in that state. Yet only CANEGROWERS is actively involved in supporting sugar tourism through its association with the Australian Sugar Heritage Center. Since deregulation of the Australian sugar industry, no individual organisation speaks for the entire industry, perhaps to the detriment of sugar-related tourism in Australia.

Finally, sugar-related tourism in Australia has a long history, dating back to at least the 1900s. Its heyday was probably between 1910 and 1980, when the presence of canefields, sugar mills and bulk sugar terminals were actively promoted in the tourist literature as tourist attractions. Since the 1970s, sugar-related attractions have been less prominent in the promotion of coastal Queensland and northern New South Wales as tourist destinations. Nevertheless, sugar-related tourism was maintained and expanded during the 1980s and 1990s and is still occurring today in Queensland and northern New South Wales. Yet a 'sweeter' outcome may have been achieved through better marketing of the current sugar attractions and greater support from the different Australian sugar industry organisations. Surely, the sights, sounds, smells and tastes associated with one of the world's most significant sugar industries with a rich heritage deserves to be presented in an informative and engaging way to the substantial numbers of international and domestic visitors who each year happen to find themselves in one or more of Australia's sugar-producing regions.

References

About Cairns. Monthly Magazine for Visitors, 1980–1987 (set located at the City Library, Cairns Regional Council).

Anon. (1910) *Railway Tours on the North Coast Line: Brisbane to Gympie*. Brisbane: Queensland Government Printer.

Anon. (c.1923) *Cairns, Centre of Australia's Sugar Industry* [Documentary Film No. 34021]. Canberra, Australia: National Film & Sound Archive.

Anon. (c.1925) *Mackay: The Sugaropolis of Queensland*. Brisbane: Queensland Government Printer.

Anon. (1937) *Illustrated Souvenir of the City and District of Mackay, the Sugaropolis of Australia, 1862–1937*. Mackay: Daily Mercury.

Anon. (1938) *Cairns: A Guide and Handbook for the Use of Tourists, Residents and Businessmen*. Cairns: E.P. Holmes.

Anon. (1949) *Cairns, Innisfail and Atherton Tableland: Visitors Directory 1949*. Cairns: Cairns Visitors' Publishing Company.

Anon. (1960) *Tours from Townsville* [Folded brochure, Box 3, Tourism – Townsville and region, Ephemera material]. Brisbane: State Library of Queensland.

Anon. (c.1960) *Bundaberg. City of Charm* [Folded brochure, Box 3, Tourism – Wide Bay Burnett and the Coral Coast region, Ephemera material]. Brisbane: State Library of Queensland.

Anon. (1962a) *Innisfail and District, North Queensland, Australia*. Brisbane: Innisfail District Brochure Management Committee.

Anon. (1962b) *Mackay and District on the Threshold of its Second Century*. Brisbane: Olive Ashworth Publicity Services.

Anon. (1964) *Townsville and District Tours* [Folded brochure, Box 1, Tourism – Townsville and region, Ephemera material]. Brisbane: State Library of Queensland.

Anon. (1969a) *ADA: Queensland Tourist Guide: Directory of Accommodation, Resorts, Essential Services and Attractions*. Brisbane: P.McNiven.

Anon. (1969b) *Tours from Townsville* [Folded brochure, Box 1, Tourism – Townsville and region, Ephemera material]. Brisbane: State Library of Queensland.

Anon. (1978) Sugar industry museum opened. *Australian Sugar Yearbook* 37, 204.

Anon. (1982) *Far North Queensland: Holidays and Travel.* Cairns: Combined North Queensland Councils and the Cairns Port Authority.

Anon. (1983) *Destination Cairns: Gateway to the Great Barrier Reef and Tropical Far North Queensland: Travel Agents Manual.* Cairns: Far North Queensland Promotion Ltd.

Anon. (1988a) Museum will preserve sugar's rich history. *Australian Canegrower,* January, 22–23.

Anon. (1988b) Tourism move at Condong Mill. *Australian Canegrower,* January, 14.

Anon. (1988c) Museum pays tribute to a great industry. *Australian Canegrower,* June, 26–27.

Anon. (1990a) *Bundaberg and the Coral Isles. Tourist Guide* [55 pp. booklet, Box 1, Tourism-Wide Bay Burnett and the Coral Coast, Ephemera material]. Brisbane: State Library of Queensland.

Anon. (1990b) *Townsville and the Magnetic North 1990 Fact Finder* [30 pp. booklet, Box 3, Tourism – Townsville and region, Ephemera material]. Brisbane: State Library of Queensland.

Anon. (1994) Sugar museum. *Courier Mail* (Brisbane), 19 July, 26.

Anon. (1995) *Bountiful Burdekin Guide 1994–1995* [58 pp. booklet, Box 1, Tourism – Townsville and region, Ephemera material]. Brisbane: State Library of Queensland.

Australian Bureau of Agricultural and Resource Economics (2008) *Financial Performance of Australian Sugar Cane Producers 2005–06 to 2007–08,* accessed 29 May 2011. http://www.abare.gov.au/interactive/08_ResearchReports/SugarGrowers.

Australian National Travel Association (1971) *Travel Industry Appraisal and Recommendations: North Queensland Region.* Sydney: Australian National Travel Association¿

Australian National Travel Association (1972) *Travel Industry Appraisal and Recommendations: Central Queensland Region.* Sydney: Australian National Travel Association¿

Australian Sugar Cane Railway, Bundaberg (2010) Accessed 26 May 2011. http://qldrailheritage.com.ascr/aboutus.html.

Australian Sugarcane Annual (2009) Toowoomba: Greenmount Press.

Australian Sugar Industry Museum (1977) *The Australian Sugar Industry: The Heritage of the Industry.* Cairns¿: Australian Sugar Industry Museum.

Australian Sugar Industry Museum (1985) *The Australian Sugar Industry: The Heritage of the Industry.* Cairns¿: Australian Sugar Industry Museum.

Australian Sugar Year Book (1963) Brisbane: The Strand Press Pty Ltd.

Barr, T. (1990) *No Swank Here¿ The Development of the Whitsundays as a Tourist Destination to the Early 1970s.* Townsville: Department of History and Politics in conjunction with the Department of Tourism, James Cook University.

Beenleigh Historical Village (2011) Accessed 19 May 2011. http://www.beenleighhistoricalvillage.org.au.

Beenleigh Rum Distillery (1982) Take a tour through the good old days: Beenleigh Rum Distillery, a fascinating taste of Queensland history [Brochure]. State Library of Queensland.

Berry, E.N. (2000) An application of Butler's (1980) tourist area life cycle theory to the Cairns region, Australia, 1876–1998. PhD dissertation, James Cook University, Cairns Campus.

Berry, M. (2000) *Refined White: The Story of How South Sea Islanders Came to Cut Sugar in Queensland and Make History Refining the White Australia Policy.* Innisfail: Australian Sugar Industry Museum.

Brian Sweeney & Associates (1996) *Brand FNQ Master Report. The Branding of Far North Queensland.* Cairns: Far North Queensland Promotion Bureau.

Briody, P. (2003) *Sunshine Sugar. Secrets of Success. The History of the New South Wales Sugar Milling Cooperative Limited*. Broadwater, New South Wales: New South Wales Sugar Milling Cooperative Limited.

Bundaberg Chamber of Commerce and Promotion Bureau (1967) *Bundaberg. City of Charm* [53 pp. booklet, Box 3, Tourism-Wide Bay Burnett and the Coral Coast, Ephemera material]. Brisbane: State Library of Queensland.

Bundaberg Rum (2011) Distillery tours, accessed 31 May 2011. http://www.bundabergrum.com.au/distillery.html.

Burnett Regional Tourism Board? (1988) *Sugar Coast/Burnett & Bundaberg Country*. Brisbane: Queensland Tourist Publications Pty.

Cecmar Enterprises (2009) Polstone Farm Tours, accessed 19 May 2011. http://www.cecmarenterprises.com/polstone.html.

Christensen, C.B. (1937) *Queensland Journey*. Brisbane: P.A. Meehan Publicity Service.

Cinema Branch (c.1926) *Sugar Industry in Cairns and a Trip to the Great Barrier Reef* [Documentary Film No. 11604]. Canberra, Australia: National Film & Sound Archive.

Cohen, K., Cook, M. and Pearce, H. (2001) *Heritage Trails of the Tropical North: A Heritage Tour Guide to Far North Queensland*. Brisbane: Queensland Environmental Protection Agency.

Cridland, S. (2008) An analysis of the winter movement of grey nomads to Northern Australia: planning for increased senior visitation. PhD dissertation, James Cook University, Cairns Campus.

Davidson, J. and Spearitt, P. (2000) *Holiday Business. Tourism in Australia since 1870*. Melbourne: Melbourne University Press.

Day Away Tours (2011) Accessed 27 May 2011. http://www.daywaytours.biz.

Environmental Protection Agency (2009) Beenleigh Rum Distillery, accessed 19 May 2011. http://www.epa.qld.gov.au/chims/placeDetail.html.

Gregory, H. (1991) *Making Maroochy. A History of the Land, the People and the Shire*. Nambour: Boolarong Publications with Maroochy Shire Council.

Griggs, P.D. (2011) *Global Industry, Local Innovation: The History of Cane Sugar Production in Australia, 1820–1995*. Berne: Peter Lang AG.

Hamilton-Wilkes, M. (1969) *What to See Round Cairns*. Sydney: Angus and Robertson.

Hudson, A. (2000) *By the Banyan. Tully Sugar, the First 75 Years*. Brisbane: Christopher Beck Books.

Joskeleigh South Sea Islander Museum (2004) Accessed 26 May 2011. http://qldrailheritage.com/cq/josk.htm.

Kennedy, V. (1933) *Cairns North Queensland Guide Book. Winter Tours*. Cairns: Cairns and Tablelands Publicity Association.

Kerr, J. (1995) *Northern Outpost*. Mossman: Mossman Central Mill Company Limited.

McKillop, B. (1997) Mulgrave Rambler narrow gauge tourist train, accessed 11 May 2011. http://www.railpage.org.au/ausrail/97july/0106.html.

Morton, C. (1995) *By Strong Arms*. Gordonvale: Mulgrave Central Mill Company limited.

Mulgrave Central Mill Co. Ltd (1940) *Notes for Visitors: On Growing and Harvesting Cane and Milling Process: As Seen on a Visit to the Mill*. Cairns?: Mulgrave Central Mill Co. Ltd.

Mullins, S. and Gistitin, C. (2006) 'Mere colloquial things'. South Sea Islanders and the memory of place. In S. Mullins, M. Danaher and B. Webster (eds) *Community, Environment and History. Keppel Bay Case Studies* (PP. 173–192). Rockhampton: Central Queensland University Press.

Navarre, E. (2007) *The Cane Barracks Story: Sugar Cane Pioneers and their Epic Feats*. Cairns: The Author.

Neville, D. (1999) *Sweet Talking: A Collection of Oral Histories from the Australian Sugar Industry*. Innisfail: Australian Sugar industry Museum.

Nixon, A. (1941) *Travel in the Tropics*. Sydney: R. Dey, Printer.

Osborne, P. (2010) Rivers and resorts: how rivers and sheltered waters influenced the location of the Sunshine Coast's resort towns. In *Journeys through Queensland History: Landscape, Place and Society*. Proceedings of the Professional Historians Association (Queensland) Conference (pp. 43–55). Brisbane: Professional Historians Association (Queensland).

Pacific Area Travel Association Development Authority (1981) *Cairns: A Review of Increased International Tourism Potential*. San Francisco: Pacific Area Travel Association Development Authority.

Proserpine Historical Museum (2011) Accessed 11 May 2011. http://www.queenslandholidays.com.au/.../proserpine-historical-museum.

Queensland Department of Lands and Queensland Department of Agriculture and Stock (1905) *Queensland: The Queen State of the Commonwealth: The Winter Paradise of Australia*. Brisbane: Howard Smith Co.

Queensland Government Intelligence and Tourist Bureau (1924) *Townsville and Ayr Districts, North Queensland: Rich Agricultural and Pastoral Areas, Picturesque Tourist Resorts*. Brisbane: Queensland Government Intelligence and Tourist Bureau.

Queensland Government Intelligence and Tourist Bureau (1927) *Mountain and Seaside Resorts of Southern Queensland: From Noosa to the Tweed*. Brisbane: Queensland Government Intelligence and Tourist Bureau.

Queensland Government Tourist Bureau (*c*.1935) *Cairns and Hinterland: North Queensland*. Brisbane: Queensland Government Intelligence and Tourist Bureau.

Queensland Government Tourist Bureau (*c*.1950) *The Sunshine Route. Along the Coast to Cairns* [Folded brochure]. Brisbane: Queensland Government Tourist Bureau.

Queensland Government Tourist Bureau (1959) *Inclusive Tours in Queensland, the Sunshine State*. Brisbane: Queensland Government Tourist Bureau.

Queensland Government Tourist Bureau (1960) *Guide to Queensland. The Sunshine State of Australia*. Brisbane: Queensland Government Tourist Bureau.

Queensland Holidays (2011) Accessed 31 May 2011. http://www.queenslandholidays.com.au.

Queensland Office of Economic and Statistical Research (2010) International tourism, accessed 18 May 2010. http://www.oesr.qld.gov.au/products/tables/international-tourism-visitors-no/index.

Queensland Railways (*c*.1913) *Tours in the Mackay District*. Brisbane: Queensland Railways.

Queensland Tourist and Travel Corporation (1983) *Mackay Whitsunday*. Brisbane: Queensland Tourist and Travel Corporation in association with the Mackay/Whitsunday Tourism Council.

Queensland Tourist and Travel Corporation (1988) *Sugar Coast/Burnett and Bundaberg Country*. Brisbane: Queensland Tourist Publications Pty Ltd.

Queensland Tourist and Travel Corporation and the Boeing Commercial Airplane Company (1981) *Tourism Potential in Queensland*. Seattle: Boeing Commercial Airplane Company.

Queensland Tourist Bureau (1936) *The Sunshine Route. Through Queensland to Cairns*. Brisbane: Queensland Railways Commissioner.

Richardson, J.I. (1999) *A History of Australian Travel and Tourism*. Melbourne: Hospitality Press.

Robinson, G. (1995) Deregulation and restructuring in the Australian sugar industry. *Australian Geographical Studies* 33 (2), 212–227.

Rotary Club of Ingham (1948) *Invitation to Ingham and the Herbert River Valley.* Ingham: Rotary Club of Ingham.

Russell, R. (1995) Tourism development in Coolangatta: an historical perspective. Unpublished B. Business (Hons) thesis, Griffith University.

Rutledge, L. (1993) *The motoring holiday to North Queensland, Australia: from Bowen to Cape York and west to the Undara lava tubes and Charters Towers.* Brisbane: Queensland Tourist and Travel Corporation and the Royal Automobile Club of Queensland.

Sarina Sugar Shed (2011) Accessed 18 May 2011. http://www.sarinasugarshed.com.au.

Stephens, W. (1936) *Bountiful Queensland.* Bendigo: Cambridge Press.

Stimson, R., Jenkins, O., Roberts, B. and Daly, M. (1998) The impact of Daikyo as a foreign investor on Cairns-Far North Queensland regional economy. *Environment and Planning A* 30, 161–179.

Sugar Cane Tourist Drive (2011) Accessed 18 May 2011. http://www.tweedtourism.com.au/accom_result1/sugar-cane-tourist-drive.

Tablelands Publicity Association (1932) *Special Land and Sea Tours.* Cairns: Cairns and Tabelands Publicity Association.

The Canecutter Way. Accessed 11 May 2011. http://www.canecutterway.com.au/index.html.

The North Queensland Annual, 1966 to 1972 (set located at the State Library of Queensland, Brisbane).

The Shed Gallery (2011) Accessed 18 May 2011. http://www.clarencetourism.com/what-to-see-do/goodwood-island/the-shed-gallery/p/1033.

Trimarchi, N. (1999) *The Sugar Trail: From North Queensland to Northern NSW: Development and Marketing Study: A Report to the Australian Sugar Industry Museum.* Brisbane?: Rainwater Productions.

Tropics: Far North Queensland, 1972–1975 (monthly magazine devoted to travel in North Queensland, State Library of Queensland).

Up North: The North Queensland Magazine, 1983–1986 (set located as part of the North Queensland Collection, James Cook University).

Wills, J. (2010) Remembering the cane: Conserving the sugar legacy of far north Queensland. In *Journeys through Queensland History: Landscape, Place and Society.* Proceedings of the Professional Historians Association (Queensland) Conference (pp. 165–182). Brisbane: Professional Historians Association (Queensland).

4 Brazil's Sugar Heritage and Tourism – From Engenhos to Cachaça

Angela Cabral Flecha and Linda Joyce Forristal

Introduction

This chapter reviews the history of sugar in Brazil as a background to exploring its sugar heritage relative to tourism. Brazil's sugar heritage is expressed in terms of its material tangible culture in the form of *engenhos* (rustic sugar mills) and great houses open to visitors, but also in terms of the intangible culture of its rich food-ways in the form of cachaça, or the 'brandy' of the sugarcane, tasted and experienced by visitors at production sites and restaurants. Additionally, this chapter introduces the development of touristic routes related to sugar heritage, such as in the province of Pernambuco where visitors can experience the 'Roteiros dos Engenhos de Açúcar' and in Rio de Janeiro and neighboring Minas Gerais, where tourists can experience the 'Cachaça Tour: The Five Senses of Cachaça'. Preparing this chapter we used both historical and contemporary sources on the history and production of sugar in Brazil. In the process of investigating the sugar-related tourism products, we interviewed key tourism stakeholders in the sugar-related tourism sectors.

Before the Portuguese occupied Brazil in the New World and started sugar production there, they produced sugar on the colonized islands of Madeira, in the Mediterranean, the Azores and São Tomé in the Gulf of Guinea off the western equatorial coast of Central Africa. In the late 1400s and early 1500s, the 'large quantity of sugar in Madeira was sufficient to influence the course of European trade' (Deerr, 1949: 100). When the Portuguese brought sugarcane to Brazil from the island of Madeira in 1502 it was the first step in influencing the course of the global sugar trade.

In the year 1500, Portuguese navigator Pedro Álvares Cabral landed at Porto Seguro (in modern-day Bahia) on Good Friday and 'took possession of Brazil for the Portuguese Crown on Easter Monday' (Deerr, 1949: 102). Because of their prior production of sugar on Madeira and São Tomé, the Portuguese readily saw tropical Brazil's potential to continue and expand their sugar production in the New World. Although the exact date of when sugarcane reached Brazil is not documented, in 1526 there was a definite record that Brazilian sugar imports were paying duties at the Lisbon Custom House (Deerr, 1949: 102), which also mentions factories on the Iguarassu River and in the state of Pernambuco as early as 1520.

However, the establishment of sugarcane production in Brazil is usually credited to Martin Affonso de Sousa, a distinguished navigator, who when exploring the coast of Brazil in 1531 discovered the harbour of Rio de Janeiro and was granted the captaincy (bequeathed land and rule) of São Vicente, the first Portuguese permanent settlement in the Americas, now located in the state of São Paulo along Brazil's southeast coast south of Rio de Janerio. A year later, de Sousa brought sugarcane to Brazil from Madeira and built a factory at São Vicente. The sugar mill at São Vicente was originally called *Engenhos do Senhor Governador.* After being purchased by two Germans, Erasmus Esquert and Julius Visnats, the name was changed to *Engenho de São Jorge dos Erasmos,* or the Mill of St George.

From São Vicente sugarcane spread to other parts of Brazil, especially along the north-eastern coast in two major producing areas, the Zona da Mata in Pernambuco, once a forest zone between the coastal plain and inland scrub, and the Recôncavo in Bahia, an extensive fertile basin surrounding the Bahia de Todos os Santos (All Saint's Bay). The Portuguese built the city of Salvador on a high bluff at the bay's northern entrance. Surrounding areas were settled and developed for sugar production due to the excellent soil and perfect climate.

After serving in the Portuguese East Indies, Duarte Coelho was granted the captaincy of Pernambuco, the area along the Brazilian coast between the Sao Francisco and Iguarassu rivers, where he founded the city of Olinda in 1537. Although Olinda and neighboring Recife are now known for their beautiful architecture and arts, the cities owe their rapid rise and notoriety to the cultivation of sugarcane in the region of Pernambuco. One of the first sugar mills in Pernambuco belonged to Coelho's brother-in-law Jeronimo de Albuquerque and was named *Nossa Senhora d'Ajuda* and later *Velho or Forno de Cal.*

The captaincy of Bahia was granted to Francisco Pereira Coutinho, who arrived in Brazil in 1536 (Pires & Gomes, 1994: 184). Before Coutinho's arrival,

Portuguese and Spanish settlers worked out a harmonious relationship with the Tupinnambá natives of the area. Taking advantage of this situation, Coutinho's colonists quickly spread throughout the Recôncavo (Pires & Gomes, 1994: 184), and devoted themselves to building sugar mills and growing other crops. From 1549 to 1763, the city of Salvador in Bahia was Brazil's first capital and as such witnessed the blending of European, African and Amerindian cultures. From 1558, Salvador in Bahia was also the site of the first slave market in the New World, the epicenter of slaves arriving to work on the sugar plantations (UNESCO, 2011). Some of the largest and earliest mills in Bahia belonged to Catholic religious orders, including the Benedictines, Jesuits and Carmelites (Schwartz, 1985, 1988). *Engenho Sergipe* is a good example.

The sugarcane the Portuguese brought from Madeira was *Saccharum officinarum*, a species recognized as noble cane or tropical cane, which is characterized by its high sugar content, large thick stalks and little fiber content. Because of these characteristics, *S. officinarum* was probably the only variety grown during the first three centuries of colonization. In the 19th century, this sugarcane was renamed 'Creoula', 'Mirim' or 'land of Cana', to distinguish it from varieties which began arriving in South America in the 19th century (Lima, 1984), such as 'Caiana', a corruption of Cayenne, which was first imported and successfully cultivated in French Guinea. Nunes (1987) reports that being more productive and richer in sucrose, Caiana began to replace Creoula from the year 1810. The 'Cayenne' cycle lasted until the year 1880 when this variety was subjected to a severe insect attack in the main sugarcane regions of the country.

Brazilian sugar production has had many ups and downs over the past five centuries, including:

- a period of Dutch occupation in the north that commenced in 1624;
- the Brazilian gold rush in Minas Gerias beginning in 1675 promulgated a southern migration of slaves from northern sugar plantations (Deerr, 1949: 110);
- the rise of the Rio de Janeiro lowland mills in the late 1700s and early 1800s, threats to Portuguese domination of the sugar trade when Britain acquired the Caribbean islands of Barbados, Jamaica and other 'sugar islands' (Mintz, 1985: 61);
- Napolean's push for the refinement of beet sugar in the mid-19th century;
- the advent of *central mills* in the 1870s to which sugarcane from surrounding farms was collected;
- the end of the first 'sugar cycle' in Brazil with the abolition of slavery in 1888 directly contributed to the industrialization of sugar production and the eventual appearance of *usinas*, sugar factories.

After five centuries, Brazil is now the largest sugar producer in the world, shipping sugar around the globe from Santos port in São Paulo, the largest port in the Americas. Sugarcane production here is dominated by the state of São Paulo in the south-east, but is mostly inland from coastal São Vicente, accounting for 60% of production; the north-east accounts for less than 20% of production with the states of Pernambuco and Alagoas dominating (Bolling & Suarez, 2001). The cultural heritage related to Brazil's rich sugar history is visible in the many engenhos, or rustic sugar mills, dotting the landscape where sugar was historically produced, and in Brazilian food-ways that incorporate sugar.

The Engenhos or Rustic Sugar Mills

It is not an exaggeration to say that sugar shaped Brazilian history and culture, starting with the social structure surrounding and supporting the sugar plantations and mills. The ancient sugar mills of Brazil are called 'engenhos', which denotes 'engine' or 'ingenuity'.

> Whoever called the mills where sugar is made 'engenhos', truly chose the name well. For whomsoever see them and consider them with the reflection they merit, is obliged to confess that they are one of the principal conceptions and birth-given inventions of human ingenuity, which, being a small portion of the Divine, reveals itself always admirable in the way of its working... A title to which so many aspire is that of 'senhor de engenho' because it implies to be served, obeyed and respected by many. (Antonil, 1711; Pires & Gomez, 1994: 9, 182)

The highest rank in the complex sugar plantation society was the lord of the mill or 'Senhor de Engenho'. Most often he had been granted a captaincy by the Portuguese government as a reward for previous service. The owner and his family enjoyed remarkable social status, often living in luxury, surrounded with the best available furnishings. In addition to the sugar mill, the plantation complex was usually composed of a big house or greathouse for the family, a chapel, slave quarters, and fields (Figure 4.1).

The 'Senhor de Engenho' and his family lived in the big house, where he fulfilled his role as mill patriarch. As revealed by this layout, a key factor in the societal web of Brazilian sugar production, just as it would be in the Caribbean, was black African slave labor. The slaves lived in slave quarters, and even though they were the 'hands and feet of the mill lord' (Antonil, 1711) and an irreplaceable element in the social structure of the engenhos,

Figure 4.1 Frans Post painting of a Brazilian sugar mill in 1650s Pernambuco
Source: Post *et al.* (2005). Reprinted with permission John Carter Brown Library, Brown University.

they were often treated like animals and exposed to the most heinous and violent punishments. The chapel was a sacred place for religious services and the social center of the plantation. To the mistress of the plantation fell the task of managing the home and overseeing the domestic slaves.

In Brazil, the mill owner was rarely also the planter. Rather, the mill owner hired a foreman who supervised the slaves working the fields and the mill, doling out privileges and punishments. Other free workers also worked in the mill, including swains men, masons, carters (ox-cart drivers), cowboys, fishermen and farmers who, besides taking care of the cultivation of sugarcane, also planted and tended plots of maize, cassava or beans, ensuring food for the big house, slave quarters and free employees.

In America the Portuguese usually adopted the method of sugar production that had been introduced by the Moors during their occupation of Spain and Portugal, with the water mill. The water mill captured the energy in the flow of a stream or river to turn the huge wooden wheel to power the sugar mill to grind sugarcane (Freyre, 2006). There were also ox-driven mills, which produced about half the capacity of water-driven ones (Deerr, 1949: 108).

The horizontal and spatial layout of the rural engenhos was probably due to plentiful land. In Salvador, Rio de Janeiro, Sao Paulo and Ouro Preto, the houses varied between one and two floors, some reaching three stories in Rio de Janeiro, rarely four or five. However, the port cities of Recife in Pernambuco and Salvador in Bahia were home to the commissioners of sugar, the lords of the trade. Their grand houses spread out vertically and reached five or six floors, and some of these are considered to be the highest expressions of sugar heritage in Brazil. There was a lookout or crown on top of the sixth floor from which one could view the blue sea, green foliage and fresh air (Freyre, 2003: 311).

Many of these grand sugar estates and houses began to crumble from neglect and lack of conservation when sugar production was industrialized. However, many remaining structures have been renovated into tourism attractions, especially churches and chapels that often out survived the big houses (Freyre, 2006).

Sugar Mill Tourism in Pernambuco

Marked by a long tradition of the sugar mills and their manifestations of popular culture, the Zona da Mata in Pernambuco is boosting the economy of the north-northeast region by promoting tourism for sustainable development. The sugar plantations still dominate the landscape, filling the green plains and mountains with the large houses that remain. Until the middle of the 1900s, sugar accounted for 60% of Pernambuco's exports, but by the year 2000 that number had dropped to 26%. The advent of bio-ethanol as an alternative fuel favors the small mills and sugarcane farmers, but the attempt to attract visitors, through ecological, historical, cultural and religious tours, is the objective of the state government, with the launch of 'Roteiros dos Engenhos de Açúcar', a tourist route which includes 19 municipalities and 90 tourist attractions in the region. This development required an investment of US$5.5 million for adaptations and improvements in rural and urban areas and creation of the new routes.

Traveling the highway that connects Nazaré da Mata, located 65 km from Recife, and the neighboring municipalities of Tracunhaém, Carpina, Vicência and Alliance, extensive sugarcane mills are still extant (with five basic elements of the great house, the mill, slave quarters, chapel and fields). The area is also headquarters to *maracatu*, a regional dance of Pernambuco, as well as a museum and cachaça factories, or *cachaçaria*, which are sugar-related specialties of the region.

In the town of Vicência, Engenho Poço Comprido, a restored 18th-century sugar mill once served as a refuge for Frei Caneca, a religious and political figure of Brazil and leader of the Confederation of Ecuador. Engenhos are a popular aspect of the historical tours, and many of them were formerly abandoned. Gradually, architects have been hired to revitalize them and some now host guided tours. For example, Engenho Poço Comprido is on the protected list of the Instituto de Patrimônio Histórico e Artístico Nacional (IPHAN), an agency of the Ministry of Culture, with the mission being to preserve the cultural heritage of Brazil. One curious feature of this engenhos is the private breezeway that joins the big house and the chapel, which allowed the family passage without mixing with the slaves. African baobab trees reveal where the slave quarters once stood.

After visiting Engenho Poço Comprido in the rural countryside, tourists can stop at the cachaçaria named Água Doce back in town. After learning about the various stages of production, tourists are offered the chance to experience sugar heritage by tasting various historical sugarcane spirits and liqueurs, as well as cold sugarcane juice.

Following the example of several European countries, where hotels and hostels are installed in old monasteries, castles and palaces, visitors who come to the Pernambuco area may want to stay in authentic mills to experience the atmosphere of sugar's heyday. Thus, in the town of Nazaré da Mata the guest rooms of Engenho Cueirinha are located in both the historic big house and new chalets.

In the foothills, decorated by the yellow-flowered pau d'arco trees, outside Vicência the tourist can visit Engenho Jundiá. Visitors can view the surrounding fields from the chapel of Nossa Senhora da Conceição, located at the top of the mountain. In the big house the period furniture (c.1882) arrangement allows visitors to view an authentic setting. The list of northern mills now open to visitors is: Engenho Trapuá, Engenho Juá, Engenho Abreu, Engenho Bonito, Engenho Santa Fé, Engenho Várzea Grande, Engenho Ventura, Engenho Tamataúpe das Flores, Engenho Cavalcanti, Engenho Conceição, Engenho Poço Comprido, Engenho Jundiá, Engenho Iguape, Engenho Cipó Branco, Engenho Jucá, O engenho Jucá, Engenho Vazão, Engenho Jaguaribe, Engenho Água Azul, Engenho e a Usina Cruangi, Engenho Xixá, Engenho Santa Luzia, Engenho Capibaribe and Engenho Patos.

This list represents only a fraction of the sugar heritage in Brazil's northeast corridor already open for tourism or that could be developed for tourism. One of the ways the area's rich history is being preserved and further explored is through the *Sugar Civilization Integrated Roadmap – Ways of The Mills*, created with the support of Ministry of Tourism (MTur, 2009), Serviço Brasileiro de Apoio às Micro e Pequenas Empresas (SEBRAE or the Brazilian System of Support of Micro and Small Enterprises) and Embratur, a Brazilian destination marketing organization responsible for promoting and marketing tourism products to the international market. This route crosses the three north-eastern Brazilian states of Alagoas, Paraíba and Pernambuco and lets tourists learn about the history of sugarcane cultivation, sugar production and the role sugar plays in the country's economy. This tour passes through 17 cities filled with cultural and natural wealth, such as Alagoa Grande, Alagoa Nova, Areia (Sand), Banana, Coruripe, Goiás, Igarassu, Itamaracá, Joao Pessoa, Marechal Deodoro, Nazaré da Mata, Olinda, Pilar, Rio Largo, Serraria (sawmill), União dos Palmares and Vicenza.

Products of Sugar Production

Sugarcane is the raw material for the manufacture of three qualities of sugar (white, muscovado and panela), molasses, and both comestible alcohol and bio-ethanol. The bagasse (the fibrous matter left over from the crushing of the sugarcane to extract the juice) was traditionally used as animal fodder, but now the vapor from burning bagasse is commonly used to power steam turbines to make renewable bioelectricity that is used in the production of sugar and also sold to the electrical grid. In 2010, 3% of Brazil's electricity was produced from sugarcane (UNICA, 2011). Bagasse is also a renewable resource used in the manufacture of pulp and paper products and building materials. It is also the source of *furfural*, a highly reactive organic compound with a large number of applications in the chemical and pharmaceutical industries.

Sugarcane juice is fermented and distilled on an industrial level to make bio-ethanol, which is used to enrich petroleum based gasoline (with up to 25% bio-ethanol). The emerging market for bio-ethanol is increasing consumer demand for flex-fuel cars. It is also used in the manufacture of polyethylene, styrene, ketone, acetaldehyde, polystyrene, acetic acid, ether and acetone. Like oil, the other industrial uses of sugarcane include the manufacture of synthetic fibers, paints, varnishes, containers, tubes, solvents and plastics, with an all-important difference: they are biodegradable and not offensive to the environment. Sugarcane juice is also fermented and distilled on a cottage or artisanal level to produce an alcohol called cachaça, a liquor that holds a special place in the cultural heritage of Brazil.

Cachaça and the Caipirinha

Cachaça, or the 'brandy' of the sugarcane, was first discovered in the mill of the captaincy of São Vicente between 1532 and 1548 in an open wooden trough for animals, coming from the pots of brown sugar. Compared to *cauí*, an alcoholic drink produced by the Indians from corn, it was considered a clean drink. By the mid-16th century, cachaça became the currency used to buy slaves in Africa (pre-dating the Caribbean triad of sugar, rum and slaves), with some mills dividing production between sugar and cachaça. The discovery of gold in Minas Gerais brought a large number of people from all over the country to cities in the cold Espinhaço Mountains. The consumption of cachaça made life more bearable and Minas Gerais remains a key cachaça-producing area.

Due to increased efforts to export cachaça and make it a globally recognized commodity 'some confusion over rum and cachaça identities has arisen' (Cardoso *et al.*, 2004). Despite some similarities, cachaça does not have the same chemical compostion as rum. Rum is a sugarcane spirit produced from the distillation of fermented sugarcane juice and molasses, while cachaça is a distillate made from fermented sugarcane juice without the addition of molasses (Cardoso *et al.*, 2004). Specifically, the levels of propanol, isobutanol and isopentanol distinguish the two products.

The manufacturing process begins with the crushing and pressing of sugarcane, which produces a juice to which water is added, resulting in the wort. With the addition of yeast, the wort goes into the short fermentation process. After decanting, which separates the sludge, distillation takes place in a still. This distillate is aged in barrels no larger than 700 liters, with the choice of wood ranging from indigenous woods to European oak, helping to distinguish one cachaça from another. The alcoholic content of a typical cachaça falls between 38% and 48% by volume.

Although efforts are being made by the Brazilian government to make cachaça as renowned and sought after as rum, including geographic protection and distinction under the auspices of the World Trade Organization, less than 1% of the more than 2 billion liters produced each year is exported, reaching more than 60 countries, including Germany, the United States, Portugal and France. However, the best way to experience cachaça is *in situ* (i.e. in Brazil). In 2008, SEBRAE noted that Brazil had 40,000 producers and 4000 brands of cachaça. With micro-enterprises dominating the sector with 99% of all production and responsibility for directly or indirectly generating over 600,000 jobs, they have the potential to develop cachaça-themed tourism experiences.

Established by the Brazilian Institute of Cachaça (Instituto Brasileiro da Cachaça or IBRAC) in 2009, 13 September is a national day for the celebration of cachaça. However, as the largest producers of artisanal and high-quality cachaça, *mineiros* (i.e. people who live in Minas Gerais) claim the paternity of this national spirit. Pre-dating the national celebration, mineiros have marked the start of the sugarcane harvest since 2001 with their own Cachaça Day on 21 May. Thus, some of the earliest tourism development in relation to cachaça is in Minas Gerais. These events have the potential for contributing to branding cachaça and its related tourism experiences.

Last, but not least, one should not forget the *caipirinha*, the national drink of Brazil, which is not only a good vehicle for introducing wider audiences to cachaça, but also serves as a liquid ambassador. The simplest recipe for a caipirinha is one lemon (quartered), two tablespoons of white sugar, one of shot cachaça and ice cubes. The lemon is smashed into the sugar to squeeze out the juice, then the cachaça and ice are added and stirred. The caipirinha is an example of a traditional Brazilian food-way and sugar's intangible heritage served in an old-fashioned glass.

The Cachaça Tour or Cachaçatur

In the states of Rio de Janeiro and neighboring Minas Gerais, the visitor can experience the five senses of cachaça with a tour that features the history, culture and local cuisine of Brazil from colonial times until today. Implemented in 2010, the two-day itinerary, centered on the capital city of Belo Horizonte, not only introduces participants to how cachaça is produced, but also to the region's history and beautiful landscapes. At the end of the tour participants receive a certificate of 'cachaça' as a souvenir.

This route consists of pubs and stores specializing in the production or selling of the artisanal cachaças of Minas Gerais, using criteria established for the project. Participating pubs and restaurants in the Cachaçatur must have a 'Letter of Cachaça', a document that indicates the name, origin, color, alcohol content, storage time and storage of individual cachaças. They also must have a bartender trained to present the options available to customers and to assist them to choose, through a personalized service where liquor is served at the table in the bottle and in the presence of the customer. The participating property (bar, restaurant, store or farm) must also provide alternative forms of consumption of the beverage. Thus, in addition to pure sugarcane brandy (i.e. cachaça), they must offer cocktails prepared with cachaça, including the quintessential caipirinha, cachaça Sauer and cachaça frozen (as aperitifs) and the premium rum. Additionally, menus must contain at least one dish prepared with cachaça produced in Minas Gerais.

For Belotour, through the Belo Horizonte Tourism Office, the Cachaçatur introduces the tourist to the heritage of Minas Gerais while attracting more investment, which ultimately generates more jobs. Each January Belo Horizonte typically receives about 15,000 attendees for conferences, events and business meetings. The Cachaçatur itinerary adds value to the destination by providing visitors with the opportunity to learn about and explore parts of the city beyond the hotel and convention center. Besides generating income for the communities involved, this new kind of tourism is designed to emphasize the social and cultural aspects of the region, which can lead to sustainable development. Tourism is a great motivation for producers of cachaça, one of the most important products in the region, who seek certification and registration of their stills. Currently, tourists can visit four venues and two producers registered with the Ministry of Agriculture, some who already export cachaça (see Tables 4.1 and 4.2).

In addition to the more formalized Cachaçatur, tourists and conference attendees visiting the state of Minas Gerais can obtain a free map from Belotur branch offices to use as a guide to explore area pubs, specialty stores and stills (i.e. businesses that distil cachaça from sugarcane). These pubs feature up to 50 regional cachaça brands distinguished by name, origin, color, alcohol content and period of aging, as well as dishes prepared with cachaça. As Minas Gerais is a leading producer of distilled cachaça, there are about 8500 stills (with 500 being registered with the Ministry of Agriculture, Livestock and Supply), which produce about 250 million gallons per year. This represents over 50% of national production and is responsible for generating US$1.4 billion a year and 116,000 direct jobs. As well as consuming cachaça, production is thus another sugar-related tourism product for visitors to experience.

Paraty Circuit of Cachaça

In 2007, the Association of Producers and Friends of Cachaça from Paraty (Associação dos Produtores e Amigos da Cachaça Artesanal de Paraty or APACAP) received geographical identification and protection (Indicação Geográfica or IG) for cachaça from Paraty from the Brazilian Patent and Trademark Office (Instituto Nacional da Propriedade Industrial or INPI). Such certification was important for the agri-business sector in the State of Rio de Janeiro and Brazil as a whole, as this was the fourth geographical indication recognized in Brazil and the first and only for the sugarcane brandy industry.

The Brazilian IG is much like the Protected Designation of Origin (PDO) issued by the European Union to certify and protect the names of locally produced products throughout Europe, or the Appellation d'Origine Contrôlée (AOC) appellation system used to designate and protect French wine. This Brazilian based appellation system aims to recognize and protect the geographical name of a region or locality, identifying a typical product or service (Tamagno & Rodrigues, 2010). The certificate that cachaça from Paraty received from INPI was the indication of origin, i.e. the exclusive right that only the cachaças produced in that municipality can exhibit on their labels the statement: Cachaça from Paraty, followed by the words 'Indication of Origin'. Only the cachaça produced in Paraty can now use the geographical name 'Paraty' on their labels, when formerly many brands, in various states, used the name 'Paraty' to denote sugarcane brandy. Paraty is thus the

Table 4.1 Minas Gerais Cachaça Tour, or Cachaçatur, founding partners working with the Belo Horizonte Tourism Office

ABIH – Brazilian Association of Hotels	The oldest organization in the domestic tourist trade; officially represents the hotel industry in the country. http://www.abihmg.com.br
ABRASEL – Brazilian Association of Bars and Restaurants	Representative of an industry now comprising around one million businesses and generating six million direct jobs across the country. http://www.abrasel.com.br
AMPAQ – Minas Gerais Association of Producers of Quality Cachaça	Protects interests of producers of cachaça, supporting the development and improvement of this sector. Created the first seal of control of quality from Brazil to rum of AMPAQ. http://www.ampaq.com.br
COOCEN/MG – Central Cooperative of Producers of Stills of Cachaça de Minas Gerais	Association of the regional singular cooperatives of cachaças stills and producers. http://www.ampaq.com.br
CLUBE MINEIRO DA CACHAÇA – Mineiro Club of Cachaça	Created to promote a genuine product of the skill and art of Brazil: Cachaça of Stills. Their events reflect its motto: Health, Cachaça and Joy.
FENACA – Brazilian Federation of Producers Association of Cachaça of Stills	Founded June 2001; aims to coordinate the regional associations representing the industry's production of cachaça still in Brazil.
SENAC MINAS – Brazilian Commercial Training Service – Regional Minas Gerais	A private educational organization, focused on professional training in the trade, services and tourism area. Since its founding in 1946 the institution has contributed to overcoming the social and economic problems of the Minas Gerais state, through professional education. http://www.mg.senac.br

(contiuned)

Table 4.1 (*Continued*)

SINDHORB – Union of Hotels, Restaurants, Bars and similar to Belo Horizonte and Metropolitan Area	Represents 306 municipalities of Minas Gerais, where there are approximately 70,000 companies in the sector generating 250,000 direct jobs. http://www.sindhorb.org.br
SINDBEBIDAS – Union of beer and beverage industries of the state of Minas Gerais	Represents the segments of cachaça, beer and refreshments in Minas Gerais state. As part of tourism, carried out the Production Program Associate to Tourism in partnership with the Estrada Real Institute (Royal Road) that structured 14 stills for tourist visitation.

Table 4.2 Minas Gerias Cachaça tour or Cachaçatur venues and producers

Institution	Category
Clube Mineiro da Cachaça	Restaurant and Bar
Restaurante Jardim de Minas	Restaurant and Bar
Restaurante Terra de Minas	Restaurant and Bar
Restaurante Xico da Kafua	Restaurant and Bar
Prazer de Minas	Producer
Alambique Cachaçaria	Producer

first Brazilian cachaça to receive IG certification. A number of producers can be visited on the tourist route referred to as the Paraty Circuit of Cachaça (Table 4.3; Figure 4.2).

Cachaça Events

In June, for the last 15 years, Belo Horizonte has hosted a cachaça expo. At the 2011 Double Shot ExpoCachaça (see Figure 4.3), experts chose the top 10 white (not aged) and aged cachaças out of a pool of 90 entrants (see Figure 4.4). At Expocachaça 2011 in Belo Horizonte, the caipirinha was cast as the 'welcome drink' and official beverage of FIFA World Cup 2014 (ABRASEL, 2010). In 2011, the state of São Paulo invited the expo organizers to put on a

Table 4.3 Paraty Circuit of Cachaça

Institution	Category	Description
Cachaça Maria Izabel	Producer	One of the most beautiful stills of Paraty is located in a rustic place by the sea. It has the capacity/production of up to 15,000 liters/year.
Cachaça Coqueiro	Producer	The largest and most modern still of Paraty, has two sugarcane grinders, a conveyor for removal of mechanical pulp, and two distillation stills with a capacity/production of up to 100,000 liters/year. First cachaça with seal of quality and excellence.
Cachaça Corisco	Producer	Has a water wheel to move the engine and two distillation stills with a capacity/production of up to 50,000 liters/year.
Engenho D'Ouro	Producer	This small still (with capacity up to 4000 liters/year) has a water wheel to move the mill for grinding sugarcane.
Cachaça Vamos nessa e Quero Essa	Producer	This still does not have any tourist attraction, but has pieces of antique stills. Production capacity of 40,000 liters/year.
Cachaça Itatinga	Producer	Stills with no further attractions. Production of up to 10,000 liters/year.
Cachaça Maré Alta	Producer	Stills with no further attractions. Production capacity of up to 30,000 liters/year.
Fazenda Murycana	Restaurant	Disabled stills located within a tourist farm with restaurant, museum and children's activities. Entry fee charged. Still exists with sugarcane brandy tasting.
Alambique São Gonçalo	Producer	Small still located in community of São Gonçalo, near a beach. No added tourist attractions. Capacity up to 4000 liters/year.

Figure 4.2 Paraty Circuit of Cachaça
Source: Brazilian Center of Cachaça.

Figure 4.3 Attendees at Expocachaça, 2011
Source: Leticia Moreira/Folhapress.

Figure 4.4 A jury member evaluates one of the cachaças at Expocachaça, 2011
Source: Leticia Moreira/Folhapress.

sister event in São Paulo, at the São Paulo Municipal Market, the Mercadão. As a result, the name Double Shot ExpoCachaça is now associated with the two cities of Belo Horizonte and São Paulo. The São Paulo expo had an audience of approximately 290,000. From 2012 on, two annual expos will take place: one in Belo Horizonte in June and the second in São Paulo in September (Mendes & Mendes, 2011).

Each January, Belo Horizonte also hosts the Cachaça Gourmet Food Festival, a joint venture of the Cachaça of Minas Gerais Club, the municipality of Belo Horizonte, Belotur, the Belo Horizonte Convention and Visitors Bureau, the Minas Gerais Association of Producers of Quality Cachaça (AMPAQ) and Krug Bier. The 2011 event had record participation from 25 restaurants, each partnered with one of 25 cachaça brands entered in the festival to create an original cachaça based cocktail and dish containing cachaça. The public and an official jury both voted for their favorite cocktail and dish. The 2011 public winners were a cachaça, shrimp, fish and crab dish from Bahia Restaurant Aracajé, made with Cachaça Caieira Muqueca, and the Coquetel Sensação (Sensation Cocktail) from Restaurant Emporium Savassi, made with Cachaça Vale Verde. The winners designated by the expert jury were Big Owl I Restaurante's Ninho da Coruja (Owl's Nest), a dish made with the Cachaça Cobiçada (Cachaça Coveted), and the Berga 8 Restaurant's Berga Caliente cocktail, made with the Cachaça Século XVIII. All winners were from Belo Horizonte. Other events dedicated to cachaça are listed in Table 4.4.

The Future is Sweet

Rural tourism is relatively new in Brazil, the result of a movement to return to origins in search for values, customs, traditions and simple behaviors

Table 4.4 Typical calender of cachaça events

Date	Name of the event	City, state
January	Cachaça Gourmet Food Festival	Belo Horizonte, MG
March	Salão da Cachaça de Qualidade	Rio de Janeiro, RJ
	Feira Mineira de Artesanato (Handicrafts Fair of Minas Gerais)	São João Del Rei, MG
	Expo QualiCachaça	Salvador, BA
April	Café, Chorinho e Cachaça (Coffee, Cachaça choro music)	Coffee Valley in Rio de Janeiro State
	TECHNOBAR – The Minas Gerais Food-Service Fair	Belo Horizonte – MG
	Brasil Cachaça	São Paulo – SP
	Internacional Cachaça Fair	São Paulo – SP
	Festa da Cachaça Mineira (The Minas Gerais Cachaça Festival	Sete Lagoas, MG
	Mel, Chorinho e Cachaça (The Honey, Cachaça choro music)	Viçosa do Ceará – CE
	Feira da Cachaça (The Cachaça Fair)	Bom Despacho (MG)
June	ExpoCachaça	Belo Horizonte – MG
	Minas Cachaça	Belo Horizonte – MG
	Congresso Mineiro da Cachaça (The Minas Gerais Cachaça Congress)	Belo Horizonte – MG
	Festival da Cachaça de Abreus (The Abreus Cachaça Festival)	Abreus – Alto do Rio Doce – MG
	Festival da Cachaça	São Lourenço – MG
July	Festival Mundial da Cachaça (The World Festival of Cachaça)	Salinas – Norte de Minas
	Festa da Cachaça (The Cachaça Festival)	Luis Alves – SC
	Festa da Cana e Festival da Cachaça (The Sugarcane Feast and Cachaça Festival)	Presidente Bernardes, MG
	Cachaça Fest Piaui (The Piaui Cachaça Feast)	Castelo do Piaui – PI
	Festival da Cachaça de Guararema (The Guararema Cachaça Festival)	Guararema – SP
August	Festa do Morango e da Cachaça (The Strawberry and Cachaça Feast)	Monte Alegre do Sul – SP
	Festival da Serra de São Bento (The Serra de São Bento Festival)	Serra de São Bento – RN

(contiuned)

Table 4.4 (Continued)

Date	Name of the event	City, state
	Festival da Cachaça do Ipê Clube (The Cachaça Festival Ipê Club)	Ipatinga – MG
	Festival da Pinga e Produtos Típicos Caiçara (The Cachaça and Typical Products of Caiçara Festival)	Paraty – RJ
	Festival da Cachaça, Cultura e Sabores de Paraty (Cachaça, Culture a Flavors of Paraty Festival)	Paraty – RJ
	Festival da Cachaça com Comida de Bar (Cachaça Festival with Food Bar)	Natal – RN
September	Festa da Cachaça (Cachaça Feast)	São João Del Rey – MG
	Encontro de Produtores de Cachaça (Cachaça Producer Meeting)	Quissamã, RJ
	Festival da Cachaça (Cachaça Festival)	Abaíra – Chapada Diamantina – BA
	Festival da Cachaça (Cachaça Festival)	Novo Cruzeiro – MG
	Festival da Cachaça e da Rapadura Cachaça and Brown Sugar Festival)	Areia – PB
	Mostra de Cachaças do Vale do Café (Cachaça Exhibition of The Coffee Valley)	Conservatória, RJ
	FEICA RIO	Rio de Janeiro – RJ
	ExpoCachaça Dose Dupla (ExpoCachaça Double Shot)	São Paulo, SP
October	EXPOPARTY	São Paulo, SP
	Salão Internacional da Cachaça (International Salon of Cachaça)	Recife, PE
	Cachaçaria Carvalheira and The Comedoria Popular accomplish the first edition of the event Mill Culture	Recife, PE
	Festival Regional da Cachaça em Taruaçu (Cachaça Regional Festival of Turuaçu)	São João Nepomuceno, MG
November	Festival da Cachaça (Cachaça Festival)	Conceição de Mato Dentro – MG
	Festival da Cachaça do Restaurante Gosto com Gosto (Cachaça Festival of Taste with Taste Restaurant)	Visconde de Mauá – RJ

that have been forgotten or replaced by the pressure of technology and competitiveness in major cities. This chapter has discussed such tourism in relation to the sugar heritage of Brazil, in the form of tours of historic sugar mills (engenhos) and tourism related to the consumption and production of a sugar-derived liquor, cachaça.

According to the Ministry of Tourism (Ministério do Turismo, 2004), rural tourism has provided some benefits. These include diversification of the regional economy; the establishment of micro and small businesses; improving the living conditions of rural families; and the internalization of tourism and diversification of tourism offerings. In addition, rural tourism can contribute to a reduction in the rural exodus and promotion of cultural exchange; conservation of natural resources; generation of new employment opportunities; improved transport infrastructure; communication; sanitation; equipment and real property; income generation alternatives that add value to rural activities; direct relationship of the consumer to the producer who can sell beyond the services of lodging; food and entertainment; fresh products (fruits, eggs, vegetables) or processed products (jams, cheeses, crafts); integration of rural properties and enhancement of community and rural practices.

In terms of products resulting from the artisanal process, cachaça can be considered a golden opportunity. The product can be consumed at the production site, providing a differentiated and varied experience to the visitor (the farm, the still and the production process), and can be taken home as a souvenir to be consumed later or to be offered as a gift. Aware of this trend, the tourism sector has incorporated cachaça and it has become an important part of travel and tours, comparable to wine tourism in the wine route in southern Brazil. Considering the possible benefits of cachaça, we can therefore identify points of synergy with tourism, including its use in culinary tourism and related rural tourism routes.

Conclusion

Brazil is an excellent position to increase its sugar tourism offerings in multiple directions. In addition to establishing historic sugar mill routes in Pernambuco and cachaça routes in Minas Gerais, the concept of the sugar mill or cachaça tour could be introduced elsewhere in the country. Interesting developments in the state of Minas Gerais, such as the Cachaça Gourmet Food Festival and ExpoCachaça, lead the way. However, in other Brazilian states where overall sugarcane production is lower, but consumption is significant, no meaningful developments have been observed. This may be due to the lack of government development policies in relation to Brazilian sugar heritage.

However, it is in Minas Gerais province where the production of cachaça flourishes. Of 80 renowned brands of cachaça in Brazil, 69 are produced in Minas Gerais. Some of these, such as Cachaça Salinas, cost as much as $100 a bottle. In addition to cachaça, several other contemporary culinary products could be tied to sugar tourism in Brazil, including brown sugar (rapadura), chocolate and rum. Like cachaça, the state of Minas Gerais is also a leading producer of distilled rum with about 8500 stills (with 500 being registered with the Ministry of Agriculture, Livestock and Supply). These stills produce about 250 million gallons per year, which is over 50% of national production and responsible for generating $1.4 billion a year and 116,000 jobs. Thus, although not discussed in this chapter, rum production is another sugar-related tourism product for visitors to experience.

The opportunity to partner with other events, such as the Jazz Festival in the Vale do Café (or Coffee Valley), located in the rolling green hills of the Paraíba River, and the International Literary Festival of Paraty, both in the state of Rio de Janeiro, could assist in popularizing cachaça tours or routes. There are also opportunities to create tours of modern-day, sugarcane and ethanol plantations in São Paulo, where the largest industrial sugarcane plantations and ethanol plants are concentrated. Partnerships with industrial sugar producers or usinas such as UNICA could be explored. Another producer with tourism potential is Usina São Francisco, owned and operated by Grupo Balbo, a century old, family owned sugar company that is producing and exporting organic sugarcane and was recently designated a 'new sustainability champion' by the World Economic Forum (2011). Its Green Cane Project (Projecto Cana Verde) is promoting sustainable sugarcane cultivation (Grupo Balbo, 2011).

Currently, a good number of sugar-related experiences await the tourists in Brazil, with others in the development pipeline or ripe for development. For example, while sugar mill tourism is well established in Pernambuco (although efforts there are individualized rather than supported by the state or federal government), there is a strong historical basis to develop and promote more sugar-related tourism in neighboring Bahia, which was a major Brazilian plantation zone for almost 300 years. As Bahian sugar plantations were established by the Catholic Church there may be an opportunity to partner with or receive development funds from them instead of the government. Salvador, the capital of Bahia, would be a natural starting point for such tours, just as Belo Horizonte has been for the state of Minas Gerais.

Acknowledgment

The authors would like to thank sugar mill expert Willem van Bergen for his review of this manuscript.

References

Antonil, A.J. (1711) *Cultura e opulência do Brasil, por suas drogas, e minas, com varias noticias curiosas do modo de fazer o assucar, plantar, & beneficiar o tabaco; tirar ouro das minas; & descubrir as da prata; e dos grandes emolumentos, que esta conquista da America meridional dá ao Reyno de Portugal com estes, & outros generos, & contratos reaes,* accessed 1 October 2011. http://www.brasiliana.usp.br/bbd/handle/1918/06000400#page/1/mode/1up. Lisbon: Deslandesiana.

Associação Brasileira de Bares e Restaurantes (ABRASEL). (2010) *Produtores querem transformar caipirinha no drinque da Copa de 2014,* accessed 1 October 2011. http://www.abrasel.com.br/index.php/noticias/541-06062011-produtores-querem-transformar-caipirinha-no-drinque-da-copa-de-2014.html.

Associação dos Produtores e Amigos da Cachaça Artesanal de Paraty (APACAP). (2011) *O que é IG?,* accessed 1 October 2011. http://www.apacap.com.br/o_q_e_ig.html.

Bolling, C. and Suarez, N.R. (2001) *The Brazilian Sugar Industry: Recent Developments.* Washington, DC: Economic Research Service, USDA.

Cardoso, D.R., Andrade-Sobrinho, L.G., Leite-Neto, A.F., Reche, R.V., Isique, W.D., Ferreira, M.M.C., Lima-Neto, B.S. and Franco, D.W. (2004) Comparison between Cachaça and rum using pattern recognition methods. *Journal of Agricultural and Food Chemistry* 52(11), 3429–3433.

Deerr, N. (1949) *The History of Sugar.* London: Chapman and Hall.

Freyre, G. (2003) *Sobrados e Mucambos: decadência do patriarcado e desenvolvimento do urbano.* São Paulo: Global.

Freyre, G. (2006) *Casa Grande e Senzala: formação da família brasileira sob o regime da economia patriarcal.* São Paulo: Global.

Grupo Balbo. (2011) Green Cane Project (Projecto Cana Verde), accessed 20 December 2011. http://www.nativealimentos.com.br/en/cana-verde/index.html.

Instituto Nacional da Propriedade Industrial (INPI) (2011) accessed 20 December 2011. http://www5.inpi.gov.br/menu-esquerdo/indicacao/listagem-dos-pedidos-de-ig.

Lima, G. A. (1984) *Cultura da Cana-de-Açúcar.* Fortaleza: Editora Fortaleza.

Mendes, J.L. and Mendes, J.V. (2011) Patrocínio do Sebrae Nacional Ajuda a Viabilizar Expocachaça Dose Dupla em Evento Inédito no Mercado Municipal Paulistano CBRC-Centro Brasileiro de Referência da Cachaça. Newsletter n° 8. 2011. Belo Horizonte, MG.

Ministério do Turismo. (2004) Livreto Turismo Rural. Ministério do Turismo (2004). Livreto Turismo Rural. http://www.turismo.gov.br/export/sites/default/turismo/o_ministerio/publicacoes/downloads_publicacoes/Turismo_Cultural_Versxo_Final_IMPRESSxO_.pdf.

Mintz, S.W. (1985) *Sweetness and Power: The Place of Sugar in Modern History.* New York: Viking.

MTur (Ministério do Turismo). (2009) Roteiros do Brasil. http://www.turismo.gov.br/turismo/o_ministerio/publicacoes/cadernos_publicacoes/05revista_roteiros.html or http://www.turismo.gov.br/export/sites/default/turismo/o_ministerio/publicacoes/downloads_publicacoes/Revista_Roteiros_do_Brasil_-_internet.pdf.

Nunes, Jr., M.S. (1987) Variedades de cana-de-açúcar. In S.B. Paranhos (ed.) *Cana-de-açúcar: cultivo e utilização* (Vol. 1; pp. 187–259). Campinas: Fundação Cargill.

Pires, F.T.F. and Gomes, G. (1994) *Antigos engenhos de açúcar no Brasil*. Rio de Janeiro: Editora Nova Fronteira.

Post, F. J., do Lago, P. C. do, Ducas. B. and Musée du Louvre. (2005) *Frans Post: le Brésil à la cour de Louis XIV. Volume 5.* Paris: Musée du Louvre.

Schwartz, S.B. (1985) *Sugar Plantations in the Formation of Brazilian Society: Bahia, 1550–1835.* New York: Cambridge University Press.

Schwartz, S.B. (1988) *Segredos internos: Engenhos e escravos na sociedade colônia, 1500–1835.* São Paulo: Companhia das Letras.

Serviço Brasileiro de Apoio às Micro e Pequenas Empresas (SEBRAE). (2008) *Cachaça Artesanal. Relatório completo. Série Estudos de Mercado.* SEBRAE: Rio de Janeiro, RJ.

Tamagno, M.B. and Rodrigues J., E.B. (2010) *Intellectual Property Law in Brazil*. Alphen aan den Rijn, The Netherlands; Frederick, MD: Kluwer Law International.

UNESCO. (2011) Historic Centre of Salvador de Bahia, accessed 22 August 2011. http://whc.unesco.org/en/list/309/.

UNICA. (2011) União da Indústria de Cana-de-Açúcar (Brazilian Sugarcane Industry Association), 'Bioelectricide/bioelectricty', accessed 25 August 2011. http://www.unica.com.br/usina-virtual/video-new/usina-virtual (in Portuguese) and http://english.unica.com.br/virtual-mill/video-new/virtual-mill.htm (in English).

World Economic Forum. (2011) *Redefining the Future of Growth: The New Sustainability Champions.* Geneva, Switzerland: World Economic Forum.

Part 3

Perspectives from Countries Transitioning from Sugar to Tourism

5 The Industrial Heritage of Sugar at World Heritage Sites in the Caribbean

Tara A. Inniss and Lee Jolliffe

The industrial heritage of sugar is part of our global heritage. This chapter reviews the sugar heritage recognized by properties in the Caribbean, historically a major sugar producing area, highlighting and discussing properties inscribed on the United Nation Educational, Scientific and Cultural Organization (UNESCO) World Heritage (WH) List and those on the Tentative List. In particular, three relevant properties will be examined: *Trinidad and the Valley de los Ingenios*, Cuba, inscribed in 1988; *Ruta de Los Ingenos* in the Dominican Republic, on the Tentative List since 2001; and *The Industrial Heritage of Barbados: The Story of Sugar*, Barbados, on the Tentative List since 2005.

This chapter draws from the literature on WH Sites and tourism and from UNESCO documents related to each property. In addition, fieldwork was undertaken for the case study of The Industrial Heritage of Barbados: The Story of Sugar, Barbados, consisting of site visits and interviews of key stakeholders. This allowed the authors to gain insights into perspectives of this tentative site from the local level.

The industrial heritage of sugar in the region is reviewed as a context for discussing the possibilities of heritage tourism, in relation to the region's WH properties. Challenges in managing world heritage related to the region's sugar heritage will be identified and discussed, then examined through case studies of the sites. In conclusion, lessons will be derived from the comparative analysis of these sites as well as from the review of how the Caribbean's industrial heritage of sugar is currently represented as WH in the region.

The World Heritage Convention and the Caribbean

The WH Convention provides a means for the recognition of sites, both natural and cultural, with outstanding universal value (OUV) that form part of the world's heritage. UNESCO's objectives for the preservation of the world's natural and cultural heritage are exemplified in the convention, which encourages the identification, preservation and protection of sites that are considered to be of outstanding value to humanity (UNESCO, 1972). Individual states are signatories to the convention; each state party is able to put forward sites for inclusion on the Tentative List, such sites are then nominated as WH properties.

This Tentative List is a list of the sites that the state party intends to nominate in the coming years. The process of submission for the list is seen as a useful planning and management tool, allowing state parties to work in collaboration with local partners in preparation for the actual nomination. Developing stakeholder relations is a major issue, as most heritage assets have multiple stakeholders.

In total, 936 properties have been inscribed overall on the WH List. According to the WH Centre it is widely acknowledged that the cultural and natural heritage in the Caribbean sub-region is underrepresented on the WH List. The region has 19 state parties to the WH Convention, with only nine having properties that have been inscribed. This number includes CARICOM member states, Caribbean dependencies and the Dominican Republic and Cuba. The Spanish-speaking Caribbean has been the most successful in getting its cultural and natural heritage recognized as WH (Cuba, for example, has nine WH properties). However, only two cultural heritage sites and three natural heritage sites have been recognized in the English-speaking Caribbean. Over the past decade there has been some improvement in the identification of sites for inclusion on the Tentative List, but several state parties have been reluctant to make the investment to produce the substantial nomination dossiers that must be evaluated for possible WH inscription (UNESCO, 1994; ICOMOS, 2004).

For the small nation states and territories in the Caribbean whose heritage is greatly related to the heritage of the present and former sugar industries there are numerous challenges in getting this heritage represented on the WH List. Many jurisdictions have limited resources for the research and preparation of tentative listings and nominations (UNESCO, 2004). Other territories as dependencies of European state parties encounter difficulties getting assistance for assessing site potential for WH. For example, the Département D'Outre Mer (DOM) of Martinique, as a dependency of

France, is considered a region in the French Republic. Sites within such territories may not be considered priorities within the larger culture portfolio of the state parties representing them, as they have no individual power to sign on to the WH Convention on their own. Timothy and Boyd (2003) cite the latter situation as one reason for the paucity of WH listings overall in the Caribbean. However, other dependencies have found support and success from their governments. The Historic Area of Willemstad, Inner City and Harbour, Curaçao was put forward by the Kingdom of the Netherlands, achieving inscription in 1997, and La Fortaleza and San Juan National Historic Site in Puerto Rico was advanced by the USA, being inscribed in 1983.

The lack of technical capacity in the development of nomination dossiers and management plans has also been identified as a reason for the small number of sites nominated in the region. UNESCO has addressed this through the development of the Caribbean Capacity Building Programme (CCBP) and other ad hoc training and workshop efforts in the region. This has led to the development of tentative lists for some state parties and increased awareness of WH at the local and regional levels.

The International Council on Monuments and Sites (ICOMOS), acting as an advisory body for WH cultural sites, has produced thematic studies to guide the nomination and evaluation process, but to date only one has been published on the WH potential of the Caribbean (ICOMOS, 2006). UNESCO has also encouraged expert meetings to explore the WH potential of other areas of the region's cultural heritage, including the 'Caribbean Fortifications Experts Meeting' in 1996 in Colombia. Historical research and archaeology have been used in assisting with the research process towards designation, for example, in the case of Barbados (Farmer, 2005). These initiatives have helped to produce expert knowledge on the interpretation and evaluation of some sites; however, similar studies have not been conducted on the region's distinctive industrial sugar heritage.

For many small states with limited financial and human resources there may be issues of stakeholder collaboration, as it is necessary to determine who will prepare a management plan and who has the day-to-day responsibility for the management of the tentative sites. Impacts of designation must be carefully considered in terms of the possible increase in visitor numbers leading to crowding, as WH Site designation is known to increase visitation (Shackley, 1998). Once designated, these sites are destined to become major attractions that can be pivotal in the tourism industries of their countries (Fyall et al., 2008). A major advantage that WH properties have in attracting visitors is that they have been branded as World Heritage.

World Heritage Sites and Sugar in the Caribbean

The Caribbean has a long history and heritage of sugar production, reflecting in particular a global process of industrialization and acting as the centre of the international slave trade, which provided the labour for sugar production, but few sites concentrate on the industrial heritage of sugar. However, there has been one WH Site directly related to the industrial heritage of sugar inscribed in Cuba, and another two are on the Tentative List (Dominican Republic and Barbados) (Table 5.1). In particular, the nomination for the Story of Sugar (Barbados) will concentrate heavily on the role African labour played in the development of Caribbean sugar economies. However, when many of the territories of the Caribbean have a strong sugar heritage, why have such few sites related to the industrial aspect of this heritage been inscribed?

The following review of the Caribbean's industrial heritage of sugar examines how such heritage might be viewed through heritage tourism. This is an approach that offers some potential for the interpretation of sugar heritage as well as the encouragement of its broader representation on the WH List, addressing in part the question above of why such few sites representing the region's industrial sugar heritage have been inscribed.

Sugar's Industrial Heritage in the Caribbean

Sugarcane production was transferred from the Mediterranean islands to the Caribbean islands in the Atlantic in the 15th century (Schwartz, 2004). Some authors (for example, Williams (1994)) have argued that the slave based sugar economies of the Caribbean contributed directly to the British Industrial Revolution. Undoubtedly, the cultivation of the crop transformed consumption patterns of the popular commodity in food and drink once it could be cheaply manufactured and sold in European markets, causing a *food revolution* of sorts. Sugar production in the region required large estates or plantations and, according to Schwartz (2004), regimented labour forces, often consisting of enslaved workers sourced from the trans-Atlantic slave trade. The intensification of using coerced labour in an industrial process has also been referred to as the 'sugar revolution' (Batie, 1976; Highman, 2000). However, even though Menard (2006) refutes some of the basic suppositions of the so-called 'sugar revolution' he does confirm that the process likely intensified under conditions in Barbados.

Sugar production in the Caribbean, using the plantation model, required both equipment and intensive labour. On a typical plantation cane was tended and then harvested in the fields, transported to the sugar mill where it was

Table 5.1 World Heritage related to the industrial heritage of sugar in the Caribbean

Site	Country	Status	Significance
Trinidad and the Valley de los Ingenios	Cuba	Inscribed on the World Heritage List in 1988	Trinidad was a sugar trading city and the nearby Valle de Los Ingenios, a living museum of the sugar industry, includes ruined sugar mills and other buildings related to the sugar production.
Boca De Nugua Sugar Mill (Ruta de Los Ingenios)	Dominican Republic	On the World Heritage Tentative List since 2001	Sugar processing complex; processing area, warehouse, guard house and distillery buildings. Typical of great Cuban and Haitian sugar mills from the end of the 18th century.
The Industrial Heritage of Barbados: The Story of Sugar	Barbados	On the World Heritage Tentative List since 2005	The nomination includes four sites encapsulating the story of sugar in Barbados; Codrington College, a 17th century sugar plantation then college supported by a sugar plantation; Morgan Lewis Sugar Mill, a restored sugar mill; Saint Nicholas Abbey; Newton Slave Burial Ground.

Source: Adapted from UNESCO (http://whc.unesco.org)

crushed, the sap then being piped into the boiling house where it was boiled off a number of times, then cooled and cured (Mintz, 1985). Some plantations also had distilleries where molasses blended with sap from the first boiling was distilled into rum. Abbott (2008: 91) reports that on some large plantations the 'cutting-milling-boiling-distilling cycle went on night and day for five months'.

This intensive process was fuelled by slave labour, for the most part by enslaved Africans, until slavery was abolished in 1834 in the British Caribbean; even then there were apprenticeship systems that assured continued labour for the plantation owners until full emancipation was granted in 1838 (Thompson, 2010). See Chapter 1 for abolition dates elsewhere in the region; for example, in Cuba slavery was not abolished until 1886.

Schwartz (2004: 3) notes that the sugar plantations were agro-industrial enterprises combining the farming of the cane and the processing of its juice into sugar, 'giving the sugar mill its distinctive, quasi-industrial character'. Cornwell and Stoddard (2001: 3) indicate that the former sugar mills are highly contested as sites of struggle over issues of nation, race and neocolonialism in the Caribbean. The mills were often powered by wind and to this day such sugar mills are a powerful symbol of the former colonial times. In fact, the sugar mill is a common and central element in the three WH properties (two tentative and one nominated) representing sugar heritage in the Caribbean.

Industrial heritage tourism involves using former man-made industrial sites for tourism, such tourism in some cases being a tool for the economic and social revival of the locales in which the sites are located (Edwards & Llurdés i Coit, 1996). In the case of the former industrial sugar sites, industrial heritage tourism provides a lens through which we can examine the possible relationship and synergies between the heritage of the sugar industry and tourism. In some of the former industrial sites in Europe such tourism has been seen as a tool of regeneration of individual industrial locales and even of industrialized regions (Hospers, 2011). Such tourism is also known in some cases to enhance local identities, providing a means for local understanding of the industrial past.

In the case of the former sugar industries of the Caribbean with their contested labour practices being represented by the history of enslavement and indentureship, interpretation of former plantations and industrial processing of sugar may provide a means for discussing the contested past for the local populations, while at the same time developing industrial heritage tourism products with the potential to contribute to the diversification of local tourism industries, creating local employment and associated benefits.

In the small territories in the Caribbean, which are in fact former industrial sites for the production of sugar, industrial heritage tourism, while forming a small part of the tourism product in the region, nonetheless has a potential that has to date not been examined in any detail by scholars or state cultural and tourism agencies. Experience from Europe has suggested that individual components of industrial heritage can be linked in routes (such as the European Route of Industrial Heritage linking industrial heritage sites across Europe). This linking of sites makes a more viable tourism product with the potential to attract tourists while enhancing local econo-mies. In Europe, industrial heritage tourism efforts have in part been a response to the economic downturn; in the case of the Caribbean it remains to be seen if the current global economic and financial crisis will influence the further development of industrial heritage tourism in the region. This process would involve a shift in the region's industrial history from places of production to places of consumption, as Hospers and van Lochem (2002) has traced in the case of Europe.

A number of authors have classified the different types of industrial heri-tage that can be utilized for tourism, identified (Table 5.2) as applied to the industrial sugar heritage of the Caribbean.

However, optimism for the use of the industrial heritage of sugar for tourism needs to be tempered with the fact that the impacts of such tourism are unproven; in reality jobs are created in the transition, but at a minimum they are miniscule when compared to the levels of employment when the industries were fully operational. However, as in the case of former mines around the world that are valued for their heritage properties (Conlin & Jolliffe, 2011), the use of such places for tourism can have direct benefits for local communities, if not in terms of significant economic impacts, in terms of strengthening local communities and their identities.

In addition to the directly industrial sites noted above, a number of mili-tary fortifications and urban centres supported the sugar industry through their mercantile activities, providing supplies and labour (both enslaved and free) for the sugar monopolies in the region. Some of those that have been inscribed as WH Sites reflect the role of fortifications and town centres in supporting the colonial sugar industry and trade; for example, Brimstone Hill Fortress in St Kitts, Historic Bridgetown and its Garrison in Barbados, and the Urban Historic Centre of Cienfuegos in Cuba.

Below we consider the representation of sugar heritage in the transition of sugar from industry to heritage to tourism for three UNESCO WH proper-ties dedicated to the story of sugar, one listed in Cuba and two on the Tentative List, one in the Dominican Republic and the other in Barbados.

Trinidad and the Valley de los Ingenios, Cuba

The WH property of the city of Trinidad and the Valley de los Ingenios in Cuba was listed in 1988. The colonial city of Trinidad, established in the 16th century and with heritage buildings from the 18th and 19th centuries, was enumerated alongside its surrounding rural Valle de Los Ingenois (literally valley of the sugar mills), as a testimony to the development of the sugar industry.

Table 5.2 Types of industrial heritage and examples from the Caribbean's WH and sugar heritage

Type	Example	Case examples
Industrial processing and production remains	Sugar mills and buildings involved in the industrial processing of sugar	*Trinidad and the Valley de los Ingenios* (Cuba) is home to numerous sugar mills. *Ruta de Los Ingenos* (Dominican Republic) includes a range of sites that were part of the industrial processing of sugar. *The Industrial Heritage of Barbados: The Story of Sugar* includes the restored Morgan Lewis Sugar Mill and other properties associated with sugar production.
Transport attractions	Cane trains	*Trinidad and the Valley de los Ingenios* (Cuba) includes a Baldwin locomotive (on a former cane train line) tourist train from Trinidad to Manaca Iznaga estate.
Socio-cultural attractions	Former plantation great houses and plantation grounds/ outbuildings	*Trinidad and the Valley de los Ingenios* includes a great house at the Manaca Iznaga estate. *The Industrial Heritage of Barbados: The Story of Sugar* includes the great house at St Nicholas Abbey, while Codrington College and the built heritage of the estates demonstrate the socio-cultural relationships between education, theology and the economy. Newton Slave Burial Ground is the only excavated communal slave burial ground in the western hemisphere and represents the lives of Africans who provided the enslaved labour required to operate the industrial complex of sugar.

Source: Types adapted in part from Edwards and Llurdés i Coit (1996).

By the end of the 18th century, under Spanish rule, the sugar industry was firmly established in the valley and the port city of Trinidad prospered due to the sugar trade, reflected by its historic core consisting of public squares and both public and vernacular buildings, some built by sugar barons. According to UNESCO, in addition to the city of Trinidad.

The nearby Valle de Los Ingenios is a living museum of the sugar industry, featuring 75 ruined 19th century sugar mills, summer mansions, barracks, and other facilities related to the field. The famous Manaca-Iznaga Tower, built in 1816, is 45 m high, and the tolling of its bells once marked the beginning and end of working hours on the sugar plantations. (UNESCO, 2011)

This property was nominated as WH under criteria (iv) as an outstanding example of a type of building or architectural or technological ensemble or landscape which illustrates (a) significant stage(s) in human history; (v) or an outstanding example of a traditional human settlement or land-use which is representative of a culture (or cultures), especially when it has become vulnerable under the impact of irreversible change. It was inscribed at the 12th meeting of the WH Committee in 1988 in Brasilia. Upon listing as a WH property, both ICOMOS and UNESCO congratulated Cuba on preservation efforts in Trinidad itself but cautioned that the surrounding valley also needed to be protected, 'it strongly recommended to protect the environment of the town sugar mills and valley which should not suffer from tourism development' (UNESCO, 1988). ICOMOS (1987) had recommended against immediate inscription because of concerns regarding the preservation of the sugar mills. It is significant that this was not a serial nomination and thus individual buildings in Trinidad and sugar mills in the surrounding valley are not listed, rather the whole of the city and valley are inscribed. ICOMOS (1987) was concerned that no perimeter of protection was suggested for the rural assets and that there was no guarantee of preserving industrial heritage assets related to historic sugar production.

The sugar heritage aspect of this WH property is significant. The sugar plantation is at the core of the Cuban identity, as asserted by Barnet and Lindstrom (1980), and many of the preserved aspects of the former plantations are symbolic, including the sugar mills and the bell towers that were used to define the workday. The intense plantation system of sugarcane farming created a situation where people of various backgrounds worked together and where aspects of the national culture developed. Sugar is still a significant industry in other regions of Cuba but, as demonstrated by this WH listing, sugar is now also valued for its heritage, and for its contribution to Cuban culture. For Cuba, tourism and more specifically heritage tourism is also a means of nation-building and instilling civic pride (Sanchez & Adams, 2008).

Heritage tourism is now acknowledged to be the main industry both in the city of Trinidad and the surrounding Valle de Los Ingenios (Pugh & Momsen, 2006). The city features outstanding colonial architecture as an asset for such tourism. The rural area surrounding the city has a landscape shaped by the cultivation of sugar, the symbolic architecture of the historic sugar mills and the railways constructed to carry the sugarcane to the factories. Rural areas such as this can provide the setting for some of the most spectacular heritage attractions (Timothy & Boyd, 2003).

Sugar-related attractions in the valley include a steam train ride and visits to the observation tower Manaca-Iznaga (used by the land owner to oversee his slaves). The adjacent Iznaga Colonial House Restaurant, located in the house of the former estate owner, now features local Cuban cuisine and live performances of traditional music and dance. The train, originating in Trinidad, makes a stop at the Manaca-Iznaga Tower. The steam train ride, on tracks laid to carry sugarcane from the farms to the centralized sugar factory, is symbolic of the transition of the sugar industry here to industrialization (Pollitt, 2004). The train reportedly makes a round trip daily from Trinidad to the valley at a ticket cost of CU$10; however, *Frommer's* reports that the 1907 steam train often breaks down (Boobbyer, 2011). The *Rough Guide* also reports that the half-hour ride on the steam train is a touristic highlight in this area (McAuslan & Norman, 2007). Additional attractions in the vicinity include horse riding tours in this valley shaped by sugar. Visitors here experience a landscape changed by sugarcane production as well as remaining sugarcane fields, along with remnants of estate houses, sugar mills and slave quarters, all in the context of an authentic sugar steam train ride.

It is significant that this is the only property currently listed as WH in the Caribbean that has such a rich and dedicated focus on the heritage of the sugar industry. It is not only linked with sugar heritage but also with the cultural identity of Cuba as a nation. The site is significant in interpreting the importance of sugar heritage to the development of Cuba as a nation and to the broader economic and cultural impacts elsewhere in the Caribbean. It is potentially part of a regional route both commemorating and interpreting the influence of the Spanish Caribbean on the sugar heritage of the region.

As an attraction however, the sugar heritage here is living and a reflection of national culture, but also rather undeveloped, at least by intent, for tourism purposes. If tourism develops in Cuba from mass tourism to more niche areas, should the US embargo on Cuba be lifted, there is potential here for the sugar valley to be not only the attraction, but also to provide increased and reliable services for tourism. However, as noted by ICOMOS prior to inscription, any increase in infrastructure for tourism and visitation will need to be carefully planned in order to respect the integrity of this historic example of sugar production.

Ruta de Los Ingenos, Dominican Republic

This property, Ruta de Los Ingenos (literally route of the sugar mills), is in the Dominican Republic (DR) on the island of Hispaniola, where Christopher Columbus introduced sugarcane during his second voyage (1493–1496) and where the first contingent of enslaved Africans to this region was received (1501). The route has a strong link to the heritage of the cultivation of sugarcane in the New World in terms of industrial heritage and associated enslavement.

This site was submitted by the permanent delegation of the DR at UNESCO as a cultural property to the WH Tentative List in 2001, and the listing was added to in 2002. This process is a prerequisite for nomination, signifying the DR's intent to put this site forward for nomination in the future. This is a serial nomination, composed of a number of sugar mill complexes and estate houses, including the Boca De Nugua Sugar Mill (2001); The Ancient Big House of Palavé (2001); The Ancient Diego Caballero Sugar Mill (2001); The Sugar Mill of Engombe (2001), Nuestra Señora de Monte Alegre or la Duquesa Sugar Mill (2002); and the Sanate Sugar Mill (2002). Many of these sites reflect early technologies in the production of sugar from sugarcane.

The WH listing process for cultural properties allows for the tentative listing and then nomination and inscription of both individual sites and groups of buildings that 'because of their architecture, their homogeneity or their place in the landscape, are of outstanding universal value from the point of view of history, art or science' (UNESCO, 1999). A UNESCO experts meeting on plantation systems noted 'the serial nomination also offers a possibility to bring elements from different geographical locations together that attain their outstanding universal value only in this configuration' (UNESCO, 2001: 8). This international experts meeting examined plantation systems in a broad sense, seeing them as mixing aspects that include cultural landscapes, industrial heritage, architecture (both monumental and vernacular) and having multicultural aspects in relation to WH. The experts identified plantation systems as places of memory, discussing the concept of a cultural tourism of memory; for example, as embodied in UNESCO's Slave Route Project.

Each of the sites in this serial tentative listing in the DR of six historic properties has a link to the former sugar industry there. Added to the Tentative List as a cultural site under the following criteria: (ii) 'exhibit an important interchange of human values, over a span of time or within a cultural area of the world, on developments in architecture or technology, monumental arts, town-planning or landscape design', (iv) 'be an outstanding example of a type of building or architectural or technological ensemble or landscape which illustrates (a) significant stage(s) in human history' and (vi) 'be directly or tangibly associated with events or living traditions, with ideas, or with beliefs, with artistic and literary works of outstanding universal significance' (UNESCO, 1999: 10) most of these properties are sugar mill complexes. They are said to be characteristic of both the Cuban and Haitian sugar mills from the end of the 18th century, but also some with elements of the earlier 16th-century sugar agriculture (Table 5.3).

According to Chardon (1984) the term ingenio has referred to a sugar-producing mill since its introduction in the early 1600s. The first sugar plantations were established here in and around Santo Domingo in the 16th century, around 35 sugar mills were built according to Dr Moya Pons (UNESCO, 2001). Sugarcane production here is acknowledged to have two distinct periods, the first in the 16th century when the ingenios were Spanish owned and the second in the late 18th and early 19th centuries, initiated by Cubans, North Americans and other foreigners (Chardon, 1984). By the 19th century a plantation economy had developed and sugar was produced on a large scale with imported labour. The sugar plantation system operated later than in other locations, although after emancipation labourers from the region were employed. While in the DR, as elsewhere in the region, the sugar mill is symbolic of colonialism and its plantation economies (Cornwell & Stoddard, 2001), today the ingenio remains the basic unit in the sugar production process.

The economy of the DR, long dominated by sugar, has now diversified to focus more on the service industries, including tourism. As such, tourism in the DR has developed quickly since the 1970s and 1980s when the government first invested in infrastructure. More recently, tourism has prospered through foreign direct investment in the construction of hotels, many of which are all-inclusive and thus do not encourage economic linkages with domestic businesses and benefits to the community. A United Nations (UN) investment policy review of the DR (2009: 34) noted that 'Other drawbacks of the all-inclusive model in its current form include few linkages with domestic business, other than in domestically provided support services and construction and small daily expenditure by tourists outside of the all-inclusive resorts.' The government has realized that diversification

Table 5.3 Properties in the Ruta de Los Ingenos tentative listing

Name	Date	Description/significance
Boca De Nugua Sugar Mill	2001	Located close to Santo Domingo (on the WH list since 1990), the sugar mill complex consists of a sugar mill, caldron and furnaces, warehouse, guardhouse and distilleries from the 18th century with a 16th-century irrigation system. Location of a slave rebellion around 1884, when the property was burned down. Abandoned for many years, restoration studies in 1978, partially restored 1979–1981 (UNESCO, 2001). On the Places of Memory of the Slave Route of the Latin Caribbean.
The Ancient Diego Caballero Sugar Mill	2001	This site includes a sugar mill and associated buildings from the 16th century with a water canal.
The Ancient Big House of Palavé	2001	Ruins of a plantation house located to the west of the colonial WH city of Santo Domingo.
The Sugar Mill of Engombe	2001	A 16th-century sugar mill and estate house.
Señora de Monte Alegre or la Duquesa Sugar Mill	2002	Sugar mill founded in the late 1880s by an American, represents the second period of sugar production here.
Nuestra Sanate Sugar Mill	2002	No information available.

Source: UNESCO, accessed 5 February 2012. http://www.lacult.org/sitios_memoria/Dominicana.php?lan=en and http://whc.unesco.org/en/statesparties/do

is required, acknowledging the potential for employment associated with ecotourism and sporting holidays (World Travel and Tourism Council, 2007). This diversification has attracted some international development support. However, Ashley *et al.* (2006: 8), examining the need for tourism diversification in the Caribbean, note 'In Dominican Republic near to Santo Domingo, there are the first three sugar mills built in the Western hemisphere, yet none of them are tourist attractions.'

Heritage tourism, employing the sugar heritage embodied in a route of properties such as in the Ruta de Los Ingenos, therefore, could hold potential for the broadening of both the types of tourism targeted and tourism's inherent benefits to local livelihoods. Sugar is still produced in the DR so it should also be possible for visitors to experience how sugarcane is grown (if even from passing sugarcane fields) and produced (if visits to sugar processing facilities are made available). This has the potential to add relevant historic assets, such as those that make up the Ruta de Los Ingenos, to the sugar heritage experience. The existence of a recognized sugar-related route therefore holds promise for heritage-related tourism diversification here. However, there may be issues interpreting the DR's contemporary sugar industry, which has been criticized by human rights advocates for labour abuses and contemporary forms of sugar slavery (Bernier, 2003) involving migrant Haitian workers.

The Industrial Heritage of Barbados: The Story of Sugar

The government of Barbados placed this serial cultural heritage nomination on the Tentative List in 2005, under the following cultural criteria:

(i) represent a masterpiece of human creative genius; (ii) exhibit an important interchange of human values, over a span of time or within a cultural area of the world, on developments in architecture or technology, monumental arts, town-planning or landscape design; (iii) bear a unique or at least exceptional testimony to a cultural tradition or to a civilization which is living or which has disappeared; (iv) be an outstanding example of a type of building, architectural or technological ensemble or landscape which illustrates (a) significant stage(s) in human history. (UNESCO, 2005)

As a tentative serial nomination, 'The Industrial Heritage of Barbados: The Story of Sugar' currently includes four sites designated as representing the industrial development of the sugar industry in Barbados: St Nicholas Abbey (Figure 5.1), Morgan Lewis Windmill (Figure 5.2), Codrington College (Figure 5.3) and Newton Slave Burial Ground. The Industrial Story of Sugar was placed on the Tentative List along with Historic Bridgetown and its Garrison (which was subsequently inscribed on the WH List at the 30th Session in 2011) and The Scotland District of Barbados.

From 1643 to the mid-20th century, sugar was central to the development of the Barbadian economy, and became a basis for English military and colonial expansion in the Caribbean region. Large amounts of land, labour and capital were required to cultivate the tropical cash crop and by the 1640s

Figure 5.1 St Nicholas Abbey
Source: Photo: Tara A. Inniss.

the island's entire economy and society revolved around the export of sugar and its by-products, molasses and rum.

The need to protect and expand the English presence in the Caribbean intensified as profits were reaped from sugar exports, ensuring the growth of empire. The decision to use enslaved African labour to produce sugar required a total reorganization of the society into a 'slave society' based on coercion and discipline. Thus, by the mid-17th century and within 30 years of English settlement, Barbados was the first European colony to be completely engaged in the 'sugar revolution', which transformed the industrial potential of the colonies and consumption patterns across the imperial British Empire.

The serial nomination for *The Story of Sugar* includes sites associated with several aspects of the socio-economic landscape of sugar production from the 17th to 19th centuries. In the Barbadian context, the heritage of sugar is not only seen as the disused architecture of the industrial complex, but encompasses all of the social, political and economic processes that are bound up in the *story* of sugar.

Figure 5.2 Morgan Lewis Windmill
Source: Photo: Tara A. Inniss.

The Tentative List sites represent the plantation great house and factory outbuildings (St Nicholas Abbey and Morgan Lewis Windmill), and the socio-cultural elements that accompanied the development of the sugar plantation society (Codrington College and Newton Slave Burial Ground), including debates regarding the care and treatment of the labour force; the life and work experiences of the enslaved African and Creole population; abolition and emancipation.

The heritage of sugar and enslavement is seen as a significant part of the genesis of Barbadian culture. The hybrid Creole culture born out of the African and European experience of acculturation in slave society, in a process

Figure 5.3 Codrington College
Source: Tara A. Inniss.

called *creolization*, is a critical part of this narrative (UNESCO, 2005). So, although the industrial heritage of sugar is often represented in great houses and industrial buildings, which represent power and profit in the sugar landscape, other elements of tangible and intangible heritage are needed to represent the contributions of those who toiled under or were silenced by the economic imperatives of sugar production.

Comparatively, *The Story of Sugar* has the potential to represent a unique period in sugar's industrial heritage, not currently reflected on the WH List and Tentative List. As an example drawn from the English-speaking Caribbean, it presents an earlier and distinctive trajectory for sugar development than in the Spanish-speaking Caribbean, which experienced the height of its sugar prosperity in the 19th century. The rapid success of 17th- century Barbadian planters and their investment in the industrial architecture of slavery and new sugar technologies made the colony a model for English colonial settlement and expansion, used in the creation of colonies throughout the Caribbean and mainland South and North America.

Barbados is known as a 'sophisticated' tourism destination that has attracted international visitors for centuries. After the 1960s, visitor arrivals from the United Kingdom and North America increased, and the tourism industry is now the major foreign exchange earner for the country. British visitors, in particular, have long valued the special relationship with Barbados, which is also known as 'Little England' to its former colonial ruler.

Repeat visitors are drawn to the sand, sea and sunshine. However, as the Caribbean tourism market is saturated with all-inclusive packages from cheaper destinations, Barbadian tourism officials are seeking ways to diversify the tourism product to offer a more enriched experience of Barbadian life and culture, adding value to the visitor experience. Heritage and cultural tourism are part of this strategy, and this has been an important motivation for pursuing WH status for the island's heritage sites (Barbados Ministry of Tourism, 2001).

The pursuit of WH status, however, must also respond to the main challenges of the protection and management of existing sites, which, although they largely remain intact, do suffer from neglect due in part to limited resources for preservation, but also from the perceived alienation of Barbadians from certain aspects of their history. Since emancipation, there has been a psychosocial distancing of Barbadians from their plantation history as they wish to forget the traumas of the slavery past and forge a new path to a modern post-colonial identity. Memorializing only the built heritage of the colonizer does little to convince many Barbadians that *The Story of Sugar* is *their* story. Therefore, emphasis must also be placed on researching and presenting both the tangible and intangible heritage of the descendants of enslaved Africans to ensure the sustainable development and protection of Barbadian cultural heritage.

Tourism and cultural officials have tried to address the conflict. However, cultural routes that trace the legacy of the slave trade and slavery have been seen as potential tourism attractions that may help to mediate the divide. Over the last two years, the Barbados Museum and Historical Society (BMHS) and the Ministry of Tourism have collaborated to produce a new island tour called 'Freedom Footprints' that takes visitors to various locations across the island (including to Newton Slave Burial Ground) to visit areas that are linked with the history of slavery and freedom. Originally conceptualized to be a popular attraction for visitors from the African and Barbadian diaspora, it has received more support from local Barbadians wishing to explore their own history (Interview, Deputy Director, BMHS, 1 February 2012). Recent public tours of Historic Bridgetown and its Garrison have also been over-subscribed by Barbadians wishing to learn more about the inscription, and audiences have been particularly enthralled with the interpretation and representation of the enslaved and free coloured experience in urban Barbados. Similarly, the owner-operator of St Nicholas Abbey, who has made significant investments in the preservation of the plantation, has been actively engaging the surrounding communities in employment to provide shared opportunities and benefits. He also plans to investigate the role of some of the surrounding communities in the history and development of the property (Interview, Larry Warren, St Nicholas Abbey, 20 January 2011).

Similar projects could be undertaken to ensure that the heritage of local communities is reflected not only for the consumption of the foreign visitor, but for the local Barbadians as well. Such experiences can help to cement heritage appreciation and preservation in management strategies needed to secure WH status for similar sites.

Conclusion

When the two cases on the Tentative List move to the nomination and, possibly, inscription stages, the WH related to the industrial story of sugar will have a more balanced representation in the Caribbean. However, there is the potential that other sites could be nominated in the future. For example, consideration could be given to the role that St Christopher (now known as St Kitts) played as a sugar-producing island with its good collection of 17th and 18th-century milling technologies.

Through regional meetings UNESCO encourages collaboration between the state parties in the region and those with sites that have either been inscribed or are on the Tentative List. The regional office in Havana actively nurtures the development of knowledge about and capacity for WH Site development and management through the CCBP. With the importance of the sugar heritage of the region and its OUV there may be a need for further training initiatives and for focused research and collaboration on how the universal culture and heritage of sugar can be recognized and commemorated through WH recognition in the Caribbean. Moreover, there is significant potential for the economic development and engagement of local communities, especially when the history and heritage of those communities is reflected in the management and interpretation of WH sites.

References

Abbott, E. (2008) *Sugar: A Bittersweet History*. Toronto: Penguin Canada.
Ashley, C., Goodwin, H., McNab, D., Scott, M. and Chaves, L. (2006) *Making Tourism Count for the Local Economy in the Caribbean Guidelines for Good Practice*. London: PPT Partnership and the Travel Foundation.
Barbados Ministry of Tourism (2001) *Green Paper on the Sustainable Development of Tourism in Barbados – A Policy Framework*. Bridgetown: Government of Barbados.

Barnet, M. and Lindstrom, N. (1980) The culture that sugar created. *Latin American Literary Review* 8 (16), 38–46.

Batie, R.C. (1976) Why sugar? Economic cycles and the changing of staples in the English and French Antilles, 1624–1654. *Journal of Caribbean History* (8–9), 1–42.

Bernier, B.L. (2003) Sugar cane slavery: Bateyes in the Dominican Republic. *New England Journal of International and Comparative Law* 9 (1), 17–45.

Boobbyer, C. (2011) *Frommer's Cuba* (5th ed.). Hoboken, NJ: Wiley Publishing Inc.

Chardon, R. (1984) Sugar plantations in the Dominican Republic. *Geographical Review* 74 (4), 441–454.

Conlin, M. and Jolliffe, L. (2011) *Mining Heritage and Tourism: A Global Synthesis*. London; New York: Routledge.

Cornwell, G.H. and Stoddard, E.W. (2001) Reading sugar mill ruins: 'the island nobody spoiled' and other fantasies of colonial desire. *South Atlantic Review* 66 (2), 133–157.

Edwards, J.A. and Llurdés i Coit, J.C. (1996). Mines and quarries: industrial heritage tourism. *Annals of Tourism Research* 23, 341–363.

Farmer, K. (2005) Annex: Presentation of the Caribbean countries and legal protections: The Archaeological Heritage of Barbados – The path towards World Heritage Nomination. In *World Heritage Series No. 14: Caribbean Archaeology and World Heritage* (pp. 91–96). Paris: UNESCO World Heritage Centre.

Fyall, A., Garrod, D. and Leask, A. (2008) *Managing Visitor Attractions New Directions*. Oxford: Butterworth-Heinemann.

Highman, B.W. (2000) The sugar revolution. *Economic History Review LIII* 2, 213–236.

Hospers, G-J. (2011) Industrial heritage tourism and regional restructuring in the European Union. *European Planning Studies* 10 (3), 397–404.

Hospers, G-J. and van Lochem, M. (2002) Searching for a missing link. *New Economy* 9 (1), 52–56.

ICOMOS (1987) *World Heritage List No. 460. Advisory Body Recommendation, Trinidad and the "Valle de los Ingenios"*. January 19, 1987. ICOMOS: Rome.

ICOMOS (2004) *Filling the Gaps: An Action Plan for the Future*. Paris: World Heritage Centre.

ICOMOS (2006) *Rock Art of Latin America and the Caribbean: Thematic Studies*. Rome: ICOMOS.

McAuslan, F. and Norman, M. (2007) *The Rough Guide to Cuba* (4th ed.). London, England: Penguin.

Menard, R.R. (2006) *Sweet Negotiations: Sugar, Slavery, and Plantation Agriculture in Early Barbados*. Charlottesville, VA: Virginia University Press.

Mintz, S.W. (1985) *Sweetness and Power: The Place of Sugar in Modern History*. New York: Viking.

Pollitt, B.H. (2004) The rise and fall of the Cuban sugar economy. *Journal of Latin American Studies* 36 (2), 319–348.

Pugh, J. and Momsen, J.H. (2006) *Environmental Planning in the Caribbean*. London: Ashgate.

Sanchez, P.M. and Adams, K.M. (2008) The Janus-faced character of tourism in Cuba. *Annals of Tourism Research* 35 (1), 27–46.

Schwartz, S.B. (2004) *Tropical Babylons: Sugar and the Making of the Atlantic World, 1450–1680*. Chapel Hill and London: The University of North Carolina Press.

Shackley, M. (1998) *Visitor Management Case Studies from World Heritage Sites*. Oxford: Butterworth-Heinemann.

Thompson, A.O. (2010) *Confronting Slavery: Breaking through the Corridors of Silence*. Barbados: Thompson Business Services Inc.

Timothy, D.J. and Boyd, S.W. (2003) *Heritage Tourism*. Harlow: Pearson Education Limited.

UNESCO (1972) *Convention Concerning the Protection of the World Cultural and Natural Heritage*. Paris: UNESCO.

UNESCO (1988) *Report of the World Heritage Committee Twelfth Session*. Paris: UNESCO.

UNESCO (1994) *Global Strategy for a Representative, Balanced and Credible World Heritage List*. Paris: UNESCO.

UNESCO (1999) *Operational Guidelines for the Inscription of World Heritage Sites*. Paris: UNESCO.

UNESCO (2004) *Periodic Report: State of the World Heritage in Latin America and the Caribbean*. Paris: UNESCO.

UNESCO (2005) *Operational Guidelines for the Implementation of the World Heritage Convention*. Paris: UNESCO.

UNESCO (2011) *Trinidad and the Valley de los Ingenios*, accessed December 1, 2011. http://whc.unesco.org/en/list/460

UNESCO World Heritage Committee (2001) *Information Document: Regional Experts Meeting on Plantation systems in the Caribbean, Paramaribo, Suriname, 17 to 19 July 2001*. UNESCO: Paris.

United Nations Conference on Trade and Development (2009) *Investment Policy Review Dominican Republic*. United Nations: Geneva and New York.

Williams, E. (1994) *Capitalism and Slavery* (2nd edn). Chapel Hill; London: The University of North Carolina Press.

World Travel and Tourism Council (2007) *Dominican Republic, Travel and Tourism: Navigating the Path Ahead*. London: WTTC.

6 Developing Sugar Heritage Tourism in St Kitts

Rachel Dodds and Lee Jolliffe

Industry on the Caribbean island of St Kitts has shifted from being mainly based on agriculture to a service based tourism economy. Sugar was the primary export from the 1640s onward, but rising production costs, low world market prices and increasing losses caused the shut down of the nationalized sugar industry after the harvest in 2005. Working with their main crop, the government briefly studied the potential of biofuel (electricity and ethanol) production on former sugarcane lands. However, the tourism, agricultural, export-oriented manufacturing and offshore banking sectors developed and are now taking larger roles in the country's economy.

Tourism has shown the greatest growth and is now one of the key foreign exchange earners for St Kitts, as evident from an 83% increase in foreign direct investment in tourism-related projects (US Department of State, 2011). Today, the economy of the Caribbean island of St Kitts is dominated by tourism, with it accounting for approximately 40% of Gross Domestic Product (GDP) (International Development Association, 2008). Tourism includes both cruise and stay-over visitors, with increased cruise arrivals, a major hotel development (St Kitts Marriott Resort) and residential real estate developments, such as Ocean's Edge Resort, geared to offshore visitors.

The Leeward Islands nation of St Kitts and Nevis is located in the eastern Caribbean's Lesser Antilles, in the southern half of the Caribbean archipelago. The two islands have a combined land area of 104 sq. miles (269 sq. km), with St Kitts (formerly Saint Christopher), the larger of the two, being 68 sq. miles (176 sq. km) (Ministry of Finance, 2004). St Kitts is volcanic and has a tropical marine climate. With a relatively small population of approximately 35,000 the island is also experiencing a negative population

Developing Sugar Heritage Tourism in St Kitts 111

growth due to migration, as is common with many small island developing states (SIDS).

As a Caribbean island, St Kitts offers sun and sand like many nearby islands; however, the island is now recognizing its former sugar industry as a potential resource for heritage tourism. An inventory of heritage sites and complexes outlined in the 1993 Organization of American States (OAS) Tourism Master Plan for St Kitts and Nevis identified 250 potential heritage tourism sites (Organization of American States in Collaboration with the Ministry of Trade, Industry, and Tourism of St Kitts and Nevis, 1993). Some of these sites are being developed as heritage and cultural attractions, but many are relatively unexploited and undeveloped. Main heritage site attractions on the island include the St Kitts Scenic Railway and Brimstone Hill World Heritage Site, which are included in popular cruise ship excursions. However, recently there has been an increasing focus on heritage tourism.

This chapter traces the evolution of tourism on St Kitts, examining sugar heritage as a potential diversification tool, identifying the long-term potential for incorporating the island's sugar heritage into the current tourism offered to the benefit of local communities and economies. Data were collected using a multi-method research approach with a combination of primary and secondary data. A field visit conducted in 2006 was followed up in 2011 by qualitative interviews with key stakeholders in heritage tourism, policy and tourism issues on the island. A snowballing approach was used to collect interviewee names. A longitudinal perspective was taken on both tourism and sugar to understand the transition that took place post 2005, after the closure of the sugar industry. Secondary information on St Kitts tourism, from the academic literature and local and regional tourist boards, was sourced to provide contextual information and for references to sugar heritage traditions and sites.

Tourism Context

According to Dodds and McElroy (2008: 4), 'The postwar economic history of many small Caribbean islands is the story of restructuring away from colonial stables (sugar, cotton) towards the most sustained engine in global commerce, tourism.' In Caribbean island destinations, the decline of traditional industries has led to the growth and development of tourism, seen as an economic driver (Briedenhann & Wickens, 2004; Graci & Dodds, 2011) and a potential contributor to both foreign exchange earnings and local employment and livelihoods (Lockhart, 1997; Giannoni & Maupertuis, 2007;

Scheyvens & Momsen, 2008). The island of St Kitts has a small population and tax base and as a consequence has limited production capabilities. Tourism development therefore has focused on foreign direct investment and programmes such as the Citizen by Investment Program (provided for in the 1984 Citizenship Act, which provides citizenship to foreigners buying a villa or land plot with a minimum investment of US$400,000), leading to development of new tourism accommodations rather than regeneration of existing infrastructure.

Formerly developing mainly as a sun and sea destination (Dodds & McElroy, 2008), St Kitts underwent rapid tourism development (1995–2006) before ultimately stagnating. The island suffered a major tourism arrivals drawback after 2001, as it was dependent on the US market. Tourism numbers recovered in 2004 and major development was seen; for example, the expansion of resort complexes. New hotel complexes, including international chains (such as the Marriott), were introduced; however, St Kitts again suffered a setback during the 2008 global economic recession. Arrivals from the US market dropped and hotel occupancy in 2008 declined by between 30% and 40%, many airlines also cut back operations.

Realizing that they could not offer many white sandy beaches (some of the beaches are black and volcanic), direct access or low cost (as many other islands, such as the Dominican Republic, do), the tourism industry in St Kitts started to investigate alternative types of tourism. Along with many other tourism destinations, concern over intense regional and international competition therefore led St Kitts to attempt to diversify (Dodds & McElroy, 2008). A new cruise ship port, marina and shopping precinct, Port Zante, were built and sports tourism was focused on. In 2007 St Kitts was a host venue for the ICC (International Cricket Council) Cricket World Cup; however, the island did not see as much benefit as it had hoped from this event and recognized that cruise visitors from limited cruise stops at that time may not have benefitted the local economy as much as originally anticipated. The government therefore attempted to shift its focus to heritage tourism, which encouraged increased cruise visitation through endeavours such as the St Kitts Scenic Railway, in which the original cane tracks have been utilized with new sightseeing trains as a tourist attraction, and its promotion of Brimstone Hill, a UNESCO World Heritage Site (WHS).

International tourism arrivals grew from 2004 to 2006 (approximately 90,000 to 140,000 respectively); however, numbers have dropped since then and stood at 121,000 in 2009 (World Bank Indicators, n.d.). International tourism receipts also dropped from a high of US$130 million in 2007 to US$120 million in 2009 (World Bank Indicators, n.d.).

Heritage Resources in St Kitts

Heritage is acknowledged as the single most important resource for international tourism (Graham *et al.*, 2000). Heritage places are thus significant locations for consumption, with heritage elements being arranged to be accessible to tourism. This may be facilitated by partnerships between governments as well as public and private entities responsible for conserving and protecting the heritage, such strategies may support the development of heritage visitor attractions (McKercher & du Cros, 2002). As with other Caribbean islands (Found, 2004) St Kitts possesses a wealth of heritage resources in the form of sites and material culture as a basis for participating in the growing trend of heritage tourism. The island is acknowledged to have strong assets for heritage tourism, especially in terms of its built heritage (Nurse, 2008).

In St Kitts the heritage resources related to the island's sugar heritage include a landscape shaped by sugarcane agriculture. There are numerous surviving great houses on former plantations and estates, the remains of sugar production facilities (for example, sugar mill ruins on former plantations), as well as the narrow gauge railway that transported cane from the fields to the central sugarcane factory. This rail line served the sugar factory in Basseterre that had been built starting in 1912 in an effort to modernize sugar production by centralizing processing. By 1926, the cane was brought from the fields by this narrow gauge railway, until the government stopped sugar production in 2005.

As noted by Conlin and Jolliffe (2011), regarding the heritage of former mining industries, the interpretation of the heritage of a former industry can be challenging. In the case of St Kitts and its industrial sugar heritage, there are no completely intact plantations to visit (some are just ruins, whilst at others some architectural elements remain) and no productive cane fields in which to witness the harvesting, although there are still, at the stage of this research, fields populated by volunteer cane. With the industry having been closed by the government in late 2005, there are no operating sugar mills or factories where processing can currently be viewed, or cane juice sampled, even if just on a demonstration basis. The former sugar factory is in a state of decay and some historic sugar mills are in ruins. Due to limited resources there is little possibility of restoration and operation of sugar mills for demonstration purposes, as the Barbados National Trust has done in Barbados with the Morgan Lewis Sugar Mill and was formerly done with Betty's Hope Sugar Mill in Antigua (personal communication, David Rollinson, Heritage Consultant). One resource still existing, if often in altered forms, is the plantation great houses, several of which have been converted into hospitality facilities, whilst others (intact or in ruins) are included as stops in tour itineraries.

National Heritage in St Kitts

National museums have a role to play in the independence of emerging small island nations in the Caribbean (Cummins, 1992). Heritage in St Kitts is governed by national legislation, including the National Conservation and Environment Act (1987), designating Brimstone Hill and its fortress as a National Park. A National Museum was established with the signing of an agreement between the government of St Kitts and Nevis and the St. Christopher Heritage Society (1999) for the preservation of the Old Treasury Building in Basseterre and its transformation into a National Museum. Some of the national collections, formerly held at Brimstone Hill, predate this agreement (Cummins, 1992). The National Museum opened in 2002 as a project of the St Christopher Heritage Society. In 2009 an act of government saw the society transition into the Saint Christopher National Trust (SCNT, 2011), establishing it with a broader mandate through the National Trust Bill 'for the purpose of administering and preserving sites, buildings and objects of historical, archaeological, architectural, environmental and artistic importance to the Island of Saint Christopher; and to provide for related or incidental matters' (http://stkittsheritage.com/). Sugar heritage is integral to the mandate of the museum. According to the SCNT, 'With the eventual closure of the sugar industry on St Kitts in 2005 the machinery at the Factory has stood idle, rusting and generally deteriorating as the elements and intrusive vegetation have taken their hold' (http://stkittsheritage.com/). The trust lobbied government regarding preservation of some of the sugar factory's equipment, with the intent being to identify these for a future sugar museum. As a result, significant equipment from the factory was identified for preservation.

Heritage here is also governed by international conventions. Saint Kitts and Nevis signed on as a state party to UNESCO's World Heritage Convention in 1986. Brimstone Hill Fortress National Park was inscribed as a WHS in 1999. Today, this site is managed by a not-for-profit voluntary organization, the Brimstone Hill Fortress National Park Society, under the terms of the National Conservation and Environment Act (1987). It is acknowledged that WHS has some currency in terms of tourism development (Shackley, 1998; Timothy & Boyd, 2003). While the former British fortress is a major heritage tourism site, its relationship to the island's sugar heritage is peripheral in that the fortress protected the island. The inscription documents mention the construction of the site by enslaved Africans, and it is cited as testimony to European colonial expansion, the African slave trade and the emergence of new societies in the Caribbean (UNESCO, 2011). Part of the challenge of interpreting this site is that some of the fortress is in ruins. Various interpretive methods are used here, including an informational leaflet, audio guides and a visitor centre with an interpretive film. The current administration holds special events to make the site relevant to the local and visiting public; for example, the Annual Sunset Recital is part of Independence celebrations. Visitation to the site is reported to have reached around 50,000 in 2006 (Nurse, 2008).

St Kitts also has a site on the WHS Tentative List, the Historic Zone of Basseterre, nominated under the category of a cultural site in 1998 (UNESCO, 2011). When inscribed, the tourism potential of this city, which was an integral part of the sugar trade, will be highlighted, strengthening its connection to the story of sugar.

Sugar Heritage and Tourism

The sugar heritage of St Kitts dates back to the 1640s. Large numbers of African slaves were imported to the island to provide the labour needed for this industry. Under British control in the early 1700s, St Kitts took off as a leader in sugar production in the Caribbean, especially after the French ceded the island to the British in 1713. By 1784, the sugar monoculture consisted of 120 plantations owned by British planters (Moya Pons, 2007), but at the abolition of slavery in 1834 profits from sugar began to decline.

Sugar production continued to dominate the island well into the early 20th century. The sugar industry in St Kitts was nationalized in the 1970s. Tourism was acknowledged as an alternative during the early 1980s to the early 1990s. This transition led to the Tourism Master Plan of 1993, noted earlier. Under pressure of increased global competition in the sugar industry (from the European Union), the government closed the sugar industry after the 2005 harvest, dismantling the main sugar factory, and a Sugar Industry Diversification Foundation (SIDF) was established by the government in 2006, 'to take care of the welfare of the displaced sugar workers and to accelerate the transformation of the country's economy' (SIDF, 2006). To help sustain alternative industries, the SIDF donated US$100,000 in 2011 to the SCNT to create a Heritage Site Management Unit to focus on the development of heritage tourism. These funds will oversee the affairs and development of historic venues, including the Spooners Ginnery, Bloody Point and Belmont Estate.

Sugar-Related Attractions

With the strong sugar history and heritage traditions in the region it is natural that some attractions will reflect this heritage. The regional attractions sector is mixed in terms of ownership and management, with some being owned and operated directly by government or not-for-profit entities and others being privately or family owned and directed. This leads to a wide variation in management styles and the quality of visitor attractions open to the public. Sugar-related attractions form various types of natural and cultural foci. Attraction experiences are in demand for consumption during cruise shore excursions; in the case of St Kitts interest from the cruise ship industry for a more diversified destination experience has encouraged investment to increase capacity and quality in the sector. There are a number of visitor attractions in St Kitts that are either specifically related to sugar or incorporate sugar heritage into their offerings; see Table 6.1, which outlines attractions that make up a large part of the tourism product on the island.

The first product highlighted in Table 6.1, the St Kitts Scenic Railway (SKSR), operates a sightseeing train on a former sugarcane train track, similar attractions are found in Taiwan (Chapter 8) and Australia (Chapter 3). However, in this case the attraction has been developed by a unique government and private sector partnership that has seen the government leasing the

Table 6.1 Sugar heritage attractions on St Kitts

Name	Product description
St Kitts Scenic Railway	Government/private partnership. Former sugarcane railway, now a purpose built tourist train tour product.
National Museum	Exhibits on the history of St Kitts located in the Old Treasury Building in Basseterre. Permanent and temporary exhibitions.
Belmont Estate	Former sugar estate, government owned, not currently open to the public but proposed as the future National Agriculture and Sugar Museum.
Wingfield Estate	Former sugar plantation, privately owned and currently under development, interpretive signage and guided tours are available.
Romney Manor	Romney Manor, site of Caribelle Batik, early plantation house for the Romney Plantation, adjoining Wingfield Estate.

track to the private company, SKSR, for a period of 35 years. The railway in St Kitts was originally built between 1912 and 1926 in order to transport cane from sugar plantations to the sugar factory in Basseterre (machinery from this factory is currently being held for the development of a sugar museum). This attraction is one of a few steam-operated tourist railways in the region, others being in Cuba, Guadeloupe and Martinique. It is popular with cruise visitors as a shore excursion and can be purchased on board the cruise ships; hotel based visitors and locals can also purchase tickets. As such it should appeal to railway heritage enthusiasts, to those who would like to experience a steam train journey and to those who would like to experience something of the former sugar industry by riding a sugarcane train. A significant part of the scenic railway experience is being able to see the former sugarcane agricultural landscape with the windmill towers of the sugar plantations of the past.

It is possible for visitors to take a three-hour, 30-mile circle tour of the island, partly by the train (SKSR) and partly by bus. Participation in this tour, developed specifically for and catering to the growing number of cruise ships stopping in St Kitts, is projected for the 2011–2012 season at 56,500 out of 600,000 cruise passengers (personal correspondence, Steve Hites St Kitts Scenic Railway Ltd.). The carriages of the purpose-built trains constructed in Seattle, USA have two levels, thus allowing passengers to have both a seat and a place on the observation deck. This increased opportunity for viewing is a unique characteristic of this sugar train, as those in other areas of the world (Taiwan; Australia; Maui, Hawai'i) do not have such viewing platforms. The SKSR represents a symbiotic partnership between the government and the private owners that could be a model for future heritage tourism development on the island. In addition, with its staff of 68 employees, many being the former employees of the sugarcane railway, this attraction is consequently making a significant contribution to local livelihoods in St Kitts.

The operation has also had other impacts on the local economy, for example, beyond the local employment impact; the traditional sugar cakes that are provided as a souvenir to visitors on board are manufactured by a local baker who has taken on additional staff to meet demand for the product. It is significant that the SKSR as an attraction contributes to encouraging cruise ships to stop in St Kitts. The president of the SKSR and his staff have also been involved in the volunteer effort to assist the SCNT in their efforts to preserve some of the designated equipment from the old sugar factory in Basseterre (personal communication, Steve Hites).

The second attraction is the National Museum, operated by the SCNT. The museum officially is in the Old Treasury Building in Basseterre. According to the Ministry of Tourism the exhibits were further revamped in 2008 leading up to the 25th anniversary of independence. The current museum displays include information on the sugar industry, community (slavery), built heritage and nature, an environment shaped by man for sugar monoculture. According to the Museums Association of the Caribbean the museum has the following objectives:

> Explore the interaction between the people and environment of the country, and the relationship of the people and environment with the Caribbean and the rest of the world, provide a resource for the country's history and culture, and cultivate among its citizens a deeper awareness of the heritage of the country, and promote among visitors an informed appreciation of the country and its people. (Museums Association of the Caribbean, 2011)

The museum has an important role to play in interpreting the national story of St Kitts, which includes its sugar heritage. In addition, the museum has the ability to host temporary exhibitions, which if related to sugar heritage could contribute to developing sugar-related heritage tourism.

The third and potential attraction is Belmont Estate (see Figure 6.1). This former sugar plantation, now owned by the government, has the potential

Figure 6.1 Tourists explore Wingfield Manor grounds
Source: David Rollinson

to be developed as a National Agriculture and Sugar Museum, a proposal that has the support of the Ministry of Agriculture. Being strategically located on the rail line now operated by the SKSR, it has a potential visitor market at hand and if developed could add value to the attractions currently available for developing packages and itineraries related to the island's sugar heritage.

The fourth attraction, Wingfield Estate see (Figure 6.1), is under development by the owners of the adjacent Romney Estate and Manor, home of the successful business, Caribelle Batik. Wingfield is the ruins of a historic sugar estate; over the last few years there have been several archaeological digs here, involving both tourists and residents as volunteers (see Figure 6.2), and interpretive signing is being installed (Anon., 2011). Some of the ruins are being revealed through the archaeological work while others are being built upon the original 17th-century foundations, creating a shop for the attraction as well as an office for a 'Zip Line' attraction based at the property. There is an opportunity on the site for interpreting the production of sugar, with remains of the estate, which produced sugar from 1640 to 1924, including the remnants and/or ruins of the various methods of sugar crushing, including animal power, a

Figure 6.2 Volunteer tourists tour Wingfield Manor grounds
Source: David Rollinson

water wheel (with an aqueduct still intact) and a steam engine (not yet in place). Archaeological work conducted through a volunteer tourism programme has revealed the remains of a 17th-century rum distillery. Guided visits provide an orientation to the conversion of cane to sugar, and of sugar to rum. With limited funding, the site is a work in progress and the owner-operator is developing the site to be 'informative, interesting, historically correct and financially self sustaining' (personal correspondence, Maurice Widdowson). The site is historically significant in terms of sugar heritage, and its continued development will be significant for furthering sugar-related heritage tourism on the island. The fifth attraction, located next door to Wingfield Estate, is Romney Manor. This manor house dates back to the 18th century and was the manor house of the Romney Plantation, which, as a sugar plantation for many years, was worked alongside Wingfield Estate.

Several of the small resorts on St Kitts are on former sugar plantation lands, as is clearly evident by their names (Ottley's and Rawlins), noted in Table 6.2. These inns are built around the extant structures and remains of sugar plantations (Nash, 2007). At both of the plantation inns, identified former elements of the sugar plantations have been incorporated and adapted as inn facilities. At Fairview Plantation a dining facility with some interpretation opened recently (see Figure 6.3). The rural settings of these plantations are suitable for the development of small-scale resorts and dining attractions.

For the visitor, these facilities evoke elements of nostalgia. One travel writer describes Rawlins Plantation Inn: 'On the drive through miles of sugar cane fields, you wonder if you are wandering into another century. Then your driver turns down a single-lane road that leads to a neatly manicured lawn rising to a 17th century plantation great house, and you know you've arrived at Rawlins' (Nash, 2007: 2). It is evident that inns such as Rawlins are part of the nostalgic heritage tourism industry. By preserving remains and repurposing former plantation structures, offering their guests

Table 6.2 Hospitality establishments in St Kitts on former sugar plantations

Name	Plantation	Sugar heritage remains/use
Ottley's Plantation Inn	Ottley's	Great House – Accommodations Sugar Boiling House – Dining
Rawlins Plantation Inn	Rawlins	Great House – Accommodations Sugar Mill Ruin – Accommodations
Fairview Great House and Botanical Garden	Fairview	Great House – Dining & Interpretation Chapel – Private Conference/Dining Room

Figure 6.3 Fairfield Inn
Source: David Rollinson

a glimpse of aspects of the former plantations, such as gardens and remains of sugar-processing buildings, these hospitality establishments contribute to developing sugar-related heritage tourism in St Kitts.

The great house was representative of the sugar plantation and the conversion of their historic remains, for both accommodation and dining, is a characteristic of inns and restaurants on former plantations. This is one way in which the remains of the material sugar heritage of the island are now being repurposed and used for tourism. Cornwell and Stoddard (2001) indicate that the former sugar mills are symbolic as sites of struggle over issues of nation, race and neocolonialism in the Caribbean. If these mills are incorporated into sugar attractions should their former significance be interpreted? When converted into luxury accommodations could their former use be acknowledged in how each particular plantation's history is interpreted for today's guests?

In addition to the attractions reviewed above there are other properties that could possibly play a role in heritage tourism development on the island. This includes, for example, Lodge Great House and Shadwell Great House, both in private hands and connected to the sugar industry, and the government-owned and SCNT-managed property of Spooners Ginnery, a former sugar plantation with remains of a cotton gin. A recently announced agro-tourism demonstration project, as a joint project between St Kitts and Nevis and Taiwan, is also related to the former sugar industry. The project proposal includes a labyrinth of sugarcane in the shape of the islands of both Taiwan and St Kitts. It would interpret the growth of sugarcane, a former production that both islands have in common. The project has been designed (late 2011) with input from Taiwanese landscape architects; the Prime Minister noted that this project will be important in diversifying the attractions of St Kitts, in particular for the growing cruise ship industry. Such an attraction, when implemented, has the potential to contribute to the development of sugar-related tourism in St Kitts. It also fits in with the Caribbean Agrotourism Strategy for 2007–2017 and with the agro-tourism cooperation agreement signed between Taiwan and St Kitts in March 2011 (Office of the Prime Minister, 2011).

Discussion

This section examines whether the potential for sugar-related heritage in St Kitts has been fully developed. A SWOT Analysis (strengths, weaknesses, opportunities and threats) is employed to address this question related to sugar heritage tourism on St Kitts (Table 6.3).

Strengths

This review of sugar-related heritage tourism in St Kitts has identified a number of significant strengths. There is strength in the inventory of heritage properties with a connection to the former sugar industry and to the heritage related to it. In terms of Brimstone Hill, recognition as a UNESCO WHS created significant marketing capital, raising the profile of the destination. In a similar way, the development of the SKSR as a unique attraction, one of the last operating railroads in the eastern Caribbean, has added to the marketing capital. Together these two sites are situated as anchors and primary attractions for a heritage industry supported by other secondary sites and attractions, including, at this stage, the National Museum and Romney Manor along with Wingfield Estate. With additional investment and development, other heritage sites, such as Belmont Estate, may be positioned to play their role in strengthening the heritage tourism brand of St Kitts. Backing up this

Table 6.3 SWOT analysis of sugar-related tourism in St Kitts

Strengths	Opportunities
• Location central to the sugar history of the region. • Inventory of heritage properties. • Government/private partnership for visitor attractions. • Private ownership and operation of key heritage sites/assets. • Integrity of landscape with government ownership. • Development of small-scale attractions with limited resources. • Marketing capital afforded by the UNESCO World Heritage designation.	• Packaging of individual sugar heritage experiences into products. • Developing a 'sugar heritage route' with a map and a brochure. • Nurturing stakeholder partnerships for cross-promotion and packaging. • Developing educational tourism and volunteer tourism markets. • Volunteer and not-for-profit organization commitment. • Agro-tourism developments.
Weaknesses	*Threats*
• Lack of funding for heritage development. • Lack of profile for significance of sugar heritage. • Slow development of the Belmont Estate. • Many other Caribbean islands are also developing sugar heritage tourism so potential overexposure may result.	• Overreliance on the cruise ship visitor market. • Impact of the global economic crisis on the tourism market. • Decline of sugarcane fields.

potential is the strong level of partnership between public and private entities, all in support of the development of small-scale heritage tourism.

Opportunities

With both a growing demand for heritage experiences from consumers and the need to diversify their tourism offerings, there may be some opportunities in terms of developing sugar-related tourism in St Kitts. Evidence of interest in sugar-related tourism is found in the growth of the number of people riding the SKSR to 56,500 out of 600,000 cruise passengers in the 2011–2012 season (personal correspondence, Steve Hites). Therefore, other approaches may be warranted; for example, there is no trail, map or route that would connect the sugar-related attractions (plantation inns, sugar plantations, etc.). This is a technique that has been used in sustainable tourism development in other parts of the world (Briedenhann & Wickens, 2004). This could be a self-guided tour, with a brochure provided online, at car rental agencies and to taxi drivers, or could be provided to tour guides, in order to address, in part, the growing demand for cruise ship products. Such a product could also be tied into the history of emancipation in St Kitts, as has been done with the Freedom Footprints: The Barbados Story tour developed by the Barbados Museum for the Ministry of Culture, Barbados. The tour links sites along the path to freedom and was piloted early in 2011.

Joint and or cross-marketing of sugar heritage-related attractions in St Kitts, which already takes place on an informal basis, could also be undertaken. For example, the connectivity of the Romney Manor and Wingfield Estate sites, in terms of location and connection to a shared sugar industry heritage, provides an obvious strength for future heritage tourism packaging. There is the opportunity to develop an inter-island sugar tour experience with the twin island of Nevis, an island that also has a similar sugar heritage, currently reflected in the ruins of sugar mills and plantations as well as their remains, some of which have been incorporated into contemporary inn operations.

The plantation inns of St Kitts while not visitor attractions per se are nonetheless important to the visitor experience, as those few who want to experience the plantation setting as part of their vacation on St Kitts can do so by staying there. In addition, these inns are positioned to take part in sugar-related tourism packaging, by providing lunches, teas and garden visits during day tours and more comprehensive packages that include overnight stays plus an array of sugar heritage activities.

Weaknesses

A recurring theme here has been the limited resources for the development of heritage tourism and it is of note that volunteer tourism and volunteers have made a significant contribution to that effort. For example, volunteer tourism efforts with an archaeological dig at Winfield Estate led to the discovery of a 17th-century rum distillery (Anon., 2011). Perhaps there is potential for the further development of volunteer tourism programmes, attracting volunteers with experience in heritage preservation, conservation and tourism. There is also the potential for other Caribbean islands to also focus on the niche of sugar heritage tourism, which may dilute the attractiveness of heritage sugar tours by cruise ship visitors as it would no longer be unique to St Kitts.

222

Threats

The overreliance on cruise ship shore excursions can be seen as both a weakness and an opportunity in that the cruise market could decline due to external factors, but at the same time innovations in shore excursion products could attract more visitors ashore or indeed could attract new cruise stops. In addition, a threat identified by one of the key stakeholders is that the volunteer sugar cane plants, descending from the sugar fields of 2005, will soon be at the end of its natural cycle and new cultivated cane fields should be planted to preserve the sugarcane landscape as a tourism resource.

Conclusion

The attractions in St Kitts therefore have a strong connection to both the colonial and post-colonial history of the island, which included sugar monoculture, for example the SKSR and the plantation inns. Sugar heritage that permeates all aspects of the history of the island is thus woven into the interpretive story of the attractions, as some remains of the industry are still quite evident in the physical landscape and architectural remains, as well as in the intangible culture of local folklore and cuisine (for example, the local sugar cakes). However, much more investment is needed than is currently available in order to tell a more complete story; for example, to complete the development of the sugar-related attractions of Belmont Estate and Wingfield Estate. Dixon et al. (2005) suggest community ownership and management of attractions is necessary for the development of visitor attractions in the region. For St Kitts it seems that with a limited population base and a rich inventory of heritage resources the way forward will involve partnership between government and private entities with community involvement.

As Graci and Dodds (2011) note, the facilities that are a legacy of the sugar industry on St Kitts are in need of upgrading and investment, and, as both natural and cultural resources, are in need of protecting in order for them to play a role in the sustainable development of tourism on the island. The government has addressed some of this need through enabling legislation (2010) to strengthen the pivotal role of the SCNT. One development that clearly has the potential to address the gap is the proposed development of the government-owned and SCNT-managed Belmont Estate as a National Agriculture and Sugar Museum. The government, through the Ministry of Agriculture, has been a proponent of this project for a number of years. Other interested parties have put forward suggestions for the development of the site but progress on this project has been hampered, perhaps by lack of support and available funding.

In conclusion, sugar heritage as a resource has potential for contributing to sustainable growth and development of the tourism industry in St Kitts. Small-scale sugar attraction development by local entrepreneurs supported by government and with the involvement of community based organizations and volunteers will be the most suitable way forward. This would ensure that the people of St Kitts directly benefit from the commodification of their heritage, while preserving this heritage for future generations. As an SIDS, this will also allow St Kitts to further develop sugar-related heritage tourism, regaining their historic domination over sugar by implementing a sweet form of heritage tourism with the potential to set them apart from other Caribbean small island destinations. As a locale transitioning from sugar to tourism, St Kitts therefore has the potential to be put forward as a prototype destination for the development of sugar heritage tourism in the region.

Acknowledgment

Daisy Mottram, secretary of the St Christopher National Turst, provided invaluable assistance in facilitating the collection of information for completing the chapter on St Kitts.

References

Anon. (2011) Wingfield Estates St Kitts, unpublished manuscript.
Briedenhann, J. and Wickens, E. (2004) Tourism routes as a tool for the economic development of rural areas – vibrant hope or impossible dream? *Tourism Management* 25 (1), 71–79.
Conlin, M. and Jolliffe, L. (2011) *Mining Heritage and Tourism: A Global Synthesis*. London; New York: Routledge.
Cornwell, G.H. and Stoddard, E.W. (2001) Reading sugar mill ruins: 'the island nobody spoiled' and other fantasies of colonial desire. *South Atlantic Review* 66 (2), 133–157.
Cummins, A. (1992) Exhibiting culture: Museums and national identity in the Caribbean. *Caribbean Quarterly* 38 (2–3), 33–53.
Dixon, A.,Letang, M., Stephens, R. and Tingle, A. (2005) Planning & managing visitor attractions in the Caribbean. In C. Jayawardena (ed.) *Caribbean Tourism: Visions, Missions, Challenges* (pp. 274–299). Kingston: Ian Randle Publishers.
Dodds, R. and McElroy, J. (2008) St Kitts at a crossroads. *ARA Journal of Travel Research* 1 (2), 1–10.
Found, W. (2004) Historic sites, material culture and tourism in the Caribbean islands. In D.T. Duval (ed.) *Tourism in the Caribbean Trends, Developments, Prospects* (pp. 136–151). London: Routledge.
Giannoni, S. and Maupertuis, M-A. (2007) Environmental quality and optimal investment in tourism infrastructures: A small island perspective. *Tourism Economics* 13 (4), 499–514.

Graci, S. and Dodds, R. (2011) *Sustainable Tourism in Island Destinations*. London; New York: Earthscan.
Graham, B., Ashworth, G.J. and Tunbridge, J.E. (2000) *A Geography of Heritage*. London: Arnold.
International Development Association (2008) St Kitts and Nevis: Supporting the Vital Tourism Industry, accessed 27 October 2011. http://web.worldbank.org/.
Lockhart, D.G. (1997) Islands and tourism: An overview. In D.G Lockhart and D. Drakakis-Smith (eds) *Island Tourism – Trends and Prospects* (pp. 3–21). London: Pinter.
McKercher, B. and du Cros, H. (2002) *Cultural Tourism: The Partnership between Tourism and Cultural Heritage Management*. New York: The Haworth Hospitality Press.
Ministry of Finance (2004) The Federation of St Kitts and Nevis National Assessment of The BPOA + 10: 1994–2003. The Planning Unit, St Kitts, accessed 22 October 2011. http://www.sidsnet.org/docshare/other/20041104160840_ST_KITTS_AND_NEVIS. pdf.
Moya Pons, F. (2007) *History of the Caribbean: Plantations, Trade, and War in the Atlantic World*. Princeton, NJ: Markus Wiener Publishers.
Museums Association of the Caribbean (2011) Accessed 10 November 2011. http://www. caribbeanmuseums.com.
Nash, K.C. (2007) The plantation inns of St Kitts and Nevis. *Caribbean Edge Magazine*, 1–2.
Nurse, K. (2008) *Development of a Strategic Business Management Model for the Sustainable Development of Heritage Tourism Products in the Caribbean*. Barbados: The Caribbean Tourism Organization.
Office of the Prime Minister (2011) St Kitts and Nevis and Taiwan Sign Agro-Tourism Farm Cooperation Agreement, accessed 1 November 2011. http://www.cuopm.com/ newsitem.asp?articlenumber=1982&post200803=true.
Organization of American States in Collaboration with the Ministry of Trade, Industry, and Tourism of St Kitts and Nevis (1993) Tourism Master Plan for St Kitts and Nevis: Economic Rationale for Nature and Heritage Tourism, accessed 15 October 2011. http://www.oas.org/dsd/publications/unit/oea78e/ch05.htm#A.
Saint Christopher National Trust (2011) Accessed 15 November 2011. http://stkittsher-itage.com/.
Scheyvens, R. and Momsen, J.H. (2008) Tourism and poverty reduction: Issues for small island states. *Tourism Geographies* 10 (1), 22–41.
Shackley, M. (1998) *Visitor Management Case Studies from World Heritage Sites*. Oxford: Butterworth-Heinemann.
SIDF (2011) About the Sugar Industry Diversification Foundation, accessed 20 October 2011. http://www.sidf.org/about/.
Timothy, D.J. and Boyd, S.W. (2003) *Heritage Tourism*. Harlow: Pearson Education Limited.
UNESCO (2011) Brimstone Hill Fortress National Park, accessed 15 December 2012. http://whc.unesco.org/en/list/910.
US Department of State (2011) Bureau of Western Hemisphere Affairs. Background Note: Saint Kitts and Nevis, accessed 16 October 2011. http://www.state.gov/r/pa/ei/ bgn/2341.htm.
World Bank Indicators (n.d.) St Kitts and Nevis: Travel and Tourism, accessed 26 October 2011. http://www.tradingeconomics.com/st-kitts-and-nevis/international-tourism-number-of-arrivals-wb-data.html.

7   The Contested Heritage of Sugar and Slavery at Tourism Attractions in Barbados and St Lucia

Mechelle N. Best and Winston F. Phulgence

Is there a story of the anglophone Caribbean without the story of sugar and slavery? Sugar as a commodity has dominated the Caribbean for most of the last 500 years, the evidence of which remains today. The production of sugar changed land use patterns in the Caribbean with large plantations and extensive cane fields superseding forests and other land cover to dominate the landscape. It also changed the economy of the region such that one main export crop became the basis for the existence of the colonies of the region. Further, the production of sugar led to drastic changes in the structure of Caribbean societies. For most of the region, the population transformed into one comprised primarily of enslaved Africans, whose enslavement fulfilled the need for a large cheap labour force. Though the sugar industry has long been on a downward spiral and sugar has lost its importance for many of the former colonies, its legacy provides the foundation for much of the region's heritage. The social structure and power dynamics that the sugar industry engendered continue to be reflected in the contentious historiography of the Caribbean region and by extension its heritage.

For many decades the sugar heritage in the anglophone Caribbean has been central to its tourism product. Indeed it is arguable that as far back as the 17th century sugar production and all it encompasses has been a pull factor in luring visitors to the shores of various colonies in the region. Yet, the story of slavery, without which this heritage of sugar could not exist, is notably absent, conspicuously silent from the interpretation of heritage sites now used as tourism attractions.

For the most part, the tangible heritage emphasized has been the plantation houses, while the intangible heritage has been the stories of the planter class. Generally absent from the tangible heritage are the slave huts, the cane fields and the sugar routes, and from the intangible heritage the voices and stories of the slaves. Not surprisingly there is disagreement as to not only how heritage is interpreted, but also whose heritage is interpreted. While the issue of contested heritage remains the subject of ongoing debate, questions arise as to whether or not this silence is apparent to visitors to the sites and if it impacts their experience and satisfaction.

Surveys of visitors to heritage sites in the region are infrequent. Where such surveys are undertaken, there is the tendency to ask questions which speak to the satisfaction of visitors with the interpretation at a site. Oftentimes this is operationalized as a single item on a list of features which respondents are asked to evaluate against a predetermined scale. To the authors' knowledge there are no studies of heritage sites that have focused on eliciting visitors' perceptions of the silence of slaves and their descendants in the interpretation at sites where they were the lifeblood. This chapter presents perceptions of tourists visiting popular sugar heritage sites in two contrasting destinations in the anglophone Caribbean: Sunbury Plantation House in Barbados, where sugar today remains the primary agricultural export, and Morne Coubaril Estate in St Lucia, where sugar production ceased decades ago.

Heritage Production on Plantations

The sugar plantation has dominated the history and psyche of the Caribbean for close to five centuries. The use of enslaved Africans on those plantations and the constant fight to destroy the regime of what many historians refer to as the plantation system have left an indelible mark on the Caribbean. Found (2004) notes that preservation of plantations has been a priority in the region, with more plantations preserved than any other type of historic site. Today these plantations, presented as heritage sites, have become major attractions in the Caribbean tourism product. This presents some difficulties because plantation heritage for many is also slavery heritage. It is a contested heritage.

The issue of contested plantation/slavery heritage has not been addressed by many in the Caribbean, with very little literature dealing with it directly. Lowenthal's (2008) critical analysis of the rise of heritage, though not focused specifically on the Caribbean, is relevant to the exploration of plantation sugar heritage in the Caribbean because it highlights the difficulties encountered in the creation of heritage in a contested landscape: Whose heritage will be celebrated? The author explores the creation of heritage and the role of power in its creation, highlighting the fact that in the creation of heritage in any specific context the marginalized or minorities are less likely to have their stories told. How much does the slavery story inform the creation of heritage in the context of the Caribbean?

While there has been a relatively rapid increase in plantation heritage tourism very little academic literature deals with the issues inherent in using the plantation as a place of leisure and pleasure considering its place in the history of the Caribbean, a concern raised by Dann and Potter (2001) that remains relevant today. Giovannetti (2006) deals with this issue by looking at the role of race and racism as central forces in the creation of the plantation and by extension the wider society. He focuses on the plantation as a space for defining racial meaning in present-day Caribbean society. This is particularly relevant as the plantation as a specific space has transitioned from being a central force in the sugar industry to one in the tourist industry, with both industries being the engines of economic growth in their respective epochs. Giovannetti (2006) highlights the inherent contradictions in the use of the sugar plantations as heritage sites and as popular representations of the past.

Seaton (2001), in an analysis of differences in silences and disclosures between slavery heritage sites in the United Kingdom and the United States, explores the role that power plays in the creation of heritage. The author explores how the perception of more powerful groups informs the preferred view of history, thus creating the silences in the heritage presented and consumed. In this study the roles of various groups are presented as shaping what is determined to be heritage with the context of power and time. This study is very relevant to the present chapter because it looks at the role of the consumer of the heritage product, an issue which is often ignored.

Dann and Seaton (2001), in an analysis of papers on slavery and contested heritage, ask pertinent questions which are also relevant to the present chapter. One of these is the question of methodology. How does one approach the study of slavery heritage? This question is relevant to the study of plantation and sugar heritage in the Caribbean. A great deal of emphasis is placed on the notion of silences, and the authenticity of the heritage presented on slavery sites and plantations is no exception. For Dann and Seaton oftentimes the questions of silence were raised by the researchers themselves. All too often the voices of both the marginalized co-owners and consumers of the heritage are absent from the studies. This continued silence may stem in part from the limitations of methodology. The popular approaches used have not lent themselves to answering such questions.

Tourism and contested heritage are explored by Roushanzamir and Kreshel (2001) in their analysis of promotional material for what they refer to as a first-rate heritage site by 'industry standards' in Louisiana. They focus on the compromised history, which has been turned into heritage, and the resultant creations which commodify and sanitize the plantation to make it a tourist attraction. Clearly the product consumed by the tourist is very different from the reality that a slave plantation represents. As is often the case, the processes which create the heritage product ignore much and consequently distort history. The authors performed a content analysis of promotional material used for a Louisiana plantation and compared it to its history. The paper is focused on the production of heritage. The silences produced and the disconnect uncovered by this analysis have little to do with those whose history is distorted or the consumers of the invented heritage. Methodology is an issue.

The issue of a disconnect between history and the heritage tourism product is also explored in Dann and Potter's (2001) analysis of heritage in Barbados. They highlight the wealth of historical texts available to inform the heritage of the country but argue that the 'tourism industry has largely ignored or been highly selective in borrowing from this rich source of material' (Dann & Potter, 2001: 51). Similarly Corkern (2004: 10) states

> The purveyors of heritage tourism ... all too often serve up a kind of lowest-common-denominator drivel that is designed to tell visitors what they already know. ... Rarely does heritage tourism challenge or surprise. Heritage tourism does not present a version of history that is dirty or controversial. It does not challenge the conventional wisdom.

In *Silencing the Past* Trouillot (1995) discusses the production of silence in history and the heritage which such silence informs. His critical analysis of history production and by extension heritage creation is particularly relevant when dealing with plantation heritage. The sugar plantation was the scene of horrific acts of inhumanity and forced labour but is today promoted as the ideal place for the pursuit of pleasure, while site managers are noticeably silent about the atrocities which took place in the same space (Dann & Seaton, 2001).

The issue of silence and authenticity in the production of plantation heritage is also raised by Giovannetti (2009) in his comparison of the plantation heritage in Barbados, Puerto Rico, Cuba and Brazil, four nations with well-documented, extensive plantation histories. Giovannetti, in addition to reviewing existing research on the subject, conducted his research through participant observation at each of the four sites studied. Using this method he toured select plantations to observe the presentations of the heritage by tour guides assigned to the respective plantations and more passive interpretation methods (e.g. pamphlets, displayed artifacts, furniture). The lack of a slave narrative on many of the tours and the role of power relations and how they affect the narrative are explored.

In much of the literature evaluated for this paper methodology was an issue, with the majority of studies based on reviews of existing literature, content analysis of promotional materials and or observation. Dann and Seaton (2001) have also raised methodology as a concern. None of the research on Caribbean sites explored the issue of silence from the point of view of the people whose history is commodified or the consumer for whom authenticity is an issue.

A gap exists in the research that has been conducted on heritage sites in the Caribbean, more specifically, on former sugar-producing, slavery dependent plantations, now used as tourism attractions. What is largely unknown is whether the silence of slavery is evident to the consumers of heritage at these sites. The research reported in this chapter contributes to the reduction of this gap in knowledge and also addresses the issue of methodology by directly eliciting the perspectives of visitors to these sites. The specific objective of the study detailed in this chapter was to therefore to determine the extent to which tourists visiting heritage sites noticed the absence of slavery focused interpretation or presentation of heritage, that is the persistence of 'silence' of slaves.

Methodology

The data analyzed and reported in this chapter are drawn from a larger, ongoing study being implemented at heritage sites in the Caribbean, which focuses on both residents and tourists. Only tourists' responses are presented here.

Convenience sampling was used to determine potential participants for the survey because of the exploratory nature of the research and the sometimes inconsistent visitation to heritage sites. In Barbados the survey was administered in three ways: onsite, on board tour buses that included the site in their itinerary, and in the check-in area of the Grantley Adams International Airport. The latter two methods were added after the first day of the survey as permission to invite participants onsite was withdrawn when the managing director read the questions that were more focused on slavery. In St Lucia the survey was administered onsite only.

The research instrument was a self-administered questionnaire, which was distributed by trained research assistants who remained on hand to provide help as necessary. The questions were primarily close-ended with a few open-ended questions used to elicit additional details. The questionnaire consisted of three sections. The main section included questions which measured variables pertaining to heritage sites visited, satisfaction, sense of connection to the site (Buzinde & Santos, 2009), heritage features evident and desired (Butler, 2001; Butler *et al.*, 2008), knowledge of slavery and source of knowledge (Trouillot, 1995), and adequacy of slavery interpretation (Heard, 2006; Strait, 2004). The remaining sections solicited feedback on travel patterns and demographics. Silence was operationalized through several focused questions on the adequacy of slavery interpretation, the level of detail or emphasis of slavery presentations and the evidence of slavery at the site.

Study Sites

Sunbury Plantation House

The *Ins and Outs of Barbados*, one of the country's oldest and most popular tourist magazines, refers to Sunbury Plantation House as 'a superb example of a Barbadian sugar estate great house' (Miller *et al.*, 2011: 203). The plantation house is over 350 years old and changed ownership many times over the course of its history. According to the plantation's website, Sunbury is 'a living monument to plantation life of bygone era, carefully restored and lovingly cherished by its owners for posterity, for the enjoyment of generations to come' (http://www.barbadosgreathouse.com: 11). One of the site's brochures further describes it as 'the epitome of old plantation life'.

Morne Coubaril Estate

Morne Coubaril is one of the oldest plantations on Saint Lucia. The literature on the plantation's webpage traces its history to the 1740s, when the original owners obtained a land grant from the French government and established the plantation. During its long history the plantation suffered from slave rebellions, which plagued the colony during the era of the French Revolution. The plantation was owned by the same family up until the turn of the 20th century. The plantation's website invites visitors to experience a working plantation and 'visit historical features of the estate and take a look inside authentic huts' (http://www.stluciaziplining.com) on the tour.

Survey Findings

A survey of visitors to the two sites was conducted from June to August 2011 on Sunbury Plantation House in Barbados and from July to August 2011 at Morne Coubaril Estate in St Lucia. There were 86 usable questionnaires: 29 collected at Morne Coubaril Estate in St Lucia and 57 from Sunbury Plantation House in Barbados. For approximately 80% of the participants their primary purpose for visiting the islands was leisure; for the remainder their primary purpose was visiting friends and relatives, meetings, business or some other purpose. Most (79%) were visiting the respective island for the first time and traveling with family (64%).

Participants were almost evenly distributed between the genders: males made up approximately 49% and females 51%. The largest percentage of participants (23%) was in the US$75,001–$100,000 household income bracket, Caucasian (58%), of non-Caribbean descent (84%), and had a Bachelor's (35%) or advanced degree (37%). The majority of participants were visiting from the United States (48%), 18.7% were from the UK, 8% from Canada and 9% from several countries in the Caribbean (Table 7.1).

To determine their sense of connectedness to the site participants were asked to indicate their level of agreement with three statements: 'this site is part of my heritage'; 'I feel a sense of belonging to this site'; and 'this site has symbolic meaning for me'. The statements were rated on a scale of one–five where one equaled strongly disagree and five equaled strongly agree. Most visitors to Sunbury either strongly disagreed (37%) or disagreed (30%) that the site was a part of their heritage. The mean rating was 2.2. Responses to the same question at Morne Coubaril were more evenly distributed with 33% of participants neither agreeing nor disagreeing. The mean rating of this statement was three. The participants' rating of the remaining two statements, 'I feel a sense of belonging to this site'; and 'this site has symbolic meaning for me', followed this pattern of distribution for the respective site (Table 7.2).

Participants were asked to rate their knowledge of slavery prior to and after experiencing the site. For both questions the rating was measured using a five-point scale, where one represented 'not at all knowledgeable' and five 'very knowledgeable'. On the variable 'prior knowledge' the mean rating was 3.15 (SE = 0.16) for Sunbury and 3.38 (SE = 0.26) for Morne Coubaril. An independent sample t-test was used to compare the responses for the two sites. When the two sites were compared there was no difference in knowledge before the participants experienced the sites ($t(76) = 0.81$, p > 0.05). After experiencing the site, the mean level of knowledge increased negligibly

Table 7.1 Visitor profile

	Sunbury Plantation (%)	Morne Coubaril (%)
Type of tourist		
Stayover	68	86
Cruise passenger	28	11
Excursionist (non-cruise)	4	3
Primary purpose of visit		
Leisure/vacation/holiday	82	89
Visiting friends & relatives	5	0
Meeting/convention	0	11
Business	7	0
Other	6	0
Gender		
Male	54	39
Female	46	61
Race		
African descent/Negro/Black	13	39
East Indian	4	0
White/Caucasian	66	43
Indigenous people (Amerindian/Carib)	0	7
Other Asian	4	0
Hispanic	9	4
Mixed race	4	4
Other	0	3
Of Caribbean descent	9	29
Education		
Less than high school	2	7
High school	16	14
Technical school	2	0
2-year college degree	6	11
4-year college degree	27	50
Advanced degree	47	18
Origin		
United States	56	48
United Kingdom	21	21
Canada	11	7
Caribbean	8	14
Other	4	10

Table 7.2 Rating of connectedness to site

	Strongly disagree	Disagree	Neither agree/ disagree	Agree	Strongly agree	Mean	N
This site is part of my heritage (%)							
Sunbury Plantation House	37	30	18	11	14	2.2	54
Morne Coubaril Estate	15	18	33	15	19	3	27
I feel a sense of belonging to this site (%)							
Sunbury Plantation House	29	33	28	6	4	2.2	54
Morne Coubaril Estate	7	18	56	4	15	3	27
This site has symbolic meaning for me (%)							
Sunbury Plantation House	30	32	19	13	6	2.3	53
Morne Coubaril Estate	7	15	47	11	19	3.2	27

for visitors to Sunbury (M = 3.17, SE = 0.13) and decreased for visitors to Morne Coubaril (M = 3.24, SE = 0.25). Again there was no significant difference in knowledge between the two groups after the participants experienced the sites ($t(76) = 0.27$, $p > 0.05$).

A paired sample t-test was used to determine whether the difference in knowledge prior to and after experiencing the sites was significant. The difference in knowledge was not significant for either Sunbury ($t(51) = 0.24$, $p > 0.05$) or Morne Coubaril ($t(23) = 0.84$, $p > 0.05$).

Eighty-two percent of participants from Sunbury indicated that the subject of slavery was not adequately portrayed at the site while 80% of those at Morne Coubaril said the same. Additionally, 90% of Sunbury participants and 88% of Morne Coubaril participants suggested that the subject of slavery should be presented with more detail or emphasis. In their explanation of the need for more detail or emphasis, participants made statements such as: 'we did not gain any knowledge on this tour about the slavery and that aspect of plantation life and colonization', 'slavery is past history and it should always be shared with other generations', 'the tour guide didn't mention slavery at all', 'didn't even get the idea of slaves being present, only owners living there', and 'it's an ugly truth that makes many uncomfortable but must be confronted unflinchingly'.

Approximately 10% of Sunbury participants indicated that they had gained insight on the relationships that existed between slaves and their masters. One participant who gained no insight about the relationship further explained that 'they just did not talk about slavery. There was no connection or feeling of the slaves to the plantation house', while another participant stated 'perhaps it was the short duration of the tour, but I got no insight about slavery'. For Morne Coubaril only 4% of participants had gained any such insight. A visitor to Morne Coubaril said that 'slaves were treated any way by their masters' when asked to describe the insight gained on the relationship between slaves and their masters.

Participants were asked to rate the historic information presented and their learning experience. Most Sunbury participants rated the historic information as good (46%), while most Morne Coubaril participants rated it as average (32%). Additionally, 25% of Morne Coubaril participants rated the historic information as poor (Table 7.3). In terms of their learning experience, most Sunbury participants rated it as average (37%) or good (35%), while most Morne Coubaril participants rated it as average (41%) (Table 7.3).

To further explain their perception of the site, participants were asked to complete the following statement: 'having experienced this site I am disappointed that/with ...'. There were 42 responses to this question. While 10 participants completed the statement with 'nothing', nine responses

Table 7.3 Rating of historic information and learning experience

	Poor	Average	Good	Very Good	Excellent	N
Rating of historic information presented (%)						
Sunbury Plantation House	2	25	46	19	8	52
Morne Coubaril Estate	25	32	21	11	11	28
Rating of learning experience (%)						
Sunbury Plantation House	4	37	35	16	8	52
Morne Coubaril Estate	15	41	26	11	7	27

directly addressed the lack of slavery interpretation and another eight responses spoke more generally of a lack of information about history, heritage, sugar and plantation life. At Sunbury the statement was finished with phrases such as: 'the connection to the slaves, there was none. How the house relates to actual slavery'; 'I did not learn more about the role of slavery in Barbados history'; 'nothing on slavery or its history'; and 'it did not talk more about the history of slaves and its contributions'. At Morne Coubaril participants completed the statement with phrases such as: 'not knowing more about the experience of slavery'; 'no effort was place on slavery'; 'the history of this site was not focus on as it relates to slavery'; and 'the lack of info an[d] the role of slaves in shaping St Lucia'.

Discussion

The profile of visitors to Sunbury and Morne Coubaril is in keeping with that of visitors to Barbados and St Lucia respectively, namely persons primarily from the United States and the United Kingdom traveling with their families for leisure purposes. Additionally, participants in this study were mainly Caucasian with no ancestral ties to the Caribbean. Despite the aforementioned factors and the limited sense of connectedness to the sites (i.e. not their heritage, limited sense of belonging and symbolic meaning), participants were overwhelmingly supportive of the position that the sites failed to give voice to the slaves and only minimally acknowledged the institution of slavery. In effect, the participants supported the dominant view extrapolated from the literature that the silence of slaves permeates the popular heritage sites in the Caribbean. Further, this silence is not what they want to experience at the heritage sites they visit.

Visitors to Sunbury Plantation and Morne Coubaril considered themselves to be moderately knowledgeable about slavery before visiting the site. After experiencing the respective sites their level of knowledge was relatively unchanged, despite them having rated both the historic information presented and their learning experience as good (Sunbury) and average (Morne). Notably, far fewer participants rated either the historic information or their learning experience as very good or excellent. These findings all suggest that the sites either provided very little interpretation on slavery, or that whatever was provided was at best not new information, or at worst superficial as has been suggested by Corkern (2004) and Thompson (2010).

Visitors to both Sunbury and Morne Coubaril, having self-rated their prior knowledge of slavery as average, indicated that they gained no further knowledge by experiencing the site. This supports Giovannetti's (2009) and others' observations that though plantations have been the focus of historic preservation in the region, and in spite of the availability of appropriate historic information, little effort has been made to extend the interpretation at sugar plantations beyond the traditional by adequately addressing the realities of slavery and the pivotal role it played in the plantation economy (see further examples in Butler *et al.*, 2008; Found, 2004; Pattullo, 2005; Thompson, 2010). Further, that such sites are mainly used as tourism attractions only serves to exacerbate the problem. In a similar vein, Dann and Potter (2001: 65) posited that:

the connoted realities which lie behind these denoted historic icons are being sanitized to suit the demands of recreational tourism. While there is a pretence to education, the entire visitor experience amounts to little more than passing entertainment.

That the survey participants' knowledge of slavery was unchanged by their experience at Sunbury and Morne Coubaril is not surprising given that most of them felt that what little interpretation there was of slavery was inadequate, with far too little detail or emphasis, in light of the fact that slaves were an integral part of plantation life. Statements such as 'the tour guide did not mention slavery at all' and 'I think it is important for people to know the history of the people that made this island famous and that sacrificed themselves for so many years' made by visitors to Sunbury and 'we did not gain any knowledge on this tour about the slavery and that aspect of plantation life and colonization' and 'it [slavery] was not really mentioned' are reflective of Giovannetti's (2009) observations about St Nicholas Abbey in Barbados and similar sites functioning as tourism attractions in the Caribbean. About St Nicholas Abbey, Giovannetti states 'slavery or slave labor is not mentioned on the tour, and the word "slavery" is not printed a single time in the five-page, single-spaced document provided as a description of the self-guided tour' (2009: 108).

The production of heritage within the plantation context is not devoid of the power relations which pervade the history of the Caribbean. The issue of whose heritage is presented is testimony to that. What is presented within the contested space is determined by who has the power to decide what is important or what is trivial, following Trouillot (1995: 115), 'power polishes the rough edges that do not fit neatly' in the plantation narrative. This is also clearly highlighted in Dann and Potter (2001) when the ownership of the plantations is looked at as an issue in heritage production. Power relations in the production of heritage are presented as part of what Seaton (2001) refers to as the Heritage Force Field, in which the goals and interests of the owner supersede those of the subject group in the production of heritage on the plantation.

Conclusion

The objective of the study reported in this chapter was to determine the extent to which tourists visiting select heritage sites in the Caribbean noticed the absence of slavery centered interpretation, or the 'silence' of slaves. From the responses to this survey it is evident that from the tourists' perspective the silence of slaves is deafening. In effect, it would appear that slavery either did not exist or was peripheral to the very existence of Sunbury Plantation House and Morne Coubaril Estate. While tourists at these sites were somewhat satisfied with their overall experience, they appeared to be quite disappointed with the sites' approach to the interpretation, or lack thereof, of this aspect of the heritage. This reinforces the notion that whilst some effort has been exerted to preserve the region's tangible heritage, the intangible heritage, which is largely what remains of slavery, is ignored. There is no doubt that the heritage continues to be contested and the argument can be made that the imbalances of the plantation society persist even in the current time. While this is without a doubt a great concern in the broader context of whose heritage should be preserved and interpreted, it is of particular concern for these sites, which depend on tourism for their survival.

Morne Coubaril and Sunbury are popular tourist attractions in their respective countries and their managers should be worried that they are not meeting the expectations of their visitors. Compounding the deficient interpretation of slavery is the fact that very few participants rated the historic information presented or their learning experience above average for either site. At a time when tourists are seeking deeper, more authentic heritage experiences, the failure to meet or exceed such expectations could result in negative publicity for the site, limited repeat business and deter potential visitors, none of which are in the sites' best interests.

The findings presented and discussed in this chapter are based on responses in the early stage of an ongoing survey of visitors to Sunbury Plantation House and Morne Coubaril Estate. The findings are based on responses from less than 100 participants and thus present a limitation to the study at this point. Though it is not advisable to generalize these findings at this stage, they nonetheless contribute to a better understanding of the silence of slavery from the perspective of the consumers of heritage and are in keeping with findings of other research conducted on these two sites and similar ones. These findings may also be important for the two site managers and could prove useful in helping them to improve their existing tourism product.

Acknowledgements

Funding for this study was provided by the Department of Recreation & Tourism Management at California State University – Northridge. Invaluable research support was provided by Mara Marcellin in St Lucia and Christina Payne, Sheena Coppin, and Sandra Sanchez and family in Barbados.

References

Butler, D.L. (2001) Whitewashing plantations – the commodification of a slave-free ante-bellum south. *International Journal of Hospitality & Tourism Administration* 2 (3), 163–175.

Butler, D.L., Carter, P.L. and Dwyer, O.J. (2008) Imagining plantations: Slavery, dominant narratives, and the foreign born. *Southeastern Geographer* 48 (3), 288–302.

Buzinde, C.N. and Santos, C.A. (2009) Interpreting slavery tourism. *Annals of Tourism Research* 36 (3), 439–458.

Corkern, W. (2004) Heritage tourism: where public and history don't always meet. *American Studies International* 42 (2–3), 7–16.

Dann, G.M.S. and Potter, R.B. (2001) Supplanting the planters: hawking heritage in Barbados. *International Journal of Hospitality & Tourism Administration* 2 (3–4), 51–84.

Dann, G.M.S and Seaton, A.V. (eds) (2001) *Slavery, Contested Heritage and Thanatourism*. New York: Routledge.

Found, W.C. (2004) Historic sites, material culture and tourism in the Caribbean islands. In D.T. Duval (ed.) *Tourism in the Caribbean: Trends, Development, Prospects* (pp. 136–151). London: Routledge.

Giovannetti, J.L. (2006) Grounds of race: Slavery, racism and the plantation in the Caribbean. *Latin American and Caribbean Ethnic Studies* 1 (1), 5–36.

Giovannetti, J.L. (2009) Subverting the master's narrative: public histories of slavery in plantation America. *International Labour and Working Class History* 76, 105–126.

Heard, S. R. (2006) *Presenting Race and Slavery at Historic Sites: Manassas National Battlefield Park*. Washington, DC: National Parks Service.

Lowenthal, D. (2008) *The Heritage Crusade and the Spoils of History*. Cambridge: Cambridge University Press.

Miller, S., Miller, K. and Wilkie, C. (2011) *Ins and Outs of Barbados 2011*. Online at http://www.insandoutsofbarbados.com/.

Pattullo, P. (2005) *Last Resorts: The Cost of Tourism in the Caribbean* (2nd edn). London: Monthly Review Press.

Roushanzamir, E.L. and Kreshel, P.J. (2001) Gloria and Anthony visit a plantation: History into heritage at 'Laura: A Creole Plantation'. In G.M.S. Dann and A.V. Seaton (eds) *Slavery, Contested Heritage and Thanatourism* (pp. 177–200). New York: The Haworth Press.

Seaton, A.V. (2001) Sources of slavery – destinations of slavery: silences and disclosures of slavery heritage in the UK and US. In G.M.S. Dann and A.V. Seaton (eds) *Slavery, Contested Heritage and Thanatourism* (pp. 107–130). New York: The Haworth Press.

Strait, K. (2004) *Presenting Race and Slavery at Historic Sites: Arlington House, Robert E. Lee National Memorial.* Washington, DC: National Parks Service.

Thompson, A.O. (2010) *Confronting Slavery: Breaking Through the Corridors of Silence.* Barbados: Thompson Business Services, Inc.

Trouillot, M-R. (1995) *Silencing the Past: Power and the Production of History.* Boston, MA: Beacon Press.

8 Transforming Taiwan's Sugar Refineries for Leisure and Tourism

Abby Liu

> *In the past few decades, Taiwan's economy has changed from one dependent on heavy manufacturing industry to one based on technology and services. What is known in Britain as 'industrial archaeology' – the study of disused factories and machinery – is coming into its own in Taiwan, as people rediscover the historical importance of landmark mines and mills.*
>
> S. Crook, 2006

Taiwan's historic sugar industry is playing a key role in this current transition from an industrial to a service based economy. Historically, development of the sugar industry in Taiwan has been closely aligned with political interests. It was first promoted by the Dutch colonial powers as early as the 1620s, slowly progressing in the imperial era of the Ming Dynasty from 1661–1683 and the Qing Dynasty from 1683–1894. Substantial industrial scale was achieved during the Japanese colonial period of 1894–1945. Destruction of sugar refineries was inevitable during World War II.

After the restoration of Taiwan to the Republic of China in 1946, a state-owned enterprise, entitled Tai-tan Corporation, was established to govern and rejuvenate the sugar plantations and production facilities. Together with the rice and tea industries, sugar was considered as one of the major economic crops in the 1960s and 1970s, contributing to approximately 70% of government revenue and 74% of the foreign income generation. More significantly, the sugar sector served as the major facilitator driving the transformation of Taiwan from a primary based economy to an industrialized one in the contemporary era.

However, the decline of the sugar industry was inevitable, largely driven by the government's economic restructuring polices from 1964 onwards.

Since then the Tai-tan Corporation has undergone a transformation, turning refineries from production centers to multi-functional establishments. Each individual refinery is unique because of the integration of local resources and stakeholders' visions. Moreover, government at all levels affords the refineries cultural meanings and functional purposes. Pictured as multi-functional venues, sugar refineries have emerged at the junction of a multitude of cultural entities, ecological conservation and production centers as well as leisure and recreational services. More significantly, the sugar refinery individually presents, in varying degrees, a combination of opportunities for industrial heritage conservation, leisure experience, culture learning, heritage tourism and a sense of nostalgia, as well as ecological integrity in its respective locality.

The sugar refinery's roles in relation to various forms of transition in Taiwan underpin the study's focus. This chapter discusses the historical and cultural significance the sugar refinery represents and reveals the impacts of corporate strategies and relevant policies that have led their transformation into current multi-functional venues. Focus will be given to an analysis of the changing patterns of interactions between the refinery space and the local community for the purposes of identifying an adequate approach for the transformation of refineries to cultural and leisure spaces – a generally concerted vision from stakeholders. Looking at refineries as cultural and leisure spaces also prompts a need to recognize the advantages and disadvantages of current policy directives and planning approaches that drive the future destiny of refineries in Taiwan.

Historical Backdrop

The earliest documentation of sugar production in Taiwan dates back to the Yuan Dynasty (1578–1650). From emergence, development, maturity and decline to recent rejuvenation and diversification, the sugar industry in Taiwan in the last 400 years has undergone drastic changes. Sugar ventures were initially operated by locals with manual milling establishments. Refineries for sugar have colonial roots, initially promoted by the Dutch in the 17th century. Central mills taking supplies from surrounding farms were set up by the Dutch colonial administration, this introduced the economics of scale to sugar production. Production was subsequently modernized and scaled up due to the Japanese's keen interest in export in the 20th century.

During colonization by the Dutch from 1624–1661, the expansion of sugarcane plantation areas was positioned as a mainstream development measure, and in that timeframe Taiwan became an important sugar export country in the world trade market. The Dutch were expelled by the Ming Dynasty, and during Ming rule, 1661–1683, sugar production was manipulated as a strategic resource that was primarily for export to Japan in exchange for metals, i.e. copper and lead, needed for building armaments. During the subsequent Qing Dynasty rule, 1683–1894, Taiwan continued to serve the sugar demands of Japan and northern China with rather limited supply capacity. In the second half of the 19th century, Taiwan experienced a good growth in sugar production, which was induced by the increasingly fierce competition between American and European traders.

The Japanese brought knowledge of sugar cultivation to Taiwan and established the first machinery based refinery in Kaohsiung in the southern part of the island in 1901. During Japan's rule, over five decades (between 1895 and 1945), the sugar sector was not only accentuated in colonial policies but also received overwhelming interest from overseas investors. By 1941 there were 50 industrialized sugar mills and refineries which had been established with a processing capacity reaching 70,120 tonnes daily. This marked the most prominent and productive period in Taiwan's sugar production history. However, the Taiwan sugar industry suffered a market slump in World War II due to the extraction of the labor force to the battlefield and the deterioration of factories and establishments by bombing. By 1945, 34 out of 42 sugar establishments were damaged (Figure 8.1).

After the restoration of Taiwan as a sovereignty governed by the government of the Republic of China in 1945, the Taiwan Sugar Corporation (TSC, locally known as Tan-tan which literally means 'Taiwan Sugar' in Chinese) was formed in May 1946 to take over the assets of the former ventures operated by the Japanese, with the status of state-owned enterprise. Another silver age of the sugar sector in Taiwan took place from 1952–1964. Sugar was Taiwan's leading export commodity, serving as the main foreign revenue earner and tax income generator. Sugarcane plantations were widely considered as being an effective means for the development of the rural economy. With sugar mills and refineries established throughout Taiwan, the magnitude of the sugar economy was vital for local livelihoods with:

- A total sugar plantation area scattered over 161,685 ha, occupying 19% of total farming land.
- Sugarcane farming reached 140,600 households, accounting for 30% of the farming households and 15% of the total households in Taiwan.
- Forty-nine refineries were in existence for production.
- Sugar production reached 1,400,000 tonnes.
- The sugar economy comprised 48% of total industrial production.
- Sugar exports accounted for 43% of total export value (Kuo, 2003).

Figure 8.1 Taiwan's Sugar Refineries. There were 42 refineries around 1942 during the Japanese occupation
Source: Reproduced with permission of the Taiwan Sugar Corporation

Over 400 years refineries emerged and, as a result of political and economic interests, proliferated under the monopoly power of the rulers. They served as a production center, which supplied a luxury commodity for the purposes of export. The sugar industry also contributed considerably to the prosperity of the rural economy and, at the same time, helped stimulate the development of other industrial sectors on the island. Since the end of the 1960s, the economic significance of the sugar industry has begun to wane because of evolving industrial structures, land use policies and demographic changes taking place in the rural communities. In the last decade the production of sugar has always lagged far behind local consumption. Taiwan started to depend on sugar imports to meet the local consumption needs of the south-east regions, a result of a shortage of more than 300,000 tonnes per annum (Chen, 2006). For the TSC, diversification at a corporate level was seen as a vital means for business rejuvenation.

Restructuring and Transformation

The rise and fall of the sugar industry over the last century vividly depicts political, economic and sociocultural transitions in Taiwan. Forces of colonial power, global market fluctuations, policy directives and, until recently, community involvement have been woven together, creating a vibrant and yet complex environment in which refineries strive to survive, adapt and capitalize on their resources.

As one of the leading sugar export regions, Taiwan's land morphology has been shaped by the sugar industry, including extensive farming distribution and extended transportation networks. In particular, the significance of the sugar economy to the locals' livelihoods shaped the cultural landscape across many rural communities. But, with government policy directives, fluctuation in commodity price, increasing labour cost and fierce competition from international markets, sugar production became TSC's heaviest financial burden. The holding of land assets of 118,206 ha by the TSC in 1947 was reduced to 57,459 ha in 1997, largely undertaken in accordance with governments' economic development policies, and a further reduction to 54,810 ha in 2000 was a response to cut corporate deficits. Refineries were reduced from 49 at their peak to only three locations in 2007, with rather limited production. By 2011, total land coverage of the closed refineries reached 122,059 m^2 and vacant premises accounted for 87,098 m^2; within a vast area of available land only as little as 0.88% and 1.24% of premises were leased out (Chen, 2007).

Abundant land assets and establishments once used for sugar plantation, production and storage were sold, leased or transformed for the construction of industrial or technological parks, or dismally left vacant or discarded. The major forces that have caused changes in the sugar industry in Taiwan over time are diverse, involving population migration, industrialization, urbanization, staple market fluctuations and, in particular, the profound influence of state power. As observed by Shih and Yen (2009), there were four transitional stages with respect to the relationship between the sugar economy and land use polices: the asset requisition and reconstruction period (1945–1949); the farmland expansion and readjustment period (1950–1989); the land diversification and transformation period (1990–1999); and the multifaceted land use period (2000 to the present).

By the late 1990s sugar production comprised less than 30% of the TSC's total business revenue (Shih & Yen, 2009). Commencing in 1997, the TSC, which used to be Taiwan's most profitable company, started an approach of 'closure of refinery, deviation from sugarcane' to help improve deficits and prepare for privatization. TSC's strategies for transformation, however, were paradoxical, as the corporate management often reverted to conventional bureaucratic practices rather than develop a critical posture to the changing business environment. The sale of TSC-owned land was conveniently used as an immediate savior for cutting deficits. Despite this heavy reliance on revenues from the sale of assets and land tenancy, exploring possible alternative markets for survival became an emergent issue as the TSC executive management's overall performance was impeached for substantial loss and inefficient management of the discarded industrial lands. The TSC was spurred into a more aggressive response to the changing political climate, dynamic social movement and fierce market competition.

In search of business alternatives, present operations at the TSC exist in a bewildering variety of forms, ranging from simple cultivation to technologically complex manufacturing systems and the rise of modern retailing and leisure services. In late 2003 and early 2004 a drastic restructuring was set forth to pursue a diverse and yet integrated business strategy. There are nine core operations, involving the:

(1) sugar sector;
(2) livestock sector;
(3) delicate agriculture sector;
(4) biotechnology sector;
(5) wholesale and hypermarket sector;
(6) petroleum sector;
(7) leisure and recreation sector;
(8) commodity and marketing sector;
(9) land development and asset operations.

In the process of organizational restructuring and business diversification controversies often arise because of polarized views concerning the refineries' future prospects. At one extreme, driven by materialistic pursuit, land development values derived substantial attention, while at the other extreme, preserving refinery remnants as heritage and integrating establishments into local cultural spaces were advocated. Better management and more efficient use of sugar refineries and land assets are goals anticipated by stakeholders, and the consequent transformations have been described in all kinds of ways. Paradoxically, TSC's past land use approaches had predominately been manipulated to meet political and commercial interests. Not until recently had the planning of land and industrial assets been afforded more cultural meanings. Refineries and supporting facilities were envisaged in part to be preserved as industrial heritage (i.e. architectural structure, rail networks, production lines and other related facilities) and, for some other less historically significant portions, to be retrofitted as recreational sites. This approach facilitates a combination of nostalgia ambiance, cultural experience and leisure and tourism opportunity to the local community. TSC began its major transformation program in 1990 as a diversified company, and for most of its entry to the service sector was primarily involved with the provision of recreation, leisure and cultural experiences to visitors. In 2004 the leisure and recreation division was established for an integrated use of existing resources of the sugar industry that is culturally significant, educationally vibrant and economically viable.

Policy Stimulus for Transformation to Tourism and Leisure

The TSC management saw the changes and challenges as having been organized and facilitated in pursuit, successively, of three goals: improved profitability, sustained growth and market leadership. It appears that the restructuring of TSC has been predominately geared towards commercial interests, while its representations that vividly depict the evolutionary process of industrialization in contemporary Taiwan history and cultural meanings embedded within, have been generally neglected.

At first, attempts were made to generate immediate income to compensate for corporate deficits, and, consequently, the solution for most of the closed refineries was to demolish production premises and equipment for quick sale. Later on this remedial strategy was replaced in part by an incremental approach to conserve and rejuvenate existing resources. Influenced by local cultural advocates, the industrial heritage significance of refineries thus has been reconsidered as a vital means not only to document industrial development history but also to raise visitors' awareness of a need for preserving past industrial resources.

Government policies promoting industrial tourism worked as a driving force, which helped prompt TSC's transformation to its present expansion into an innovative cultural operation for tourism and leisure services. Public agencies at all levels directly and indirectly contributed to the transformation of TSC's operations from a production based commodity to a service based one, as illustrated by the following points:

- National land revitalization plan: central government carried out integrated planning for public land in 1999 with a special focus on the effective management of idle lands. This land planning approach prompted TSC to take several measures for the effective use of land assets. In particular, special attention was given to closed refineries and farmlands discarded from sugarcane cultivation. Amongst other land development approaches, leisure service was seen as a vital strategy for invigorating TSC's operations.
- Tourism Factory Project: in 2003, the Ministry of Economic Affairs (MOEA) aimed to promote innovative concepts and value-added services to declining manufacturing establishments. The project encouraged factory operators to identify the potential vitality of a traditional manufacturing industry through exposure to production processes, space and end commodities in order to reinforce an industrial theme or a culture to varied segments of visitors who could potentially be satisfied both by a mixture of nostalgia or novelty. The MOEA's tourism factory procedure offered traditional industries such as the sugar sector an alternative for transformation into the service economy by venturing into the provision of tourism and leisure experiences.
- Revitalization project for industrial culture assets: administered by the Council of Cultural Affairs, industrial culture assets were recognized as an important factor contributing to the vitality and robustness of local society. Among others, the sugar refinery was postulated as one of the mainstream assets deserving due attention and adequate action for preservation and promotion.

Sugar refineries represent a 400-year-old cultural landscape that vividly depicts industrial movements changing local livelihoods and lifestyles. The policy supports outlined above have helped create a favorable climate in which cultural spaces with both leisure and educational entities could be nurtured. In particular, as far as the industrial heritage statute is concerned, government at different levels intervenes through its differing policies, as the commercialization of this heritage is frequently an issue due to the profit motives of the enterprises involved. Given the abundant land holdings and rich cultural embedment, the future development of sugar refinery premises and lands is more than just an issue of economic pursuit. Rather, a holistic and yet incremental approach integrating cultural significance, productivity requirements and ecological sustainability is seen as more desirable.

On the Road to Leisure and Tourism Services

Current status

Industrial tourism as defined by Frew (2008) involves visits by tourists to operational industrial sites where the core activity of the site was not originally tourism oriented. When a need to preserve and promote industrial culture and heritage is envisaged, the concept of industrial heritage tourism serves a pathway to achieve desired goals. Edwards and Llurdés i Coit (1996: 342) viewed industrial heritage tourism as being associated with 'the development of touristic activities and industries on man-made sites, buildings and landscapes that originated with industrial processes of earlier periods'.

In the process of corporate restructuring, the TSC manipulated resources derived from a 100-year-old sugar production industry and a vast amount of land assets to create leisure and tourism opportunities. Industrial tourism offers visitors an experience regarding the product, production process, application and historical background. But current revitalization approaches for sugar refineries have been predominately geared towards a focus on a narrowly defined industrial past. Narrow-gauge train rides, viewing historical architecture and product sampling have become standard offerings available at almost all the sugar refineries operated for leisure and tourism purposes. Simplistically viewed, an agglomeration of the industrial elements of sugar production will result in the creation of attractive venues in which visitors' recreational expectations and cultural pursuits can be met simultaneously. Presently there are 23 such establishments providing leisure and tourism services. Amongst these, 13 locations are centered on sugar production-related themes and generally share very similar attraction attributes (Figure 8.2).

Table 8.1 summarizes the development approaches of existing resources related to sugar refineries, ranging from tourism factory, cultural leisure park, exhibition and sales center, resort and hotel, and golf courses. Industrial relics, nostalgia atmosphere, experiential activities, innovative merchandise and service learning opportunities are commonly available at every former sugar refinery site. An agglomeration of undifferentiated elements has inevitably led

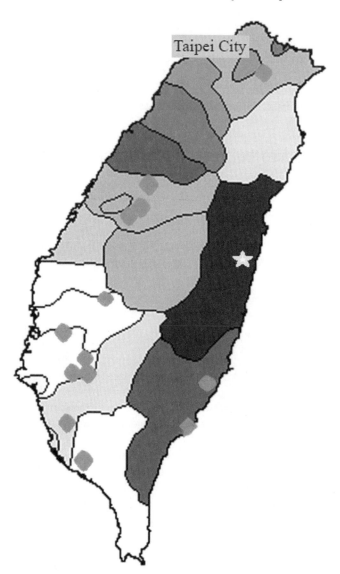

Figure 8.2 Taiwan Sugar Corporation Current Recreational Sites. The star denotes the only case of a sugar factory as a form of industrial tourism, exposing tourists to learning about industrial culture and practice, recreational experience and production promotion. It has been promoted by Taiwan's Ministry of Economic Affairs since 2003

Table 8.1 TSC's involvement in tourism and leisure services

Type	Operation unit	Offerings
Tourism factory	Yuan Mei	Sugar industry time tunnel, battlefield remnants, recreational facilities
	Huan Lien	Sugar industry historical museum, Japanese-style architecture premises
	Nan Chou	Train-driving experiential camp, tourism narrow-gauge railway train
	Chi Shan	Refinery park, popsicle products
Cultural leisure park	Si Hu Flora Cultural Park	Tourism narrow-gauge railway train
	Hsin Yi Railway Cultural Park	Railway cultural park, tourism narrow-gauge railway train
	Suan Tou Sugarcane Cultural Park	Sugarcane cultural park, railway cultural museum, tourism narrow-gauge railway train
	Nan Yin Tzung Ye Cultural Park	Historical red house, level-3 heritage
	Wu Shu Ling Leisure Park	Thematic leisure area, orchid house, tourism narrow-gauge railway train
	Nan Jing Leisure Park	Flora exhibition area, wholesale center, sugar industry cultural museum
	Kaohsiung Flora Garden Centre	Agriculture experiential area, recreation experiential area, tourism narrow-gauge railway train
Exhibition center	Taiwan Sugar Industry Museum	Railway recreational area, sugar industry cultural museum, tourism narrow-gauge railway train
	Taitung Specialty Products Exhibition Centre	Sale of sugar and popsicle products, historical architecture
Resort and hotel	Jian Shan Pi Jian Nan Resort	Leisure, recreational and MICE business
	Chr Shang Mu Ya Resort	Leisure and recreational business
	TSC Evergreen Hotel	Accommodation
Golf course	7 locations	

Source: TSC official website, http://www.taisugar.com.tw

to an unfavorable situation in which each individual attraction competes for the same market segments.

Challenges

The state-owned operator and the government have largely seen refinery restructuring as the appropriate means of land development for various income generating functions in the locality. Developing a robust cultural leisure program requires commitments, in the form of policy endorsements, financial resources, partnerships and the building of a sound base of human resources, including visionary leadership. Early approaches to refinery closure largely involved demolishing, discarding or leaving plants dilapidated. Idle refineries have often represented a problem to local communities, resulting not only in a deteriorated cultural landscape but also causing security concerns. Consequently, not every refinery site can successfully render a well-preserved industrial heritage or a combination of cultural and leisure programs. Substantial efforts are therefore required to nurture the cultural functionality of refineries, developing solid attractions that will lure visitors. The enthusiasm of local cultural advocates for enriching meaningful representations of sugar refineries is marked by a lack of awareness as to best practice in Taiwan. This is exacerbated by an absence of clarity as to the status of sugar refineries, which serve as a significant representation of Taiwan's industrial development history.

The quality of human resources and employment effects presents another impediment. Refinery staff employed at the attractions often exhibit foreignness to leisure and tourism services because their former experiences were primarily in manufacturing and production. Train drivers who spent almost their entire lives responsible for sugarcane transportation found it difficult to adapt to the new job assignments of serving and guiding visitors. Also, from the point of view of employment the effects are rather disappointing, as the number of jobs created in such cultural heritage sites is limited when compared to the employment capacity the refineries were originally able to generate for the local communities.

Opportunities

Every refinery experiences times when a broader context is addressed to embrace the local community. These could be in the form of organized events, i.e. festivals, exhibitions, performances or markets where visitors and residents can gather, interact or celebrate in the settings of the former sugar refineries. More recently, successfully or not, the refineries as cultural spaces have been promoted through processes of local participation. The capacity for communities to formulate aspirations and to realize the potential of these spaces, reflecting their expectations, is not guaranteed. It needs to be developed and nurtured. Hence, depending upon the geographical characteristics and social background of the given refinery being visited, visitors expect to experience a diverse range of attractions depicting aspects of its respective industrial past and modern evolutions. The realm of refinery attractions does not only reside in the search for nostalgia meanings but also in creative expressions. And a lot of creativity is expressed in the daily lives of people in the process of living, in the production and maintenance of dwellings and habitats. This is often ignored by developers and policy-makers, and results in a state of spatial, sociocultural and psychological alienation in which many communities adjacent to the refineries find themselves today.

Summary

Over the last two decades, the TSC has undergone a series of organizational reforms within a highly bureaucratic state-operated entity as a means to improve efficiency and to eventually enhance market competitiveness. The TSC's reforms have opened up a wide range of market opportunities and helped expand its existing primary economy based on sugarcane farming, milling and refining operations transitioning to tertiary oriented services for leisure and recreation. The refinery property projects which have transformed locations for leisure and tourism purposes were initially driven by commercial interests, and also prompted by policy interventions with dual goals aiming to revitalize discarded lands and to conserve industrial heritage. A realignment of economic and cultural interests has subsequently been a focal issue in the current transformation and reform of sugar refineries in Taiwan.

Diversification, innovation and conservation continue to be sought out as vital mechanisms for sustaining the former refineries in an integrated way that is economically viable, socioculturally appropriate and environmentally sound. Until recently, a campaign to conserve industrial vestiges was on the rise, receiving increasing attention. Ceased operations in refineries across Taiwan represented multi-faceted structural change, economically, socially and culturally. Refineries have undergone drastic transformations into leisure, tourism and cultural entities that have emerged at junctions of a multitude of drives of political agenda, commercial interest, utilitarian value and, more recently, a search for cultural meaning. Positing refineries as cultural spaces affords rich opportunities for us to connect with the spatial interventions that generations of predecessors generated over time. Moreover, it also renders plenty of opportunities for people to engage themselves in the appropriation of the spaces in various ways, whether it is for leisure, educational or nostalgic purposes.

Today the sugar refinery in Taiwan presents a combination of leisure experience, cultural exposure, ecological sensibility and a sense of nostalgia. In transitioning from sugar as industry to sugar as heritage the industrial assets of the formerly dominant sugar industry have been employed as sugar industry culture parks and sugar heritage sites. To an extent there has been some local employment generated and the leisure complexes based on sugar heritage have addressed the increased need, since the introduction of the two-day weekend, for facilities and spaces for the Taiwanese populace at leisure.

References

Chen, W. (2006) A study of predicting the international sugar price and calculating the domestic sugar price. *Master's thesis*, Taiwan University of Science and Technology, Department of Industrial Management, Taipei, Taiwan.

Chen, M. (2007) *Sugar Industry in Taiwan. Walkers Culture*. Taipei: Sinobooks.

Crook, S. (2006) Suantou Sugar Mill – factory turned tourist attraction. *The China Post*, 20 October.

Edwards, J.A. and Llurdés i Coit, J.C. (1996) Mines and quarries: Industrial heritage tourism. *Annals of Tourism Research* 23, 341–363.

Frew, E.A. (2008) Industrial tourism theory and implemented strategies. In A.G. Woodside (ed.) *Advances in Culture, Tourism and Hospitality Research* (Vol. 2; pp. 27–42). Bingley: Emerald Group Publishing Limited.

Kuo, H.W. (2003) Taiwanese's Taiwan History, accessed 20 March 2011. http://www.taiwanus.net/history/4/109.htm.

Shih, C. and Yen, S. (2009) The transformation of the sugar industry and land use policy in Taiwan. *Journal of Asian Architecture and Building Engineering* 8 (1), 41–48.

Part 4
Consuming Sugar and its Heritage

9 Sugar in Tourism: 'Wrapped in Devonshire Sunshine'

Paul Cleave

For many years 'Wrapped in Devonshire Sunshine' was the tagline on the packaging of Bristow's fudge, produced in Devon and especially popular with the tourist market. This chapter utilises the county of Devon in the south-west of England to show how food and tourism are connected to local dairy products and sugar confectionery. Together these have contributed to the enduring popularity of one of its most popular food souvenirs, fudge. The rapid growth of tourism in the 20th century is an important feature in the historiography of consumerism, and the tourist as a consumer. Tourism and holidays stimulated the demand for new products associated with the pursuit of leisure. Watson and Kopachevsky (1994: 650) indicate that through the procedure of commodification consumers are entwined in a process that begins and ends with 'money and exchange value' (Watson & Kopachevsky, 1994: 653). It is suggested that tourists cultivate meaning attached to objects, service and experience at the level of exchange, not at the level of production. However, the sugar based culinary examples utilised in this chapter show how the meaning and value of production have acquired nostalgic and ethical meanings for many tourists.

Pimlott (1976) and Stevenson (1984) suggest that tourism and holidays have become one of the principal objects in 20th-century life, and are frequently enjoyed in retrospect when they are over. This is an important observation as food, whether the specialities enjoyed and consumed at the destination, or the souvenirs taken home, contributes to the memory of the holiday. Gnoth (1997: 295) indicates that a 'biogenic need' for food may motivate tourists, and subsequently is important in expectation formation Wood (2002). For many tourists this physiological requirement is associated with place, for example the lush agricultural landscape of Devon is connected to both food and tourist destination. Burnett (2004) observes this in the context of holidays and leisure suggesting that there was a change in the tourist market, noting that by the early 20th century, when holidays were still a luxury for many, 'day outs provided a popular leisure activity for the lower working classes' (Burnett, 2004: 126–130). Important features of the popular resorts were stalls selling traditional gingerbread and toffee apples alongside the newer ones with ice cream, candyfloss and fizzy drinks. These were considered something of an indulgence and a holiday treat for children. The holiday, even an annual 'day out', was a special occasion, a break from routine, and the holiday-maker looked forward to eating out and eating differently. In this way the relationship between food and the experience of leisure can be observed.

Attracting the Tourists

For many tourists food is a motivation to visit a particular destination, and contributes to the enjoyment of the holiday. In the context of food-related tourism people travel to experience the food and drink at a particular destination, whether haute cuisine restaurant meals or regional specialities, and frequently to take home a taste of the holiday, according to Hall *et al.* (2003). Food has played an important part in this process, in the context of tourism it is associated with pleasure and leisure where, by eating away from home, tourists frequently experience the food and culinary specialities of another region.

The history of food is inextricably linked to travel. Travellers and explorers introduced many foods to Europe and the ways in which food travels is a story of culinary travel, mobility and evolution. This is observed by Drummond (1957), Spencer (2002) and Tannahill (1973), who suggest that, for example, the history of sugar is one of travel, and its status is as an ingredient and trading commodity. Tourists continue this tradition as they bring home new foods and ingredients.

Food for Thought

Food is frequently shared, distributed or given and symbolises much about our place in society, including holidays and leisure time. It is symbolic and encodes social messages; for example, food as a gift, or when associated with holidays and ritual events (Douglas, 1971).

Many of the popular sweet foods associated with the tourism experience are classified as comfort foods. These are described by Wansink *et al.* (2003) as foods whose consumption evokes a psychologically comfortable and pleasurable state for an individual. A preference for confectionery as a snack food, it is suggested, may be associated with connotations from childhood food and the family; for example, home cooking and the special treats of ice cream, candyfloss and confectionery. However, tastes for comfort foods may change over time. This can be illustrated by young people's preference towards saltiness and intense sweetness, the pronounced tastes often found in snack foods. Collins (2009: 28) asserts that these so-called comfort foods can be categorised as 'nostalgic, indulgent, and convenient', in addition to their significance in providing physical comfort. In the context of tourism, the four criteria are identified with the inclusion of experience and place. For example, ice cream cones for countless tourists are synonymous with seaside summer holidays, the rich yellow ice cream particularly evoking images of cream and dairy goodness. Although comfort foods are readily available and physically satisfying, particular brands often carry nostalgic associations with an era, resort and holiday experience.

Food and Tourism

This chapter investigates the phenomenon of tourism from a culinary perspective. Food is an integral part of tourism, whether eating out, experiencing local food and culinary customs, or taking home food as a souvenir. It presents the popularity of food as a souvenir and demonstrates how the addition of local ingredients (e.g. in Devon butter and clotted cream) may confer localised authenticity on an imported food. An important component of the tourism experience for many is the purchasing and consumption of souvenirs. Food is frequently taken home as a souvenir gift, an edible memento. The production of most confectionery traditionally relies on sugar and thus links consumption with a much earlier history. From this historical background, place and product become interlinked in the context of tourism. Strong (1954: 46) states that the history of sugar spread by gradual stages from the remote islands of the southern Pacific to the Asian continent 'and from there by the widening web of trade routes to all over the world'. Its story is suggested as being 'interwoven in the migrations of primitive races and bound up in the great empires of the East, it moves in the surge of Islamic conquests it colours the fearless and ruthless lives of the adventurers and seamen of the West'. As the centuries passed, its importance grew and its part in human affairs developed beyond the satisfaction of a basic need in nutriment and bodily growth. It became a means of livelihood for entire communities, both in its production and its processing. Its consumption supported legions of sugar bakers, pastry cooks and confectioners and it became a staple part of the currency of many countries. Sugar's history is grounded in travel and exploration. This may be extrapolated into the phenomenon of tourism, where travel often introduces consumers to new foods, many derived from sugar.

The Significance of Sugar in the Experience of Tourism

Sugar appears to be a vital ingredient in 20th-century tourism and is associated with numerous activities, from eating out and other culinary holiday treats to the confectionery souvenir. Whittaker (1998: 90) alludes to the association of leisure activities with the marketing of confectionery; for example, motoring chocolate and picnic chocolates. Prior to the era of mass tourism, Richardson (2003: 197) states that until the 19th century sweets were an expensive luxury, 'a status symbol of the nobility', but were transformed into an everyday product to be enjoyed by all. The key to this change in status was due to the availability of the principal ingredient: sugar. Sugar confectionery is synonymous with tourism and the holiday, something special and associated with the experience of tourism, linking place with product. The opportunities for eating out and taking home food as a souvenir evolved during the 20th century. The tea room, cafe, shop and Michelin star restaurant reflect prevailing interests in food production and local produce.

For many tourists food is an important dimension of that experience. Whether ice cream or candyfloss, cream tea or fine dining, much of the food associated with tourism relies on sugar. For countless tourists, enjoying a slice of rich chocolate *Sacher Torte* in Vienna or a cream tea in Devon, place is often synonymous with food and the experience of tourism Pine and Gilmore (1998). The evolution of confectionery souvenirs and foodstuffs associated with tourism reveals a reliance on sugar; ice cream, candyfloss, confectionery and preserves – jams for the ubiquitous cream tea. These foods are for many tourists products associated with place and holidays. Some too are evocative and emotive, stimulating the 'Proustian effect' in evoking strong nostalgic memories in many tourists (Waskul *et al.*, 2009).

Tourists' Interests in Food

The attraction of food has evolved throughout the 20th century, reflecting interests in health, the demand for food away from home and the emergence of food tourism. Croce and Perri (2010) suggest that all places are shaped by social, economic and cultural factors and that these evolve over time. In terms of food, these indicate how food and wine tourism have advanced throughout the 20th century with tourists' interests in food ranging from those described as novices to multi-interest visitors.

Tourists' interests in food are further developed by Smith and Xiao (2008: 290), who classify culinary tourism resources as 'facilities, activities, events and organisations'. Culinary resources, it is proposed, include raw ingredients and prepared dishes. The dairy produce of Devon, butter and cream, provide an example of both raw ingredient and dish. In the example of sugar confectionery, the addition of local food products produced in the region is a means of demonstrating strong imagery, regional identity and association with place and finished product – *fudge*.

Background to Devon's Tourism in the 20th Century

Devon has attracted tourists from the early days of seaside resorts and spas in the 18th century. The climate and scenery of the county drew countless visitors and Fraser (1939: 333–334) describes its landscape and coastline as one 'on which the sun always seems to shine'. Many tourists and authors refer to the food eaten and observed in Devon as memorable and distinctive, Corelli (1896), Harris (1907), Morton (1927) and Green (1993) indicate that food is a reason for visiting the region and that it contributes to the enjoyment of the holiday. Their examples demonstrate not only the growth in popular tourism through the 19th and 20th centuries but also the escalating popularity of sugar confectionery. It is frequently the cream tea, with its scones and homemade jam, or confectionery that are described, specialities dependent on sugar. These provide a foretaste to food tourism and the specialised interests of the early 21st century. Quan and Wang (2004) propose that food consumption in tourism can be a peak or daily experience but emphasise that in tourism consumption it is not a repeat of daily eating habits and routines. Tourists are looking for something different.

Popular Food Souvenirs

Taking home an edible or potable reminder of the holiday is an important part of tourism. It is a way of sharing and reliving the experience of place, recreating elements of the holiday. Morgan and Pritchard (2005: 35–36) describe souvenirs and mementos as, 'signifiers of self, displaying the taste and extent of the tourists' travels and are objects of transition and trajectory touchstones of memory'. Many souvenirs, it is proposed, have the capacity to bring the past into the present, whether through nostalgic packaging and marketing or the product, which may evoke a particular era. It is also possible to look at the biographies of souvenirs and the way in which they pass through different hands, uses and contexts and, in the example of food consumption, leave little other than a souvenir tin or container. Food, unlike durable pottery and ornaments, is perishable. In the example of Devon clotted cream or confectionery, souvenirs associated with the county provide an edible and affordable reminder and way of sharing the experience of tourism.

Sutton (2001) suggests that shopping for food may be regarded as a utilitarian ritual and for some a daily event, but when on holiday it becomes for many an activity, an excursion leisure pursuit and experience associated with place and the ritual event of shopping for others, taking home a souvenir, a memento. Food is also associated with season and the culinary cycle of the year, in that particular foods are connected to holidays. For example, the United Kingdom summer seaside holiday, characterised by its seasonal specialities, confectionery, ice creams and candyfloss (Sutton, 2001: 28). There are, for many, foods that are normally only eaten on holiday, just as there are foods bonded to celebrations and festivals (Christmas, Easter, Carnival) and season (winter or summer). Food gifts are regarded as bonds of reciprocity, a gift of exchange (Sutton, 2001: 45). A food souvenir is perhaps a special gift and a means of exchanging or sharing something of the experience of the holiday and a particular place and time.

For countless tourists Devon is associated with food and this is often chosen as a souvenir and memento of a visit. Perhaps the most well known food in Devon is the rich clotted cream, which was often sent by post and is firmly associated with its place of production. Food provides a means of sharing elements of the tourism experience, whether factory or farm visits and purchases from farm shops or outlets. Sugar based food souvenirs have evolved from the sticks of seaside rock popular at the beginning of the 20th century to the locally made artisan fudge of the early 21st century.

Throughout the 20th century confectionery provided an affordable, transportable and appealing product associated with Devon through an imported recipe and a combination of global and local ingredients.

The Qualities of Sugar in Confectionery

From the days of marzipan, confits and sweetmeats, and their move from luxury status to mass-produced confectionery to satisfy our craving for something sweet, Mintz (1997) suggests that sugar was one of the first edible luxuries to become a proletarian commonplace and a necessity. Large-scale factory production enabled confectionery to reach high volume sales and a public travelling for the first time to holiday resorts such as Devon, its seaside and countryside.

In sugar confectionery, sugar (sucrose) confers sweetness, preserves and has the quality, when boiled as a sugar solution, to change texture and consistency, enabling tablet, individual pieces and decorative shapes to be produced. Using one versatile ingredient numerous products can be made, each with different textures and eating qualities: smooth and chewy, granular, brittle and soft.

Sugar allows rich flavours and colours to be developed and enhanced when cooked, and it can also be coloured and flavoured. Different types of sugar add flavour, for example through the use of molasses in brown sugars. Caramel and toffee is made by boiling a sugar solution to develop an amber colour with a distinctive aroma. In the United Kingdom sugar became relatively inexpensive once the sugar tax was abolished in 1874, and sugar beet production in the United Kingdom and elsewhere in Europe ensured a plentiful supply. During the 19th century boiled sweets such as toffees and fruit drops were sold at seaside resorts, but sticks of rock – rods of boiled sugar, usually peppermint flavoured, brightly coloured and embedded with the name of the resort – became synonymous with the 'day out' or holiday. Sticks of rock were an early form of food based souvenir that targeted the seaside tourist market. In contrast, fluffy voluminous clouds of coloured spun candyfloss soon became a popular ephemeral attraction at the fairground and seafront, eaten at the point of production.

As most boiled sugar confectionery products have a relatively long shelf life they could be taken home if required. Therefore, they proved to be the ideal souvenir gift or memento.

Devon and Sugar

Sugar was imported into Devon from the Caribbean from the 17th century, providing a link with the slave trade (Gray, 2007). However, close to Topsham, a busy port near Exeter, a small sugar refinery was established by the 18th century. Imports of raw unrefined sugar syrup were boiled and transformed into its glistening crystalline form in numerous small refineries throughout the country.

Twentieth-Century Devonshire Clotted Cream Fudge

Devon's history of confectionery production is characterised by numerous small factories or 'homemade' operations which produced boiled sweets for visitors and holidaymakers. As the county attracted larger numbers of tourists the potential for souvenirs grew. Devon had the advantage of a landscape that attracted tourists and also produced high quality dairy produce: milk, butter and clotted cream. *Cream by post*, whereby tins or jars of clotted cream were sent as souvenir gifts, was popular with generations of visitors to the county. The combination of dairy products and confectionery added a local speciality and quality to the otherwise ubiquitous and commonplace. In this instance sugar confectionery provides an example of localisation (Cowell & Parkinson, 2003), where the addition of local ingredients supports local industry. The growth of the confectionery market in the late 19th and early 20th centuries draws parallels with the expansion of mass tourism and day trips and is synonymous with seaside excursions and holidays.

Why was clotted cream used in confectionery? A product readily associated with a county well known for its dairying, Devonshire clotted cream was often sent by post as a souvenir gift, its rich golden crust a luxurious and indulgent adjunct to fruit, junket (a milk based dessert) or scones. Russell (1932) and Morton (1927) typify the travel writers' descriptions of Devon in drawing clotted cream to their readers' attention, emphasising its associations with the county.

Clotted cream is a form of rich dairy fat with a minimum 55% butterfat content. It is also a product with an element of mystery and myth; traditionally made in the farmhouse by the farmer's wife it is a product derived from the rich and fertile Devonshire landscape. Lovatt (1938: 3) suggests that the process of scalding milk to clot cream was introduced to the West Country by Phoenician tin traders 'long before the invasion of Julius Cesar'. However, Clunie Harvey and Hill (1937) describe the qualities of clotted cream in terms of health. Although regarded as a luxury and exceedingly rich, they state that it 'is now being widely recommended by the medical profession as an excellent fatty food' and is 'unusually digestible' (1937: 123–127). These comments suggest that from this period the addition of butter and cream to confectionery enhanced its food value. For example, butter toffees were enriched by the addition of butterfat to enhance flavour, smoothness and taste.

Fudge as a Tourist Souvenir

Why fudge? In other parts of the United Kingdom tourists could also buy regional sugar confectionery products, such as brittle grainy tablet in Scotland and Kendal Mint Cake in Cumbria, the peppermint-flavoured confection beloved by generations of mountaineers and climbers. A possible advantage was that fudge presented consumers with something new and innovative. Similar in consistency to other forms of sweets, like the Mexican-Spanish fudge-like confection *penuche*, it provided consumers with a different taste and texture from traditional seaside rock, toffee and butterscotch. Fudge, ice cream sundaes and the soda fountain, another 20th-century import from America, represented the new, modern and transatlantic. All depended on sugar and demonstrated how food ingredients, dishes and customs travel along with the tourist (Funderberg, 2002). Fine *et al.* (1996) state that sugar consumption grew from the late 19th century when its sweetness and other organic properties were added to something else, leading to its innovative use and helping to produce many new manufactured food products, including confectionery.

Recipes for fudge appear from the late 19th century. Commercial and domestic publications provide numerous recipes for homemade fudge alongside instructions for penouche, caramels and toffee. Most of these are American in origin, for example Fannie Farmer's *Boston Cooking School Cook Book* (1924) and *The American Woman's Cookbook* (1943). Marion Harris Neil's (*c.*1913) *Candies and Bonbons and How to Make Them* includes a chapter ('All Sorts of Fudge', pp. 102–118) comprising some 30 fudge recipes, including Whipped Cream Fudge. Cane sugar is recommended, as beet sugar, Neil suggests (*c.*1913: 18), 'will not produce so palatable a sweetmeat'. Sugar is recommended for its healthy qualities, especially in the diets of children, 'these white crystals feed the ever-burning flame of the body' and for its antiseptic properties in preserving animal and vegetable substances from decomposition (Neil, *c.*1913: 18). Recipes used during childhood, for example Goaman's (1941) *Judy's Book of Sweet Making*, are important in the story of fudge as a commercial souvenir for they may evoke nostalgic yearnings for sweets produced in the home. Davidson (1999: 324) describes fudge as a sweetmeat made by boiling milk, butter and sugar and then beating to produce its 'characteristic grainy texture'. It is described as a favourite confection for home sweet-makers (1999: 324). Baker *et al.* (2005) suggest that recipes are often passed down from one generation to another and are frequently linked to happy and memorable events in childhood, which may include holidays. Food, it is proposed, has the ability to, 'engage multiple senses and transport consumers back in time' (Baker *et al.*, 2005: 402). It may be a shared meal, the colour, flavour or aroma of a foodstuff or the place where it was consumed.

Food associated with a tourist destination has the potential to evoke a yearning for the past, perhaps an idealised and romantic bygone age. Numerous food products target the tourist market and use nostalgic imagery in their marketing. See Figure 9.1 with its tempting nostalgic image showing a bowl of clotted cream.

In Devon it is the image of the farm and countryside that are widely used. For many years Bristow's Clotted Cream Fudge carried the tagline

Figure 9.1 Tuckers Devon clotted cream fudge, *c.* 1960
Source: Authors collection

'Wrapped in Devonshire Sunshine', alluding to the climate of the county. Glucose, a monosaccharide regarded as an efficient and healthy way of getting energy, was noted as an ingredient in addition to the dairy products, but not the sugar – sucrose (Davidson, 1999; Stryer, 1975). The sugar and glucose content in barley sugar and Kendal Mint Cake offered consumers, especially hikers and ramblers, a convenient way to carry a source of energy and sustenance.

In contrast to the functional qualities of rucksack confectionery, fudge appears to be a souvenir and speciality. It provided a culinary opportunity for a fashionable food to become localised, with the addition of dairy products connecting it with its place of production. It represents a change in consumer tastes from the harder varieties of hard-boiled sweets, toffees, butterscotch and sticks of seaside rock.

Confectionery has been produced in Devon for many years. Freeth's in Exeter, Cleave's and Auther's in Crediton, Tucker's of Totnes in South Devon and Thornbury's of Barnstaple in the north of the county demonstrate the extent of relatively small-scale family business production. Devon Cream Toffee and Devon Butter's are typical examples of the evocative products they produced and were popular with generations of tourists and residents alike. The 1963 *Hotels and Restaurants in Britain* (Anon., 1963: 44) in its *Touring Notes* described Crediton in Devon as a pleasant old market town 'with flourishing cider and sweet industries', a reference to Bristow's of Devon. These were family businesses and part of the local community, names that for many were associated with place, season and summer holidays.

Bristow's of Devon was established in 1932 after the family acquired Cleave's Palace Works, a long-established confectionery firm in Crediton. Cleave's had made *Chohone* – a well-known speciality similar to chocolate-coated Turkish delight made with honey. Bristow's continued trading as a family firm until 2009 when, due to effects of the global financial crisis, the business was sold to a confectionery manufacturing company in Scotland. In the 1930s prevailing tastes were for butterscotch, toffee and what were known in the industry as hard-boilings, for example barley sugar and fruit drops (Bristow, 2011).

During the post-war era consumer tastes were changing and confectionery with a chewy consistency became popular. The American Mars Bar, with its soft eating nougat and caramel filling enrobed with chocolate, was introduced to the British public by Mars Inc. in 1932, heralding the changing taste for richer, softer-textured confectionery products. Confectionery giant Cadbury had introduced a chocolate-coated fudge bar in 1948, and when sweet rationing ended in 1953 demand for confectionery was high. Bristow's introduced bars of fudge similar to tablet in the 1950s. Clotted cream was added to some products by the 1960s and Devonshire cream toffee evolved into Clotted Cream Toffee (Figures 9.2 and 9.3).

It is important to note that although the additions of Devonshire butter and Devonshire clotted cream are acknowledged on the packaging, the source and type of sugar remained virtually anonymous until the late 20th century when it was usually labelled as Fairtrade, organic, or by its source and type, for example, raw cane demerera from Mauritius and Plantation Reserve from Bridgetown in Barbados. This represents a trend for consumer information regarding ethical trading, food sourcing and the provenance of foods (Croce & Perri, 2010: 142).

Figure 9.2 Bristow's Devonshire Butters, c. 1960
Source: Authors collection

Figure 9.3 Bristow's Devonshire Butters, *c.* 1960, a food-sweet
Source: Authors collection

Many confectionery products were sold as souvenirs, gifts personalised with the addition of rural imagery and packaging associated with Devon. Confectioners, tobacconists and newsagents were the main sales outlets, although Auther's of Crediton opened a sweet shop on the sea front in Paignton targeting the holiday market. Bristow's fudge was made in batches of 150 kg. The semi-automated process begins when the sugar bolier loads steam jacketed pans with the ingredients sugar, glucose syrup, milk powder, cream, butter or hydrogenated fat and flavourings. The mixture takes about 20 minutes to reach the soft ball temperature of 235–240 F. The cooked fudge is then stirred to encourage the fine crystals to form. Once cool and malleable the batch of fudge is machine cut into 10 g portions, individually wrapped, weighed and packaged in boxes or packets ready for despatch to wholesalers and retailers.

Artisan Fudge *Premium Quality, Exceptional Taste*

Devon Cottage Organic Fudge, shown in Figure 9.4, started life in the heart of the Devon countryside in the 1990s. Richard, its creator, decided to make something he could sell directly to the public and discovered that home-made fudge appealed to consumers as it is organic, ethical and combines local ingredients with imported ones, as shown in Figure 9.4. The fudge is made daily in 20 kg batches by hand in his Devon cottage. The organic and Fairtrade ingredients, unrefined cane sugar, butter, double cream, milk powder, wheat syrup and clotted cream, are cooked in a copper pan over a furnace. The batch of fudge takes Richard about one hour to cook, reaching a temperature of 240 F, and then about one hour to beat to develop the characteristic grainy texture, before decanting into trays and allowing to cool. Richard's basic recipe is frequently varied by the addition of organic flavourings, for example rum and vanilla, and with luxurious chocolate-coated versions. Some fudge is pre-packed for sale at local tourist attractions, but it is the thick bars of crumbly fudge sold from Richard's stall directly to the customer that provide an interface between the producer and the product.

Devon Cottage Organic Fudge is a personalised product, artisan, handmade and closely connected to the Devon countryside through its ingredients and production.

Figure 9.4 Devon Cottage Organic Fudge, 2011
Source: http://www/devoncottageorganicfudge.co.uk

Devonshire clotted cream fudge continues the tradition of outlets at resorts and attractions providing a souvenir and product for holiday consumption.

Conclusion

This chapter has utilised Devon, a county in the south-west of England, as a case study and example of a region with a long tradition in tourism and food production. It has demonstrated how over a timescale of the 20th century food products have evolved and have been influenced by changing culinary tastes and fashions. The example of fudge has shown how consumer tastes for confectionery and the tourists' relationship with sugar are influenced by holiday consumption and are associated with place.

Sugar is connected to tourism through its history, travel and consumption associated with holidays and leisure. It is a story of the relationship of product and place, and the melding of local and global ingredients. From the early examples of localisation with the addition of dairy products, the example of fudge has shown how re-localisation has evolved to include the principal ingredient, sugar.

The example of fudge has shown how one fundamental ingredient (sugar) enabled three major dairy products (milk, butter and clotted cream) to become a leading food souvenir. Evocative and relatively inexpensive, Devonshire clotted cream fudge allowed producers to make a product that became the quintessential holiday confection associated with a county famous for its dairy produce and tourism.

References

Anon. (1963) *Hotels and Restaurants in Britain, 1963: Touring Edition.* London: British Travel and Holidays Association.
Baker, S.M., Karrer, H.C. and Veeck, A. (2005) My favourite recipes: Recreating emotions and memories through cooking. *Advances in Consumer Research* 32, 402–403.
Berolzheimer, R. (1943) *The American Woman's Cook Book* (Victory Binding). Chicago: Culinary Institute of America.
Bristow, F. (2011) *Sticky Stories From the Toffee Factory.* Crediton: Crediton Area History and Museum Society.
Burnett, J. (2004) *England Eats Out 1830–Present.* Harlow: Pearson.
Clunie Harvey, W. and Hill, H. (1937) *Milk Products.* London: H.K. Lewis & Co. Ltd.
Collins, J.H. (2009) Comfort foods in long term care. *Dietary Manager*, 27–30.
Corelli, M. (1896) *The Mighty Atom.* London: Hutchinson.
Cowell, S.J. and Parkinson, S. (2003) Localisation of UK food production: An analysis using land area and energy as indicators. *Agriculture, Ecosystems and Environment* 94 (2003), 221–236.

Croce, E. and Perri, G. (2010) *Food and Wine Tourism*. Wallingford, Oxfordshire: CAB International.

Davidson, A. (1999) *The Oxford Companion to Food*. Oxford: Oxford University Press.

Douglas, M. (1971) Deciphering a meal. *Daedalus, Journal of the American Academy of Arts and Sciences* 103 (1), 61–81.

Drummond, J.C. (1957) *The Englishman's Food, Five Centuries of British Diet*. London: Jonathon Cape.

Farmer, F.M. (1924) *The Boston Cooking School Cookbook*. Toronto: McClelland and Stewart.

Fine, B., Heasman, M. and Wright, J. (1996) *Consumption in the Age of Affluence*. London: Routledge.

Fraser, M. (1939) *Holiday Haunts 1939*. London: Great Western Railway Company.

Funderberg, A.C. (2002) *Sundae Best: History of Soda Fountains*. Ohio: Bowling Green State University Press.

Gnoth, J. (1997) Tourism motivation and expectation formation. *Annals of Tourism Research* 24 (2), 283–304.

Goaman, M. (1941) *Judy's Book of Sweet Making*. London: Faber and Faber.

Gray, T. (2007) *Devon and the Slave Trade*. Exeter: The Mint Press.

Green, H. (1993) *Food Lover's Guide to Britain*. London: BBC Books.

Hall, C.M., Sharples, L.D., Mitchell, R., Maconis, N., and Cambourne, B. (2003) *Food Tourism around the World*. Oxford: Butterworth-Heinemann.

Harris, J. (1907) *My Devonshire book*. Plymouth: Western Morning News.

Lovatt, E. (1938) Clotted cream. *Supplement to the Farmer and Stockbreeder*, 5 November. London: Farmer and Stockbreeder.

Mintz, S.W. (1997) Time, sugar and sweetness. In C. Counihan and P. Van Esterik (eds) *Food and Culture: A Reader* 357–369 (359 in text). New York: Routledge.

Morgan, N. and Pritchard, A. (2005) On souvenirs and metonymy: narratives of memory, metaphor and materiality. *Tourist Studies* 5, 29–53.

Morton, H.V. (1927) *In Search of England*. London: Methuen.

Neil, M.H. (*c*.1913) *Candies and Bonbons and How to Make Them*. London: W. & R. Chambers, Limited.

Pimlott, J.A.R. (1976) *The Englishman's Holiday, A Social History*. Hassocks, Sussex: Harvester Press.

Pine, B.J. and Gilmore, J.H. (1998) Welcome to the experience economy. *Harvard Business Review*.

Quan, S. and Wang, N. (2004) Towards a structural model of the tourist experience: An illustration from food experiences in tourism. *Tourism Management* 25, 297–305.

Richardson, T. (2003) *Sweets: The History of Temptation*. London: Bantam Books.

Russell, H. (1932) *The Delectable West*. London: G. Bell and Sons Ltd.

Smith, L.J.S. and Xiao, H. (2008) Culinary tourism supply chains: A preliminary examination. *Journal of Travel Research* 46, 289–299.

Spencer, C. (2002) *British Food an Extraordinary Two Thousand Years of History*. London: Grub Street, with Fortnum and Mason.

Stevenson, J. (1984) *The Pelican Social History of Britain, British Society, 1914–1939*. Harmondsworth: Penguin.

Strong, L.A.G. (1954) *The Story of Sugar*. London: George Wiedenfield & Nicholson.

Stryer, L. (1975) *Biochemistry*. San Francisco: W.H. Freeman and Company.

Sutton, D.E. (2001) *Remembrance of Repasts; Anthropology of Food and Memory*. Oxford: Berg.

Tannahill, R. (1973) *Food in History*. Frogmore, St Albans: Paladin.

Wansink, B., Cheney, M. and Chan, N. (2003) Exploring comfort food preferences across age and gender. *Psychology and Behavior* 79, 739–747.

Waskul, D., Vannini, P., and Wilson, J. (2009) The aroma of reflections, nostalgia and the shaping of the sensuous self. *The Senses and Society* 4 (1), 5–22.

Watson, G.L. and Kopachevsky, J.P. (1994) Interpretations of tourism as commodity. *Annals of Tourism Research* 21 (5), 645–660.

Whittaker, N. (1998) Sweet talk: The secret history of confectionery. London: Victor Gollancz.

Wood, M.E. (2002) *Thornbury's Confectioners of this Town, Barnstaple*. Bideford: Edmund Gaskell.

10 Sugarcane and the Sugar Train: Linking Tradition, Trade and Tourism in Tropical North Queensland

Leanne White

Linkages between heritage, tourism and trade in Australia's most northern sugar-producing region, the Daintree Coast, are examined in this chapter. This area used to be referred to as Far North Queensland but the marketers now refer to it as Tropical North Queensland (TNQ). The chapter ties in with a number of the overarching themes of this book including: recognition of the heritage and culture of sugar; the interconnectivity of sugar and tourism in terms of origin, use and consumption; why, where, when and how sugar-related attractions are developed; and the potential for communities with a sugar heritage to benefit from sugar-related tourism.

The chapter will explore the sugar-related heritage of the region and examine the sugar industry in the area. During the harvesting and crushing season, cane trains and trucks are a familiar sight in TNQ. Of particular interest is the historic tourist steam train (formerly used for carting sugarcane to the factory) known as the Bally Hooley. Sugar heritage, tourism and trade, and the ways in which the sugar-tourism-heritage relationship is communicated in this prominent tourist region of Australia, will be examined here.

Tourism, Heritage and Popular Culture

As early as 1979, Peter Spearritt and David Walker recognised that popular culture in Australia had been largely ignored as a subject worthy of academic analysis. Spearritt argued, 'The battle for Australia's symbols was really won or lost in tourist pamphlets and encyclopaedias' (Spearritt & Walker, 1979: 58). Many studies in tourism have considered the role of heritage attractions in helping create a national identity. Pretes (2003) notes that tourists receive messages sent to them by the creators of the sites they visit, and these sites of significance, presented as aspects of a national heritage, help to shape a common national identity or imagined community among a diverse population. He also argues that a shared identity is often an official goal of countries comprised of many different cultures where there exists a common urge to create a national identity to overcome diversity and difference within the nation state. He adds that monuments in particular represent something shared by all citizens, helping to 'popularize a hegemonic nationalist message of inclusion' (Pretes, 2003: 127).

Rojek furthermore argues 'most tourists feel they have not fully absorbed a sight until they stand before it, see it, and take a photograph to record the moment' (1997: 58). If tourism sites can help create a common identity or imagined community, can images of these destinations on the websites of family and friends represent aspects of a culture and help to develop a better understanding of a destination or even a possible desire to travel to that place? Morgan et al. argue that travel for the purpose of leisure is 'a highly involving experience, extensively planned, excitedly anticipated and fondly remembered' (2004: 4). The photographs that capture the highlights of the travel occasion constitute a vital element of both remembering the event and sharing the experience with others. Urry argues that visual images generated by travellers provide a strong basis for potential tourists to select places to visit. He argues that when tourists gaze they effectively become semioticians 'reading the landscape for signifiers of certain pre-established notions or signs derived from various discourses of travel and tourism' (1990: 12). Pitchford further argues that tourism promotional materials 'speak to tourists in a language that creates a set of expectations about a destination' (2008: 98).

As Laurajane Smith argues, heritage is a 'cultural and social process' that is 'ultimately intangible' (Smith, 2006: 307). This chapter aims to demystify the ways in which the concept of Australia's often intangible heritage has been imagined. The tourist is able to rethink their understanding and 'awareness of the role' that heritage plays 'in our everyday lives' (Waterton, 2010: 206). Sean Gammon argues that heritage has the ability to 'guide and cement national identities' (Gammon, 2007: 1).

Tourism in Tropical North Queensland

The destination that is TNQ incorporates many scenic landscapes, towns and cities, including: The Great Barrier Reef, the Daintree (the world's oldest rainforest), the Atherton Tablelands, Cairns, Port Douglas, Palm Cove, Cape Tribulation, Cooktown and Cape York. Most interstate tourists fly into Cairns and either base themselves in the city or head further north to popular towns such as Port Douglas. Overseas visitors can fly direct to Cairns from a number of countries including: Japan, Hong Kong, Singapore and New Zealand. To cater for the needs of a growing number of tourists, more than 600 tours depart the region each day. A number of annual events are also staged in TNQ in order to both attract visitors and keep locals entertained. Some of the more well known festivals and events include: the Port Douglas Carnivale, the Cairns Ukulele Festival, Taste of the Tablelands, the Port Douglas Marlin Challenge, and the Great Barrier Reef Marathon Festival where long-distance runners explore scenic trails, run along the historic cane train tracks and follow 'leave nothing but your foot prints' environmental guidelines.

Another festival with a sugar connection was a three-day festival entitled *Romancing the Cane* (http://www.karnakplayhouse.com.au/Romancing-The-Cane.25.0.html) held by Karnak Playhouse in 1992. The playhouse is a spectacular amphitheatre and artistic retreat on the edge of the World Heritage Daintree National Park, built by former actor Diane Cilento in the 1980s. The festival included installations, performances and public forums. Oral histories from the local cane cutting community and an exhibition, which captured the spectacle of blazing canefields, were also part of the unique festival. Brought together to discuss 'Progressive Agricultural Diversification' at the historic event were farmers, canegrowers, scientists, futurists, community members, interest groups, the media and government departments.

Also performed at the festival was a theatrical fantasy entitled *Doll Seventeen*, based on Lawler's landmark play *Summer of the Seventeenth Doll*, which portrays much about Australian popular culture and the sugarcane industry. *Summer of the Seventeenth Doll* by Ray Lawler has been described as 'the greatest Australian play' (Burrows & Morton, 1986: 204). The 'Doll' (as it is popularly known) tells the story of canecutters Barney and Roo who spend the winter months working on the Queensland canefields and return each summer in their non-harvesting months (known as 'the slack') to their female friends in Melbourne. Each year is marked with the gift of a souvenir kewpie doll. On the 17th visit, work and relationship changes cause the otherwise 'convenient' situation to take a dramatic turn. The key themes of the production are the conflict between illusion and reality and the loss of youth. Lawler's popular play was first performed in Melbourne in 1955, and by 1957 had made its way to London's West End. The play was also made into a movie starring John Mills and Ernest Borgnine. Honouring the famous play, giant kewpie dolls were incorporated into the closing ceremony of the Sydney 2000 Olympic Games.

The city of Cairns is a major gateway city and attracts many tour groups and backpackers, while Port Douglas – located one hour by road to the north – attracts a larger proportion of higher spending tourists. The Port Douglas area claims to be the world's only region where marine and terrestrial World Heritage Sites meet – the Reef and the Daintree Rainforest (Mylne, 2005: 93). The Wet Tropics region represents an important merging of the national park and the marine park (Zell, 2006).

Though the Reef retains its status as the richest marine habitat on earth, coral bleaching has become an increasing challenge in the face of global awareness about the risks of rising sea temperatures. The more alarmist projections anticipate the virtual elimination of the Reef as a living organism over the next decade or so. Activities undertaken outside the park boundaries constitute another threat to the sustainability of the Reef. The extensive use of chemicals on the 42 million ha adjacent to the mainland is a major concern, notably in the case of nitrogen, phosphorus and potassium, which are applied for sugar cultivation and for fruit and vegetable growing. Historical data reveals that in 1990 alone, 83,000 tonnes of nitrogen was added to the land adjacent to the Reef – an amount equivalent to what had been applied cumulatively from the beginnings of farming until 1945 (Pulsford, 1993). Since 1990, the situation has continued to worsen as evidenced by the findings of a 1997 report on chemical pollutants caused by agriculture that included sugar cultivation (Bowen & Bowen, 2002: 407).

Sugar is Big Business in Australia

Australia produces around 5 million tonnes of sugar each year and, as reviewed in Chapter 3, leads the world in the exporting of raw sugar. Approximately 80% of Australia's sugar product is exported. The major destinations for the Australian product are Japan, China, Malaysia, South Korea and Canada, with new markets opening up in the Middle East and Eastern Europe. Of the sugar that is produced for the domestic market, around 80% is purchased by the large soft drink and confectionary companies. The remaining 20% is purchased by consumers as refined sugar on the supermarket shelves (Grice et al., 2005: 11). While Australians consume more than 50 kg a year of sugar, more than 70% is consumed through manufactured foods which contain sugar (Sheales et al., 1999: 95).

The processing of sugarcane into raw sugar is one of Australia's oldest and largest rural industries (Brumby et al., 2008: 3). The Colonial Sugar Refining (CSR) Company Limited was founded in 1855. Australia's sugar industry consists of around 5000 sugarcane businesses supplying product to 27 sugar mills. Five main sugar refineries are located across the country in Mackay and Bundaberg (Queensland), Harwood (New South Wales), Melbourne (Victoria) and Perth (Western Australia). Australia boasts more than 400,000 ha of cane-growing land (see Figure 10.1). Sugar is grown along the coast of north-eastern Australia with crops extending approximately 2100 km from northern New South Wales to northern Queensland. Around 94% of the nation's sugar crop is grown in Queensland. While cane farms or fields vary in size, the average farm is about 80 ha and these businesses are largely owned and operated by families. During the harvesting season, most mills crush around 10,000 tonnes of cane per day and employ about 150 people.

Queensland's sugar railway line connects the sugar mills that can be found along the state's coastal strip. Around 4000 km of narrow-gauge railway lines transport about 36 million tonnes of freshly harvested sugarcane to the nearest mill for processing each season (Browning, 2007). The trains are essential for the efficient movement of the cane from farm to factory in as quick a time as possible and normally within 18 hours of cutting. The use of rail also avoids the double handling which is inherent in other methods of harvesting. It is also the most economically efficient way to handle the sugar and can be up to 50% cheaper (Dyer & Hodge, 1988: 1). At harvesting time trains up to 1 km in length can operate 24 hours a day, 7 days a week for up

Figure 10.1 Australia's tropical north provides the perfect climate for growing sugar cane

to 26 weeks of the year (normally from June to December). Other countries have also adopted a similar system for moving fresh sugarcane from the field to the processing mill in this efficient manner. They include: South Africa, Mauritius and Australia's Pacific neighbour Fiji (where a very similar field-to-mill system has operated since the 1880s) (Dyer & Hodge, 1988: 1).

Queensland's cane railway system, sometimes referred to as a tramway, is symbolised by the sight of a powerful locomotive that hauls many large bins (metal or strong wire mesh wagons) of sugarcane. There are currently around 250 diesel locomotives and 52,000 cane bins operating in Australia.

Marketing Queensland's Sugar Country

Sugarcane has been produced in TNQ since the 1870s (see Figure 10.2). Until 1904, when legislation was introduced to ban the practice, around 60,000 South Sea Islanders (referred to as Kanakas) were forcibly brought to Queensland to work on the sugar plantations. Japanese and Indian workers replaced the Kanakas, who were later replaced by Italians after World War II. Sugar produced in the Mossman region was originally harvested by hand (see Figure 10.3) and transported by horse-drawn carriage. The cane was cut

Figure 10.2 Photographs of Port Douglas displayed at Anzac Park include the sugar train – bottom right

by hand after burning and this was clearly an arduous task for the men who worked the fields. Australia subsequently pioneered the use of mechanical harvesters, which made the back-breaking work much easier. The progressive Mossman Central Mill began mechanical cane crushing operations in 1897, introduced computerised machinery in 1971, and continued operating until 2003. The cane was shipped from nearby Port Douglas (later carried by road) and transported an hour south to a bulk sugar terminal in Cairns. However, once the railway lines were in place, rail (or tramway) proved to be the most efficient and cost effective means for moving the sugar cane to the processing mill.

Port Douglas, once a sleepy fishing and holiday village, has since the 1980s slowly grown to become a well-known tourist destination, attracting a wide variety of tourists including world leaders and high-profile celebrities. The Sheraton Mirage Resort on Four Mile Beach (a scenic stretch of beach where Charles Kingsford-Smith once landed his 'Southern Cross') and the nearby Marina Mirage shopping complex were built in 1987 and forever changed the small town of Port Douglas – known to many locals and tourists simply as 'Port' or 'PD'.

Figure 10.3 More photographs of Port Douglas include cutting cane by hand – middle image

Tourism Revised by Historic Sugar Train

Like similar ventures around the world, such as the leisurely paced cane train in the historic town of Lahaina in Maui, and the children-friendly long cane train of Hsi-Hu County in Taiwan, the Queensland town of Port Douglas has benefitted culturally, socially and historically from the revival of the Bally Hooley Steam Railway. The historic train operates on just over 4 km of narrow-gauge railway line in the resort town of Port Douglas – 67 km north of Cairns. The venture is financially supported by local business personality John Morris and the Port Douglas Steam Train Company. The train line or tramway between the sugar plantations and mills in Mossman and the wharf at Port Douglas was built in 1896. The Bally Hooley train line now provides a unique and attractive journey for tourists and in addition has ample room for cyclists and pedestrians along most of its length. The name of the train is thought to have originated from the Irish town north of Cork (spelt Bally Hooly), which has the distinction of being the first settlement in Ireland. The name translates to 'ford of the apples' as the first settlers were said to be impressed by the apple trees they found there. It is also said that the phrase 'Faugh a Ballagh' was the fearful battle cry used by clan fighters in Ireland. The Gaelic translation of the phrase is 'Clear the Way' and was made into a patriotic song in 1842.

The first steam locomotive used here was supplied by the well-known English engine manufacturers John Fowler and Company, based in Leeds, England. From there, Fowler locomotives were exported around the world. The locomotive history of sugar trains can be divided into two distinct eras – steam and diesel. The 'steam era' (1882–1955) can be divided into the Fowler period (1882–1911), then the Hudswell Clarke period (1911–1955). The Hudswell Clarke Company was also based in Leeds (Dyer & Hodge, 1988: 87). The diesel era was known to have started in some places as early as the 1920s. However, steam was generally the preferred mode until being phased out in the 1950s.

The Bally Hooley service commenced in 1900 and was operated by the Douglas Shire Council until 1958. The service was used to move both sugar-cane and passengers between Mossman and Port Douglas. After it ceased operations as a sugar train, the Bally Hooley was displayed in Anzac Park opposite the 1878 Courthouse Hotel as a reminder of the importance of the tramway to the town. Restoration of the train began in the 1970s but it was not until 1994 that the Douglas Shire Tourism Association and the Mossman Central Mill developed a formal restoration project to commemorate the Mill's centenary.

The train was originally owned and operated by the Mossman Mill, where tours began in the 1980s. When the train first began catering for tourists, it operated on a longer route in the Mossman area north of Port Douglas. After a tour of the Mossman Central Mill, the tourist train took a 10 km sightseeing journey through the canefields in the surrounding area. The three-hour tour offered a unique insight into aspects of Queensland's significant sugar industry.

Catering for the needs of many more tourists and possibly those with less interest in the sugar refining process, the Bally Hooley train now runs shorter trips (just under an hour for a return journey) out of the Marina Mirage station in Port Douglas every Sunday and on public holidays. The steam engine hauls eight coaches, which can potentially carry up to 200 passengers. Adults can purchase an all-day pass for AU$10, while a similar ticket for children costs AU$5. Lower fares apply for those wanting to make shorter trips. Each Sunday many locals and tourists are attracted to the nearby Anzac Park to stroll around the 'Port Douglas Sunday Markets' with more than 800 stalls (see Figure 10.4). Looking out over the Coral Sea, the picturesque market includes local produce, jewellery, arts and crafts and a variety of unique souvenirs. The Sunday market and historic steam train combine to provide a unique family friendly day trip.

Figure 10.4 The Port Douglas Sunday Market at Anzac Park

Anzac Day (April 25) is a respected and solemn day of the year. On this day, Australians and New Zealanders pay tribute to fallen war heroes. Anzac Day services are held at historic Anzac Park in Port Douglas (and at parks and memorials just like it around Australia and New Zealand) (see Figure 10.5). The Douglas Shire have installed a range of plaques, statues and other interpretation sites into the peaceful surroundings of Anzac Park so that visitors might make better sense of the rich history of the area. While the political genesis of Australia can be traced to the events of 1901, some historians have argued that it was the Anzac (Australian and New Zealand Army Corps) landing at Gallipoli on 25 April 1915 that marked the emergence of Australia, the nation.

The Bally Hooley train journey passes through picturesque lush vegetation, Dickson's Inlet (with mangroves and occasional crocodile sightings), holiday villas and a golf course. There are five train stations along the 4 km journey. The first is Marina Mirage – where an old canecutters' barracks has been converted into the station and where yachts, boats and other vessels are moored (see Figure 10.6). In 2010 the station at Marina Mirage was refurbished to also become the home of 'Arthouse Port Douglas' – a venue where classes and exhibitions can be held. Next along the route is Dougies Backpackers – a popular accommodation choice for younger travellers– followed by the Country Club (a convenient stop for passengers staying at the Sheraton Mirage). The train then stops at another

Figure 10.5 The Anzac Park memorial

Figure 10.6 Marina Mirage – the departure and return site for the Bally Hooley

accommodation place – Rydges Sabaya Resort – before finally making its way to the final station of St Crispins. The stations are located approximately five minutes apart. When the train arrives at St Crispins Station, passengers are asked to alight from the train while the locomotive is uncoupled from the carriages and turned around by two of the crew with the aid of a historic turntable in a pit for the return journey to Marine Mirage.

The Bally Hooley train is powered by two coal-fired steam locomotives, named Speedy and Bundy. These two locomotives were reproduced in Queensland's sugar town of Bundaberg in 1952 having obtained permission to do so from the Fowler group in England. Other engines built in the same manner were known as 'Bundaberg Fowlers'. The steam locomotives were used to cart sugar in the region until they were eventually replaced by diesel engines.

Has the Bally Hooley Run Out of Steam?

The Bally Hooley train has an uncertain future. As costs for running the tourist train are extremely high, all proceeds from ticket sales and donations go directly into paying for the coal (which is sourced from a town 900 km away), hefty insurance levies, registration costs and regular line maintenance. To assist with the expensive running costs of the venture, the train can also be chartered for private events such as birthdays and weddings. Prices for the private hiring of the train start from AU$600 for a four-hour charter to AU$1,000 for eight hours.

Like many similar initiatives around the world, the railway is operated by a small group of enthusiastic and dedicated volunteers. However, regularly operating the train is not an easy task. Each train journey requires the services of a volunteer driver, fireman (who shovels the coal into the engine), conductor and guard. Consequently, the historic tourist train is something of an endangered species. The marketing of the attraction could be significantly strengthened. In some respects, the train seems to symbolise a lost opportunity for the promotion of the rich heritage of the region.

In 2008, *The Cairns Post* reported that the train may have to cease operations due to a lack of volunteers. Driver Peter Lloyd explained, 'Unfortunately, we're not going to be able to run the train. The way the situation is, without volunteers, we can't carry on' (*The Cairns Post*, 2008: 11). The consulting company who wrote *The Port Douglas Waterfront Master Plan Transport and Traffic Review* acknowledge that the Bally Hooley operation requires financial investment from the town if it is to maintain its operations. The report states, 'Residents and tourists alike would miss this piece of history and the enjoyable journey experience if it was to cease its current operations' (Goodall & Kwok, 2008: 26). The train is thus a fragile reminder of Australia's sugar history, past and present.

Conclusion

As reviewed in this chapter, sugar is part of the popular culture, heritage and identity of Australia. This is reflected in particular in the sugar producing area of North Queensland by festivals and events that have included performances about the life of the seasonal cane cutters in which theatre-goers can reflect on this heritage, exhibits at Anzac Park where visitors can learn more about the heritage of sugar agriculture and processing in the region, and a former sugar cane train attraction that provides visitors with a glimpse of the sugar landscape and industry. It is interesting to note that there does not seem to be any coordinated interpretation of the area's rich sugar heritage and related traditions. Rather, events taking place within a limited time frame (theatrical performances during a festival, a visit to a park and a train ride) all offer a hint of the scope of this heritage.

This chapter has thus revealed how Australia's intangible and tangible sugar heritage is experienced and has been imagined by visitors. There are signs that the country's sugar heritage has become part of the national identity, as noted earlier, with giant kewpie dolls honouring the play *Summer of the Seventeenth Doll* included in the closing ceremony of the Sydney 2000 Olympic Games. Despite numerous management and operational challenges, the fact that the sugar-related Bally Hooley steam train attraction is still operating with the support of local government, business and volunteers is evidence that locals value the sugar heritage of the area and desire to share it with visitors. Another factor to consider is that with the region's sugar industry still in operation visitors can experience aspects of it through sightseeing (canefields, contemporary cane trains and sugar factories). Sugar heritage, although recognised as part of national identity in Australia, is thus both historic and contemporary, integrated into the tourism gaze not only through heritage-related tourism opportunities but through the visitors' overall experience of the sugar trade in the region.

References

Bowen, J. and Bowen, M. (2002) *The Great Barrier Reef: History, Science, Heritage.* Cambridge: Cambridge University Press.

Browning, J. (2007) Queensland sugar cane railways today, accessed 31 October 2011. http://www.lrrsa.org.au/LRR_SGRz.htm.

Brumby, S., Martin, J. and Wilder, S. (2008) *Living Longer on the Land: Case Studies of the Sustainable Farm Families Program in the Sugar and Cotton Industries.* Barton: Rural Industries Research and Development Council.

Burrows, G. and Morton, C. (1986) *The Canecutters.* Carlton: Melbourne University Press.

Dyer, P. and Hodge, P. (1988) *Cane Train: The Sugar-Cane Railways of Fiji.* Wellington: New Zealand Railway and Locomotive Society Incorporated.

Gammon, S. (2007) Introduction: sport, heritage and the English. An opportunity missed? In S. Gammon and G. Ramshaw (eds) *Heritage, Sport and Tourism: Sporting Pasts – Tourist Futures* (pp. 1–8). Abingdon: Routledge.

Goodall, S. and Kwok, R. (2008) *Port Douglas Waterfront Master Plan Transport and Traffic Review.* Milton: Maunsell Australia.

Grice, J., Paton, S. and Blines, D. (2005) *Organic Sugar: End-User Support and Grower Perception.* Barton: Rural Industries Research and Development Council.

Lawler, R. (1957) *Summer of the Seventeenth Doll.* Sydney: Angus and Robertson.

Morgan, N., Pritchard, A. and Pride, R. (2004) *Destination Branding: Creating the Unique Destination Proposition.* Oxford: Elsevier.

Mylne, L. (2005) *Frommer's Portable Australia's Great Barrier Reef* (3rd ed.). Hoboken, NJ: Wiley Publishing.

Pitchford, S. (2008) *Identity Tourism: Imaging and Imagining the Nation.* Bingley: Emerald Group Publishing.

Pretes, M. (2003) Tourism and nationalism. *Annals of Tourism Research* 30 (1), 125–142.

Pulsford, J.S. (1993) Historical nutrient usage in coastal Queensland river catchments adjacent to the Great Barrier Reef Marine Park (Research Publication No. 40). Townsville: GBRMPA.

Rojek, C. (1997) Indexing, dragging, and social construction. In C. Rojek and J. Urry (eds) *Touring Cultures: Transformations of Travel and Theory* (pp. 52–74). London: Routledge.

Sheales, T., Gordon, S., Hafi, A. and Toyne, C. (1999) Sugar: International policies affecting market expansion (Research Report 99.14). Canberra: Australian Bureau of Agriculture and Resource Economics.

Smith, L. (2006) *The Uses of Heritage.* Abingdon: Routlege.

Spearritt, P. and Walker, D. (eds) (1979) *Australian Popular Culture.* Sydney: George Allen and Unwin.

The Cairns Post (2008) Volunteers running out of puff. *The Cairns Post,* 9 April, 11.

Urry, J. (1990) *The Tourist Gaze: Leisure and Travel in Contemporary Societies.* London: Sage Publications.

Waterton, E. (2010) *Politics, Policy and the Discourses of Heritage in Britain.* Basingstoke: Palgrave Macmillan.

Zell, L. (2006) *Diving and Snorkelling Great Barrier Reef* (2nd ed.). Melbourne: Lonely Planet.

11 From Sugar as Industry to Sugar as Heritage: Changing Perceptions of the Chelsea Sugar Works

Jane Legget

New Zealand does not immediately come to mind in the context of the sugar industry, but the Chelsea Sugar Works in Birkenhead on Auckland's North Shore is a distinctive landmark on the Waitemata Harbour. Unrefined sugarcane, currently imported from Queensland, Australia, has been processed there since 1884, when the sugar works operated as the Colonial Sugar Refining Company. Today the Chelsea Sugar Works stand at the heart of the Chelsea Heritage Park, still operating as New Zealand's only sugar refinery and probably the best preserved in Australasia. This case study traces the transition of the site from sugar as industry to sugar as heritage. This includes the progress towards the recognition of the site for heritage status and securing public access, and the concept of the Chelsea Heritage Park as an urban amenity and visitor destination in a city keen to attract tourists but notable for its dearth of accessible heritage attractions. The pathway to heritage recognition involved a range of champions and stakeholders and a formal national designation process. The sugar works as heritage remains a work-in-progress, especially with the advent of a new local government now responsible for the whole of Auckland City. The chapter concludes by suggesting potential futures, including options as a visitor attraction.

Industrial Heritage in New Zealand

The concept of heritage in New Zealand continues to expand. Initially the focus was on nature, endemic species and wilderness; 'environmental heritage' identified the flora, fauna and landscape as unique and important to conserve. The customs and material culture of the indigenous Maori first attracted the attention of academic ethnographers and museum curators, before becoming the drawcard for the early tourism industry and later more broadly valued as distinct cultural heritage (McLure, 2004). It took longer for both New Zealanders and the government to recognise early European buildings and artefacts as 'heritage'. The New Zealand Historic Places Trust was founded by an Act of Parliament in 1954 and focused initially on preservation of civic buildings or important residences, but now it encompasses a greater diversity of architecture, archaeological sites and cultural landscapes. The tourism sector has only relatively recently appreciated that alongside the scenic wonders and Maori culture there is much else to interest the heritage tourist, whether domestic or international. While museums, art galleries, historic houses, churches and other landmark civic buildings now feature regularly in visitor itineraries and destination marketing, the industrial heritage still has ground to make up. Warren and Taylor (2001) reported 61 (3%) industrial heritage-themed tourism sites from a sample of 2266 operators. Their definition was broad and included workplace tours, farm stays, craft potteries, open-air museums, mining sites and mills.

The first comprehensive survey of New Zealand's industrial heritage was published in 1982 (Thornton), with a more current catalogue compiled by Smith (2001). Thomson (1981, 1991) noted several museums collecting industrial heritage material. More recently, the national online directory, NZMuseums (2008), categorised industrial heritage collections under 'technology' and 'transport'. Smith's observation (2001: 12) still holds true:

> The words 'industry' and 'heritage' do not readily trip off the lips of Kiwis and certainly not in the same sentence. Ours has been a predominantly agricultural society, not the Southern hemisphere's cradle of industrialization. Ask about the heritage of our industry and the usual response is just a quizzical look and a few fading folk memories.

Heritage legislation (e.g. Historic Places Act 1993 and Resource Management Act 1991) now governs the identification and regulation of recognised heritage sites and landscapes. The official Register of Historic Places includes records of industrial sites, assessing their significance through a complex and thorough process. Designation on the register does not, however, automatically provide protection, and industrial sites are often at risk, handicapped by a lack of the aesthetic qualities that can more easily attract supporters, especially in an urban setting. However, these sites are gaining greater recognition in specialist circles through the efforts of the engineering profession. The Institution of Professional Engineers (IPENZ) celebrates its own achievements, with a programme of installing markers at engineering landmarks including bridges, mines and factories, formalised in its Engineering Heritage Strategy 2011 (Engineering Heritage New Zealand, 2011). IPENZ's activity has led to industrial monuments featuring more often in regional heritage trails (e.g. those produced through the New Zealand Heritage Trails Foundation) and regional guidebooks (e.g. Hayward *et al.*, 2008). Nonetheless, New Zealand's persistent imagery of sheep, dairying, fruit growing, forestry and fishing eclipses the grittier concepts of industrial heritage with scarred landscapes, rusting iron, pollution, smells and noise (Bell, 1997).

When it comes to New Zealand's engineering heritage associated with food production, recognised buildings relate to the primary industries: dairying, historic farms, and the meat trade: the Belfast Freezing works in Christchurch (1883) and the Totara Estate (1850s). The Chelsea Sugar Refinery (1884) represents an exception as the raw materials processed there are imported, rather than home-grown, but it has received the attention of IPENZ (La Roche & Aitken, 2011).

The Chelsea Sugar Refinery

Visitors crossing the Waitemata Harbour always ask about the striking salmon pink buildings on the Birkenhead waterfront. The Chelsea Sugar Works is hard to miss from the seaward side but is less visible from Birkenhead itself (see Figure 11.1). Bulk shipments of raw sugarcane have been processed here for some 125 years and the refinery still operates from the original premises. The complex has heritage building status, fully designated in 2009 as a Historic Place Category I by the New Zealand Historic Places Trust. Its site today includes native bush, dammed ponds and a deep-water dock, as well as historic structures, including the industrial buildings, the manager's house and cottages that housed the workers. The Chelsea Sugar Estate sits on the edge of parkland and wilderness, some now publicly owned and managed by the local authority. As such, it is a rare survival of an industrial complex in New Zealand, one that reflects the heritage of sugar; in the 1900s it was the largest sugar refinery operation in Australasia. Today, Chelsea Sugar is an iconic food brand in New Zealand, and its products can probably be found in every kitchen across the country.

Figure 11.1 The sugar works today, from the landward side, fenced off from the public. The central tower is the cistern house, still operating after 125 years

A Brief History

The original 76 ha site of the sugar works was chosen for its natural resources and its location, allowing a high degree of self-sufficiency. Fresh water from Duck Creek was essential for its refining processes, while the surrounding bush and natural clay provided timber and clay for construction (Verran, 2010). Its deep-water anchorage and its relatively easy access across the Waitemata Harbour to the main port of Auckland served for receiving supplies and distributing its products to the growing market within New Zealand. By 1883 the Australian based Colonial Sugar Refining Company had developed new sources of sugarcane in Fiji, and New Zealand was geographically more convenient for processing these crops (Jones & McKenzie, 2009). The venture required considerable capital, with local businessmen joining the Australian investors, encouraged by New Zealand government subsidy. Construction alone required a large workforce camped on the site to dig, prepare and fire the 1.5 million bricks used for the principal structures.

A Scottish engineer, James Muir, already experienced in designing specialised production facilities in Great Britain and Ireland, had built refineries for the company in Australia. His Chelsea creation incorporated a number of innovative design features. Much of the heavy mechanical equipment came from suppliers in Scotland and England, 400 tonnes worth being shipped in from Greenock alone (La Roche & Aitken, 2011).

Land on the site was set aside to house employees, with up to 100 workers resident in a small 'company town' of 35 wooden homes each with its own large garden, supported by a school, an Anglican church and an independent store. While not exhibiting the degree of paternalism and philanthropy of English industrialists exemplified at Cadbury's chocolate factory at Bourneville or the Lever Brothers' Port Sunlight soap factory, the company nonetheless actively supported a healthy lifestyle for its employees, but retained ownership of the properties. By 1905, some 250 were employed, but new health and housing regulations required the wooden houses to be removed as they were now deemed unsuitable, so the company town was dismantled. Only four pairs of semi-detached brick homes were built in 1909 as replacements, soon afterwards difficulties between the trade union and the company evaporated when the company offered low interest loans for workers to buy or build their own homes. These workers' new homes contributed substantially to the development of the North Shore suburb of Birkenhead and supported the growth of community life with shops, schools and churches. By the 1950s a third of local residents worked at the sugar works (c. 450). The grounds of the Chelsea Estate were landscaped over the former company housing area and planted with both native and exotic trees, providing a pleasant local amenity. A meadow remained for grazing and exercising the company's workhorses.

External factors affected the sugar works throughout the 20th century. Strikes in New Zealand, the end of the indentured labour scheme which had brought many Indians to Fiji's sugarcane fields, competing sugar sources internationally, the introduction of women to the workforce during World War II and the opening of Auckland's harbour bridge each had its impact, along with greater mechanisation and the introduction of supermarkets (Jones & McKenzie, 2009). In the 1960s the company developed its distinctive brand identity, using the Cistern House with its 'pagoda tower' between two palm trees as its logo in a strategic move to foster customer loyalty (Jones & McKenzie, 2009). The company has changed its name over the years, but it continues to operate in its original complex, producing white sugar, with brown sugar, golden syrup, treacle and molasses made from the residual syrup.

Having previously acquired additional land to protect the quality of its catchment area for its vital freshwater supply in Duck Creek, the company found itself with landholdings surplus to requirements once the refinery was connected to the public water system in 1960. It sold off several hectares on its north-western boundaries in 1966, creating a subdivision for 1000 homes and contributing further to Birkenhead's expansion as a residential suburb. Bordering Kauri Point Centennial Park to the south-west and the botanically rich Chatswood Reserve on the north-west, the Chelsea Estate still represented a central component of the largest continuous stretch of native bush in the central Auckland area, regularly visited or settled by 31 native bird species. Its larger role is as a significant wildlife corridor between the islands of the Hauraki Gulf to the east and the Waitakere hills to the west. The company filled some of the park's gullies with refinery waste until the 1970s when that area was landscaped (Jones & McKenzie, 2009). In 2008, following a long campaign, much of the estate's parkland was transferred to the then local authority, North Shore City Council, to be managed along with the brick workers' houses and the former manager's home sited on it. These heritage properties are leased to residential tenants who are required to abide by heritage requirements.

Description

A brief account of the elements of the complex will indicate the extent and diversity of the operations on the site. The main activity still takes place on two level hectares on the waterfront. For the refining process itself, the complex comprised:

- the cistern house – the most striking building surmounted by a pagoda-like feature, which housed the water cisterns;
- the four-storey char house, including the kilns;
- the small bone house;
- retorts, gasometer, coal-fuelled boiler with a 120-foot chimney.

Adjacent were the substantial sugar stores for both the raw sugar and the refined products. Supporting operations were housed in other premises on site, including offices for the manager and customs officer, bag making shop, printing house, cooper's shed, bale shed, sack shed, sack maker's house, stabling for the workhorses and water tanks. The water supply eventually required four dams, with ponds as features of the estate's parkland. Two separate wharves, one for the sugar and one for the coal and other supplies, echoed the separation of the site into 'clean' and 'dirty' operating zones. Before the opening of the Auckland Harbour Bridge in 1959, the refined products were shipped over to Auckland by a fleet of six lighters. These 'sugar boats' were built and maintained by an on-site shipbuilding operation, including a slipway. There was also briefly a passenger wharf, also rendered redundant by the Auckland Harbour Bridge and subsequent road access.

Much of this industrial complex survives in use, although mechanisation has made the operation more efficient and less labour intensive. The intro-duction of natural gas power in 1960 reduced the need for coal, so the coal wharf was dismantled, and more recently the 120-foot chimney has gone. Most of the operational area is off limits to those using the Chelsea Heritage Park, as the sugar refinery is not geared up for visitors. However, local people walking in the park can see the exterior from the fences and enjoy the exten-sive grounds, with native plantings along the foreshore, managed lawns, attractive ponds, wilderness areas of both mixed hardwood forest and regen-erating and well-established specimen trees now old enough to merit their own heritage status (Jones & McKenzie, 2009).

Towards Heritage Recognition

As the population in the greater Auckland conurbation grew dramatically in the 1990s, pressure on housing increased, creating strong demand for new building land. The Chelsea Estate was (and is) one of the largest undeveloped landholdings in private ownership close to Auckland's central business district, a fact which had not escaped the notice of Birkenhead residents. Many appreci-ated the generous public access that the company had long granted locals but they also were aware of the company's track record of selling off its land for housing. Environmental lobbyists, the Chelsea Heritage Park Association (CHEPA), began organising in 1997 when it emerged that the company had plans to capitalise its land bank without public consultation. The Local Government Act of 2002 required local authorities to be more consultative and to promote the social, environmental, cultural as well as economic well-being of their communities, a situation which actively encouraged greater public engagement in a range of local decision-making and further community action.

CHEPA and other groups actively campaigned, objecting to various development plans put forward by the company. By 2005 the Chelsea Park Trust, a separate organisation set up to protect the parkland, had obtained a conditional agreement for the purchase of 37 ha, dependent on a 'satisfactory outcome' from the company's own submissions to the local planning process for residential developments. This accelerated local advocacy efforts, with considerable public opposition to the company's subsequent plans submitted for 'resource consent'. The movement to secure as much as possible of the estate for the public good ultimately drew in a wide range of stakeholders, taking different degrees of prominence in the process towards its acquisition and its later recognition as 'heritage'. Table 11.1 summarises these stakeholders, and some are discussed further below.

It was the potential loss of a local recreational amenity and threats to the environment which initiated the campaign to secure a sizable portion of the parkland and fund-raise through a charitable trust, the Chelsea Park Trust. The main objections to the company's development plans, mostly coordinated by the Birkenhead Residents Association, were: ecological effects; archaeological loss; heritage loss; cultural and identity loss; effects on local infrastructure (e.g. traffic); effects on visual amenity. At the local and national government levels, the City and Regional Councils and the Historic Places Trust also opposed the company's initial plans, the latter on heritage grounds, although it did not confer high-level heritage recognition until June 2009. While IPENZ acknowledged the importance of the sugar works, it does not appear to have contributed to these debates.

The resource consent process was long and drawn out and relationships were tense. Finally, Chelsea Park Trust negotiated with the company, arriving at a price of NZ$20 million for 37 ha, which North Shore City Council agreed to manage within its parks network once acquired. In return the company achieved a change of zoning status for part of its remaining property, permitting some contained residential development, subject to minimising impacts on the natural environment, the built heritage and the community. This resource consent remains in place, but as yet no building plans have been pursued. Using a range of local fund-raising strategies and tactics, including active liaison with local and central government as well as various community trusts and foundations, the Trust raised the full amount from central and local government contributions, community grants and other sources, a significant achievement.

The purchase and handover was made with great ceremony, launching the Chelsea Heritage Park in March 2009 as a public amenity with strong heritage flavour, both natural and historic. To mark the event, the company commissioned a public sculpture incorporating a redundant four-metre high sugar grab holding a giant sugar lump (see Figure 11.2). North Shore City Council has since provided improved walkways, public toilets, picnic areas, limited interpretive signage and lookouts.

Achieving National Heritage Status

Various external circumstances thus conspired to progress formal achievement of heritage status for the industrial complex. Undoubtedly,

Table 11.1 Stakeholders and their interests in the Chelsea Sugar Works complex

Stakeholder category	Stakeholder	Nature of interest
Commercial	CSR Ltd (parent company of Chelsea Sugar)	Current owner and operator of the sugar works, which made available 36.7 ha for the park.
Community	Chelsea Regional Park Association (CHERPA)	Action group established to advocate for the acquisition and development of the Chelsea Estate and adjacent land as a substantial regional park.
	Chelsea Park Trust	Charitable trust established as the organisation to raise the NZ$20 million to acquire company land for the community as the Chelsea Heritage Park.
	Birkenhead Residents Association	Residents' interest group, independent of the local authorities, coordinated action opposing company plans for residential developments.
	Birkenhead and Northcote Community Facilities Trust	Independent charitable trust which supports local community facilities, services and events.
	ASB Community Trust	A major regional charitable trust which supports community initiatives such as arts, culture, heritage, sports, recreation and health in the Auckland and Northland regions. Contributed NZ$6 million.
	Birkenhead Historical Society	A small membership organisation with a museum and modest documentary resources but little energy or other resources among its volunteers to lead any campaign.
	Uruamo Ecological Society	Local naturalists' group established to work with the local authority, the Royal New Zealand Navy and the community to restore urban habitats in Birkenhead, including the Chelsea Estate.
	Royal Forest and Bird (North Shore branch)	National nature conservation group (local branch) advocated for protection of the inner-city wilderness aspect of the Chelsea Heritage Park. Works in partnership with other groups to protect the environment on the ground and through lobbying.

(continued)

Table 11.1 (*Continued*)

Stakeholder category	Stakeholder	Nature of interest
Central government	Department of Conservation (DoC)	Central government department responsible for environmental and historic heritage and conservation. Contributed NZ$1 million.
	Department of Internal Affairs	Central government department which manages substantial community development grant aid. Contributed NZ$1 million.
	New Zealand Historic Places Trust	A Crown Entity, the leading national heritage agency, funded through an annual operational from the Ministry of Culture and Heritage, responsible for identifying and registering historic places and fostering public interest in heritage.
Local government	North Shore City Council (NSCC)	Territorial local authority elected by the residents and business ratepayers of North Shore City, one of four city councils governing the greater Auckland area until November 2010. Principal local planning authority, managing the District Plan. Contributed NZ$10 million and took on management of the Chelsea Heritage Park within its portfolio of local parks.
	Birkenhead Community Board	Local sub-committee of the NSCC.
	Auckland Regional Council (ARC)	Regional local authority, with responsibility for environment and regional parks.
	Auckland Council	Successor unitary Local Territorial Authority to NSCC and ARC from November 2010, now responsible for management of the Chelsea Heritage Park. Still developing comprehensive policy for heritage and culture.

Figure 11.2 Sugar grabber. This public art work incorporating an original sugar grabber was sited on one of the high points of the Chelsea Heritage Park to mark its opening in March 2009

uncertainty over the long-term operation of the sugar works and the attractively high premium on unbuilt land in Birkenhead concerned wary local residents. Quite separately various advocacy groups for wildlife and the natural environment were actively interested in preserving the important natural resources from at least 1998. The sugar works already featured in the North Shore City Council's District Plan in 2002, a place secured in the 2009 revision, by which time the council had its own local heritage strategy. National recognition, by contrast, appears more reactive than proactive, partly a function of the limited resources of the Historic Places Trust.

Creating the Chelsea Heritage Park involved strategic negotiations with the North Shore City Council. The company retained 14 ha for its current operations, although it is not known how long these will continue. Possibly anticipating change, the refinery was allowed to 'rezone' its site for future use as apartments and offices, including new buildings, with the park forming a buffer zone for suburban Birkenhead. This, together with the establishment of the park, hastened action by the New Zealand Historic Places Trust (NZHPT) to investigate the state and significance of the sugar works complex, designating it as a Category I historic place (record no. 7792) in June

2009. Category I status recognises a site as of 'special or outstanding historical or cultural heritage significance or value' (Jones & McKenzie, 2009). The process involved a formal report and significance assessment, although achievement of this, the highest level of recognition, does not ensure its protection. All planning and resource consent approvals are managed through local authorities (now Auckland Council), which must include all NZHPT-registered sites on their District Plans. Category I status means that any planning changes proposed for the sugar works must be notified to the NZHPT as an 'affected party' and it becomes involved in any decision-making. Although protection is neither automatic nor guaranteed, this process requires that full account is taken of the national and local significance of the site and its various features in determining any proposals for alterations or additions.

The complex meets the formal NZHPT 'physical eligibility' criterion as a historic place, comprising 'land and buildings and structures that are affixed to land that lies within the territorial limits of New Zealand' (Jones & McKenzie, 2009: 6). There are also nine 'significance criteria', which must also be considered for a site to first qualify for the Register of Historic Places. Table 11.2 summarises those seven met by the sugar works. No spiritual or traditional significance or value was identified for the sugar works.

To satisfy the government's investment in the Register of Historic Places, through the Ministry of Culture and Heritage, achievement of full Category I status requires a historic place to embody a high level of relevance on a number of key dimensions, mostly with practical outcomes such as education or research potential. A strong case was made on behalf of the sugar works, with the site meeting eight of the 13 possible criteria, as summarised in Table 11.3.

The Sugar Works and the Chelsea Heritage Park Today

The Chelsea Sugar brand is one of the significant intellectual assets of the company, capitalising on its heritage iconography. Through over 125 years of continuous operation, the company has endeavoured to be a good corporate citizen, continuing to support activities in Birkenhead, although its immediate future under a recent change of ownership is unclear. It promotes its long history on its website, illustrated with fascinating early photographs, and acknowledges public curiosity about the sugar refining process through provision of a virtual tour. While users of the park can view buildings from the outside, the best views are from the water. The startling pink buildings are the first landmarks to be encountered as tourist boats pass under the Harbour Bridge from their embarkation point in downtown Auckland. In the 'City of Sails', eight local tour operators run harbour cruises which feature the Chelsea Sugar Works as a point

Table 11.2 Summary of the significance criteria that contributed to the eligibility of the Chelsea Sugar Works to be formally registered as a historic place

Significance/value factor	Summary
Aesthetic	Visual qualities of building and landscape setting. Distinctive landmark qualities especially when seen from the waterfront. Ornate external and internal details.
Archaeological	Site is unique in New Zealand in including extensive physical remnants of factory complex and ancillary structures (dams, wharves and workers' housing) and buried remains of the company town, and possibly pre-refinery European farming and evidence of earlier Maori activity.
Architectural	Only sugar refining architecture in New Zealand, and rare in Australasia. Brickwork design of manager's and workers' housing illustrates Australian design influence in New Zealand.
Cultural	Close visual and manufacturing association between Chelsea sugar products and their place of production through the iconic brand's logo design of the cistern house.
Historical	International and local historical associations, including with the international sugar trade, global commerce and diet, Australasian business, sugar plantation development in Fiji, the sugar industry's tendency to operate as large industrial estate. Nationally it relates to expanding colonial markets, labour and gender history, the early settlement of Auckland and suburban Birkenhead.
Social	Important as a workplace for 125 years, the company's development and support of the community, and public amenity for recreation.
Technological	The range of industrial engineering in developing and operating the site, and uniqueness in New Zealand as a complex of sugar refining technology and food processing, supported by technologies for bag- and sack-making, coopering, boat-building and brick-making.

Source: Summarised from Jones and McKenzie (2009)

Table 11.3 Summary of the significance criteria which contributed to the eligibility of the Chelsea Sugar Works for formal designation as a Category I historic place

Dimension	Key factors
Reflects important or representative aspects of New Zealand history	Colonial links with Australia and Great Britain; New Zealand as colonial market and producer; labour history; changing industrial processes over 125 years; Auckland business.
Association with events, people or ideas important in New Zealand history	Includes: Frederick Whittaker (later Prime Minister) as investor and director; James K. Baxter (poet) briefly employed, composed a poem; a national strike; Maori settlement activity.
Potential to provide knowledge of New Zealand history	Topics include: manufacturing, trade, transport, labour history, residential life.
Community association with/public esteem for the place	125 years of local employment, plus popular amenity, taken into public ownership after a major campaign.
Potential for public education	Excellent state of preservation; proportion in public ownership; located near population centres, attractive surroundings; association with well-known product. Unique resource for telling story of sugar production and associated role in local and global history.
Technical accomplishment or value or design of the place	Quality and endurance of the complex, with much in continuous operation and specialist technology unique in New Zealand.
Importance of identifying rare types of historic places	Only sugar refinery in New Zealand, rare survival in Australasia and one of the best preserved.
Extent to which the place forms part of a wider historical and cultural complex or landscape.	Integral to understanding the urban development and landscape of Birkenhead, part of extensive historical and cultural landscape along the Waitemata Harbour shoreline, including adjacent sites.

Source: Summarised from Jones and McKenzie (2009)

of interest. Two of these specifically target senior citizens, for whom the site has nostalgic associations. During the 1930s Depression – the 'sugar bag years' (Simpson, 1997) – the sturdy bags made at the sugar works epitomised the 'make do and mend' ethos, being re-used in many ways, including as clothing.

Today, with the sugar works as a backdrop, the park is principally a place for local recreation (Figure 11.3), affording sweeping views across the harbour towards Auckland. Birkenhead residents mostly work in the city centre and other suburbs, so their attachment to the Chelsea Heritage Park is principally as an amenity. It is popular all year round with local joggers, dog walkers, family picnickers and children feeding ducks. The former company

Figure 11.3 This peaceful pond, nearest to the sugar works, is home to a pukeko, a native swamp hen

residences are very desirable for tenants. The council maintains the publicly owned grounds and walkways well. Its response to park management issues resulted in a liquor ban being introduced following some youthful disturbances. There is room for more informative interpretive signage to highlight the history and significance of the sugar works as well as the ecology. Ironically, a higher level of historical interpretation about the refinery can be found 300 km north at Waitangi in the tourism mecca of the Bay of Islands. Here the *Tui*, the last of the six lighters that shipped the sugar across to Auckland until 1961, is moored. It served as a shipwreck museum for 30 years until 2000, then from 2002 until 2011 as a restaurant called The Sugar Boat.

Outlook for the Future

The Chelsea Heritage Park remains a work-in-progress as the new Auckland Council works out how to fulfil its management obligations inherited from the North Shore City Council, including a commitment to buy the former horse paddock from the company for inclusion in the park. In 2011, another group, the Great Chelsea Gardens Trust, had been lobbying the Auckland Council to amalgamate another small reserve to develop as a formal garden, although to date this has been declined as incompatible with the emphasis on preserving native bush. The environmental interest groups are still lobbying for the amalgamation of several adjacent reserves into a single larger urban wilderness.

The operational status of the sugar works themselves may change under its new (mid-2011) Taiwanese ownership. If refinery operations cease, there may be pressure to convert some of the heritage buildings to other uses, including apartments, cafes and compatible commercial enterprises. There are overseas examples of residential development in sugar refineries, e.g. Philadelphia and Brooklyn, USA, and another former colonial sugar works in Brisbane, Australia, but it is clear that the local community will carefully monitor developments. The Category I heritage status will ensure active participation by the Historic Places Trust in any proposals, and strengthen the case for minimising alterations to the heritage structure. The Auckland Plan (a strategic document addressing future growth) to be finalised after the time of writing in 2012 anticipates the city accommodating a further million inhabitants by 2040, with 'urban intensification' likely to increase demand for building land. Birkenhead includes the Birkenhead Point Heritage Conservation Area, with many charming examples of 'the New Zealand villa', an architectural style of wooden residences that New Zealand claims as its own (Stewart, 2002). This legacy from a hard-fought campaign in the

1970s and 1980s is a point of pride, and local residents are already gathering their forces to defend it and the waterfront from any threats of future development. While the new council's planning department has yet to establish its credentials in heritage protection and management, there are promising signs. It has just published a two-volume *North Shore Heritage Thematic Review Report* (Heritage Consultancy Services, 2011) to provide an overview of heritage stock for future planning, which features the sugar works and its contributions to Birkenhead.

The city's recently published *Auckland Visitor Plan* identifies a need for more 'attractors that leverage and showcase things that are interesting and unique to Auckland' (Auckland Tourism Events and Economic Development Ltd, 2011: 56). It cites the distinct flavours of its suburban villages, and the 'heritage character' of certain areas, such as Birkenhead. The timing could be auspicious to realise the potential of both the natural and built environment for the sugar works and its surroundings by enhancing Birkenhead's appeal to tourists. Options could include moving the Birkenhead Museum (Figure 11.4) (housed in another former manager's home) onto the Chelsea Park as an interpretation centre, bringing The Sugar Boat south to be moored at

Figure 11.4 Birkenhead Historical Society's museum. The museum is operated by volunteers in a modest villa, which once belonged to an employee of the sugar works and was moved to its present site beside a sports ground in 1993

Chelsea as a restaurant or café featuring dishes using Chelsea Sugar products (such as New Zealand's iconic pavlova dessert), reinstating the passenger wharf, enhancing the harbour tours with Chelsea as a destination, and merchandising souvenirs which reflect the sugar heritage. In the event of sugar production ceasing, heritage accommodation on the waterfront location with harbour views might be a development option for part of the complex, incorporated into an urban eco-museum, with a passenger wharf included in the harbour ferry routes.

Conclusion

As a cultural landscape variously incorporating manufacturing and processing, residential buildings, waterfront transport structures and now civic amenities and facilities as public parkland, the Chelsea Heritage Park represents a significant heritage resource unique in New Zealand. The heritage dimension of the Chelsea Sugar Works itself remains a 'work-in-progress'. The profile of the industrial building complex as 'heritage' is less likely to be driven by former employees and their descendants or the management of the company that still operates the site. Rather, others with different perspectives and initiative are likely to take the lead if the industrial heritage monument is threatened by development. Personal (and financial) interests of residents will seek to retain the park as an amenity and contributor to the value of their properties, especially those living in the Birkenhead Point Conservation Area who may also be the most articulate in arguing for retention of the sugar works complex as heritage. This heritage lobby may recruit the engineers of IPENZ to support their cause. The Category I status will place greater pressure on the Historic Places Trust to be proactive, which in turn may engage the vocal support of architectural heritage activists in greater Auckland and beyond. The natural environment lobby continues to seek a safe haven for native plants and wildlife in the park and adjacent reserves. It will take an effective strategic alliance of the disparate interest groups and their diverse motives to defend the sugar works as heritage. While undoubtedly there are many real challenges ahead if and when operations cease, the Chelsea Sugar Works is now better placed for a second life as heritage, with a range of interested parties prepared to speak up for it and a more promising openness to the value and special character of industrial heritage.

Acknowledgement

The author would like to thank Joke Medhorst for assistance with the research for this chapter.

References

Auckland Tourism Events and Economic Development Ltd (2011) *Auckland Visitor Plan*. Auckland, New Zealand: Auckland Tourism Events and Economic Development Ltd.

Bell, C. (1997) The 'real' New Zealand: rural mythologies perpetuated and commodified. *The Social Science Journal* 34 (2), 145–158.

Engineering Heritage New Zealand (2011) *Engineering Heritage Strategy 2011*. Wellington, New Zealand: Institution of Professional Engineers New Zealand Inc.

Hayward, B., Murdoch, G. and Cameron, E. (2008) *A Field Guide to Auckland: Exploring the Region's Natural and Historic Heritage*. Auckland, New Zealand: Godwit.

Heritage Consultancy Services (2011) *North Shore Heritage Thematic Review Report. Compiled by Heritage Consultancy Services for Auckland Council*. Auckland, New Zealand: Heritage Consultancy Services.

Jones, M. and McKenzie, J. (2009) Chelsea Sugar Refinery and Estate, Birkenhead, North Shore City (Registration Report for a Historic Place). Wellington: New Zealand Historic Places Trust.

La Roche, J. and Aitken, A. (2011) *Chelsea Sugar Refinery*. Wellington: Institution of Professional Engineers New Zealand.

McLure, M. (2004) *The Wonder Country: Making New Zealand Tourism*. Auckland, New Zealand: Auckland University Press.

Simpson, T. (1997) *The Sugarbag Years: A People's History of the 1930's Depression in New Zealand*. Auckland, New Zealand: Godwit.

Smith, N. (2001) *Heritage of Industry: Discovering New Zealand's Industrial Heritage*. Auckland, New Zealand: Reed.

Stewart, D. (2002) *The New Zealand Villa: Past and Present*. Auckland, New Zealand: Penguin Books.

Thomson, K.W. (1981) *Art Galleries and Museums of New Zealand* (1st ed.). Wellington, New Zealand: Reed.

Thomson, K.W. (1991) *A Guide to Art Galleries and Museums in New Zealand*. Birkenhead, New Zealand: Reed.

Thornton, G.G. (1982) *New Zealand's Industrial Heritage*. Wellington, New Zealand: A.W. & A.H. Reed.

Verran, D. (2010) *The North Shore: An Illustrated History*. Auckland, New Zealand: Random House.

Warren, J.A.N. and Taylor, C.N. (2001) *Developing Heritage Tourism in New Zealand*. Wellington, New Zealand: CRESA.

Websites

Birkenhead Historical Society, http://www.historicbirkenhead.com
Chelsea Sugar (New Zealand Sugar Company), http://www.chelsea.co.nz/
Engineering Heritage New Zealand, http://www.ipenz.org.nz/heritage/
Institute of Professional Engineers (IPENZ), http://www.ipenz.org.nz/ipenz/
New Zealand Heritage Trails Foundation, http://www.heritagetrails.org.nz/
New Zealand Historic Places Trust, http://www.historic.org.nz/
NZ Museums, http://www.nzmuseums.co.nz/

12 Sugar Heritage at the World's Museums

Lee Jolliffe

This chapter examines the extent to which the history and heritage of the global sugar industry is exhibited and interpreted by museums. According to the International Council of Museums 'A museum is a non-profit, permanent institution in the service of society and its development, open to the public, which acquires, conserves, researches, communicates and exhibits the tangible and intangible heritage of humanity and its environment for the purposes of education, study and enjoyment' (International Council of Museums, n.d.). This definition is used here when considering the role of museums in representing and interpreting both the tangible and intangible sugar heritage of the world. Museum objects are noted to constitute an important part of human heritage, and to have the ability to give their beholders a feeling of continuity and cultural pride (Alexander, 1979). The same author notes that objects can be used to bring understanding and appreciation to contemporary life.

The changing societal role of museums is reflected in the ways in which the heritage of sugar is communicated and interpreted to visitors. Influenced by the 'new museology', museums have moved from a perspective of seeing the contents and the meanings of the museum as fixed to a view where they are seen a contextual and contingent (Macdonald, 2006). The role of museums in the transition of sugar from industry to heritage is therefore pivotal, as museums can act as the gatekeepers of heritage (McKercher & du Cros, 2002) as they have in the past, and in a contemporary context as places at which the heritage of sugar can be contextualized. It is thus helpful to examine how existing museums are preserving, studying and interpreting heritage related to sugar, inevitably linking sugar's transition to tourism through their role as visitor attractions. Museums with a sugar-related mandate and or collections thus have the opportunity to employ heritage assets related to sugar to reinforce the identities of communities and to discuss related contested heritage, whilst developing heritage products for tourism (Timothy & Boyd, 2003).

This chapter therefore identifies, classifies and profiles a number of what could be termed sugar-focused museums or exhibitions within museums that act as attractions for sugar heritage tourism. It considers the role of local and national museums in representing and interpreting sugar heritage to various publics. To accomplish these goals the work draws from the literature on the history and development of museums as well as on the development and operation of visitor attractions, museums being one type of attraction. While the author visited several sugar based attractions in the Caribbean (Barbados, Trinidad, Tobago and Curacao) as part of the research for this enquiry, in addition, secondary sources including museum directories and guidebook listings were employed. The chapter builds upon and expands the discussions of references to the sugar museum attractions identified in earlier chapters of the book in the Caribbean, Latin America, Asia and Australasia.

The Story of Sugar

The 'story of sugar' is one of global significance. Like cobwebs, the many threads of the story are bound up with filaments that include colonization, the slave trade, world trade and commerce, industrialization, world agriculture, souvenir and culinary traditions, and art. Aspects of the history of sugar have been covered elsewhere in this book (see especially Chapter 2 and Chapter 3). Without an extensive historical review it can be simply stated that the intensive sugar monoculture of sugar production has transformed both the landscapes and the cultures of many locations around the world (Abbott, 2008).

The industrial processing of sugar was closely related to the industrial revolution and has both driven economies and led to their downturn. This has been documented elsewhere, as in the case of Cuba (Peters, 2003; Pollitt, 2004). This downturn of the industrial processes of sugar has left a legacy of the material culture of sugar, consisting of sugar-related artifacts, including the equipment used to process sugar, such as the copper sugar boiling pans, and objects related to life on sugar estates in the case of Cuba and sugar plantations elsewhere.

Many cultures have been shaped by sugar, especially where whole societies were built on the plantation model, as white planters and enslaved Africans mingled to create a new creolized society at many locations in the Caribbean. This is vividly illustrated by Barnet and Lindstrom (1980) who indicate that the history of Cuba is intimately linked with that of the sugar industry. The authors suggest that it was on the sugar plantations that the culture of Cuba was created.

Sugar heritage is, in addition, part of the history of transportation, as enslaved people from Africa were transported in slave ships to work on the sugar plantations of various colonies. After emancipation, indentured workers were transported to colonial locations to work on sugar plantations. In addition, during a later period in the history of sugar when the sugar industry transformed from the plantation/estate model to the centralized factory model, it was cane trains that brought the sugarcane from the farm to the factory, and these trains for some countries, such as in Cuba (Pollitt, 1997), symbolize this transition. Railways in sugar-producing countries are therefore symbolic of the sugar industry, as they transported cane to the factory, and a metaphor for progress, the resultant train ride attractions that now exist at some locations (such as Maui, Hawai'i; St Kitts; Australia; Taiwan) can be seen as a glimpse of this past symbolism.

However, one challenge in terms of sugar plantation-related artifacts is that whereas many plantation houses and their furnishings have survived, the everyday objects related to the lives of the enslaved and indentured sugar workers have not. Many of the buildings related to historic sugar processing have not survived, those that have, such as the sugar mill, are significant as a symbol of both colonization and enslavement (Cornwell & Stoddard, 2001). The story of sugar, with its strong relationship to the slave trade, is a sensitive one to interpret. Some of the related heritage is contested, as discussed earlier in this volume (see especially Chapters 5 and 7), which brings challenges for museums in terms of ensuring objectivity from a curatorial perspective.

The use of sugar permeates our global culinary heritage and, from a tourism perspective, at many locations 'sweets' and 'confectionary' have become traditional souvenirs, such as Devon fudge, rock candy, etc., particularly when purchased and consumed on vacation (as noted in Chapter 9). Here, the material culture includes the artifacts related to confectionary production as well as containers and implements related to the domestic use of sugar (such as sugar tongs and sugar bowls).

Some contemporary museums have hosted exhibits of sugar-related art. Sugar art is collectable; however, the physical make-up of sugar and its deterioration provides a challenge for museum conservators, as in the case of the preservation of the sugar art related to Mexico's Day of the Dead (Daniels & Lohneis, 1997).

The complex heritage of sugar briefly identified here is reflected by permanent museums related to the story of sugar and by temporary exhibits related to the theme. The following sections elaborate on this evolving role of museums in exhibiting and indeed interpreting the rich story of sugar.

The Role of Museums in Exhibiting the Story of Sugar

Sugar-related museums generally have the purpose of acquiring, conserving, researching, communicating and exhibiting the tangible and intangible heritage of sugar. Challenges in terms of interpreting the world's sugar heritage include the paucity of collections consisting of artifacts and objects related to the agricultural and industrial processes related to sugar, as well as the nature of the subject (including the contested heritage regarding slavery). There are issues of access to the intangible heritage of sugar, which is in many ways still embedded in the culture and heritage of former and current sugar-producing locales.

For the enquiring visitor, insights into the story of sugar can be gained through visiting museums, both those dedicated to an aspect of the story of sugar and those permanently or temporarily focusing on some parts of the story. Museums can be thought of as special places in which to reflect on the story of sugar and to learn more about it, as in the case of the museum where original objects (artifacts) are presented in context for consideration and discussion (Gilmore & Rentschler, 2002; Alexander, 1979).

The traditional role of the museum has been custodial in terms of collecting, preserving and exhibiting objects. This is reflected in the terminology of the keeper of collections or the curator. Museums were often established either by individuals who had amassed collections or groups that had formed collections for either the purpose of trade (as in international exhibitions), education (as in library services) or research (as in research institutions). Some examples of early sugar-related collections can be cited from the international exhibitions, where sugar was exhibited for trade purposes; however, the general public had access to these collections so there was moreover a promotional and educational function, and it is known that such exhibitions were influential in terms of the establishment of the modern museum.

The traditional role in the case of sugar-related museums is reflected in their mission statements. Each museum needs to encapsulate its purpose within a mission statement (Moore, 1994). Today, however, the institutional mission statement as a part of the approach of modern museum management needs to be meshed with marketing approaches to attract audiences that will make the operation of the museum, as a not-for-profit entity, viable (Alexander, 1979). This need to operate within a mission and yet at the same time to be viable by attracting audiences can create conflict within a museum (Gilmore & Rentschler, 2002).

An example of the mission of a sugar-related museum can be taken from the Alexander & Baldwin Sugar Museum, located in Maui, Hawai'i. In an area with a rich sugar history and heritage the mission of the museum is stated as being:

> To preserve and present the history and heritage of the sugar industry, and the multiethnic plantation life which it engendered, for residents and visitors. (http://www.sugarmuseum.com/)

This mission statement thus addresses the curatorial aspect (preserve and present history and heritage) and the museum's obligation to its audience (for residents and visitors). The activities of a museum flow from the mission statement and in the case of this museum in Maui the desire to preserve and present the 'multiethnic plantation life' engendered by the history and heritage of sugar is reflected in one of the museum's central projects, The Plantation Sugar Camp Registry, a listing of the names of all of the people who worked in the sugar plantation camps in Maui. The creation of this list has been interactive, with the museum collecting the names from former camp residents and their families, who after viewing a map of the sugar camps were asked to submit the relevant names. To date the registry includes information on those who lived in the following plantation camps: Pu'unēnē, Sprecklesville, Pā'ia, Hamakua Poko, Kihei, Wailuku and Lahaina.

As with the example above, gradually the role of museums has thus changed in relation to society and their audiences (Gilmore & Rentschler, 2002), as museums have needed to be more audience focused in order to be sustainable. This transition has involved museums balancing a custodial with a marketing focus in order to attract visitors, while being more responsive to their audiences. Another example of this changing role of museums is that some of these institutions have partnered in telling some of the story of sugar, for example through the Understanding Slavery Initiative, a national learning exchange partnership of six UK museums. This collaboration supports 'the teaching and learning of transatlantic slavery and its legacies using museum and heritage collections' (http://www.understandingslavery.com). One of the legacies that the partnership has dealt with is the involvement of slavery in the production of sugar, particularly on plantations.

In order to be viable, the sugar-related museums and exhibitions of the world therefore need to have visitors. There are different ways in which the markets for museums can be identified and segmented. Swarbrooke (2002) identifies the visitor attraction market as being segmented by the factors of geography, demographics, psychographics and behaviour. Other ways of segmenting the attraction market include visit party composition, visit type and purpose, and how people travel to the attraction.

Sugar-Related Museums and Attractions

A number of types of sugar-related museums have therefore emerged. Some are either technical museums, such as the Sugar Museum in Berlin, Germany, associated in some way with the sugar industry or its development, or museums *in situ*, at sites of growth and processing and/or refining. A typology can be a useful way to view the types of sugar-related museums that exist today. If viewed as industrial heritage sugar-related museums and sites could be characterized according to the typology of industrial attractions as: productive attractions; processing attractions; transport attractions and sociocultural attractions (Edwards & Llurdés i Coit, 1996). Using an adaptation of this typology, sugar-related museum types identified for this research are listed in Table 12.1. In addition to museums, some attractions are included here to cover the broad range of industrial attractions noted by the authors. An additional category of special purpose attraction has been added to the original typology proposed by the authors to cover the technical museums that have developed in relation to the sugar industry.

Table 12.1 Typology of sugar-related museums and attractions

Type	Museum/attraction	Description
Productive attractions	Alexander & Baldwin Sugar Museum, Maui, Hawai'i	Located adjacent to a sugar mill, preserves and presents history and heritage of Maui's sugar industry.
Processing attractions	Redpath Sugar Museum, Toronto, Canada	Located adjacent to a historic operating sugar refinery.
Transport attractions	St Kitts Scenic Railway	A contemporary sugar train attraction using a leased cane rail line.
Sociocultural attraction	City of Sugar Museum, Madiera, Portugal	Interprets city development from sugar trade wealth.
Special purpose attraction	Australian Sugar Industry Museum, Mourilyan, Queensland, Australia	Interprets the sugar industry in Australia.

Source: Adapted from Edwards and Llurdés i Coit (1996) with information from: http://www.sugarmuseum.com/; and http://www.madeira-island.com/museums/sugar_museum; http://en.wikipedia.org/wiki/Sugar_Museum

The few examples listed here illustrate the sugar-related museum as a type of museum and industrial attraction. The fact that several additional sites are proposed as sugar museums (for example, Brechin Castle Sugar Factory in Trinidad and Belmont Estate in St Kitts) and or nominated or listed as tentative nominations as sugar-related World Heritage Sites (for example The Industrial Heritage of Sugar's tentative nomination in Barbados) reflects the fact that sugar heritage is still in the process of being recognized by the institution of the museum and related sites, as well as by both the public and private proponents of such projects.

Sugar-Related Exhibitions and Events

The role of small local museums in preserving and interpreting sugar history and heritage should be noted, as many established in locales where sugar was or is produced will surely have collections related to sugar, even if they are not classified specifically as sugar museums. An example is that of the Montserrat National Trust Museum, located on the island of Montserrat, a British Overseas Territory in the Eastern Caribbean. The museum is located in the remains of an 18th-century wind (sugar) mill and includes sugar-related exhibitions, for example a working scale model of a sugar mill. In addition it is inevitable that many of the small local museums in former colonial countries (such as the UK, the Netherlands, etc.) will hold materials related to the slave trade, which will by association be part of the story of sugar, as noted by documentation of the Understanding Slavery Initiative identified earlier.

The role of national museums in countries associated with the sugar trade is of note. For example, the Barbados Museum has a small gallery dealing with the story of slavery and sugar production. In addition, the Barbados Museum has recently (2010–2011) developed (at the request of the Ministry of Tourism, Barbados) and launched an interpretive tourism product, Freedom Footprints, which includes highlighting the journey of the enslaved population of Barbados, most of whom were on sugar plantations, after emancipation to freedom. This product includes a visit to the Newton Abbot Burial Ground where many of the slaves from the Newton Abbot Plantation were buried. This site has been the subject of archaeological investigation, which has revealed much about how the former slaves lived and were buried. While this Freedom Footprints product is not positioned as the story of sugar per se, this story is an integral part of the tour, due to both the island's strong history and heritage based on sugar production using the plantation model and its position as a centre of the Atlantic slave trade, which provided labour for the slave trade throughout the British Caribbean. Slavery focused museums thus tell the story of sugar because the story is intertwined with that of slavery. An example is the Sugar and Slavery Museum at Docklands in London, England.

Recent Developments in Interpreting Sugar Heritage

In both Trinidad and St Kitts, locales where the nationalized sugar industries have been terminated within the last decade, the heritage of sugar has been recognized and is being interpreted through museums and potential visitor attractions. This section briefly examines these recent developments in sugar heritage interpretation. At both locations (Trinidad and St Kitts) there are national museums that include sugar heritage and history in the narratives; however, what is of note is the movement to preserve and interpret former elements of the sugar industries *in situ*, at former sugar factories and sugar estates, environments where interpretation will be more immediate in connection to the land that produced the sugarcane and the industrial heritage of sugar production.

In Trinidad, where the government terminated the sugar industry in 2003, a former government-owned sugar factory and its estate, the Brechin Castle Sugar Factory, have been designated as a future sugar heritage attraction (Ramnarine, 2010), dedicated to preserving the heritage of sugar and sugar-related labour history on the island. Part of this complex, Sevilla House, is designated to be a sugar museum. Visited in early 2012, this project has blossomed as a Sugar Heritage Village and Museum project that will see a number of other facilities being developed around the focal point of the sugar museum in Sevilla House (built by Tate and Lyle Limited around 1948). The proposal, according to promotional material issued by the Ministry of Tourism of Trinidad and Tobago, includes a reconstructed sugar heritage village, an archive and documentation centre, a small functioning sugar factory, a handicraft and artisan centre as well as supporting leisure facilities to include an expanded golf course, sporting facilities, a recreational park, an auditorium, a conference centre, a guest house and a visitor information centre. At the project announcement in May 2011 the Prime Minister suggested that 'the establishment of the sugar heritage village and museum will preserve the legacy and hard work of our ancestors' (Dookie, 2011). Stating that citizens of Trinidad and Tobago are all children of the sugar industry, the Prime Minister reflected that the closure of the industry in 2003 affected the lives of thousands of citizens.

While the project appears to be ambitious in terms of the broad range of facilities to be developed, it has a number of advantages in that it involves in some cases the upgrading of existing facilities and the project committee has valuable expertise, enthusiasm and commitment amongst its members in terms of project management, as well as in the history and operation of the former sugar industry. It is planned that public-private partnerships will be employed to implement aspects of the project. The National Museum is developing the framework for the sugar museum, and as a focal point of the project it is hoped that this will be open within three years, that is by 2015. As a first step, Sevilla House is getting a new roof (from European Union (EU) funds, to support the restructuring of the sugar industry and the diversification of the economy). A small team of researchers is doing oral interviews with the sugar workers who formerly worked for Caroni 1975 Inc., and at the same time identifying small items that these individuals might like to donate to the museum.

The sugar museum under development in Trinidad will tell an important story of labour history from the sugar industry, where plantations were tended by first the Amerindians and after by the Europeans, Africans, Chinese and Indians. According to early promotional material on the sugar museum, the industry was significantly impacted upon by the utilization of enslaved African labour during the 18th and 19th centuries and, following the emancipation of slaves in 1838, by East Indian indentured workers from 1845–1912 (Ministry of Tourism, Trinidad and Tobago, 2011). Providing insights not only into the industrial sugar industry but also into the connected labour history, the sugar museum could thus develop as a flagship attraction for Trinidad, as a reflection of its national heritage and a heritage tourism product.

In St Kitts the government exited from their nationalized sugar industry after the harvest in 2005. There does not appear to have been any focused plan about how to preserve the heritage associated with the former industry; however, a number of initiatives have ensured that at least some of the heritage assets have been either identified for reuse or preservation. These initiatives are enumerated and discussed below.

First, the Saint Kitts Scenic Railway Inc. project, launched before the industry was terminated, has ensured the preservation and sustainable maintenance of the rail lines associated with transporting the sugarcane from the field to the central factory. This has been made possible by a unique public-private partnership, which has seen the government lease the rail lines to an entrepreneur (a specialist in tourist railways) who has developed a heritage railway experience that is now one of the signature attractions in St Kitts (along with the UNESCO World Heritage property of Brimstone Hill Fortress). Preservation has not only been of the tangible rail line, which has been maintained and might otherwise have been removed (as in other locations, such as Trinidad), but by employing the former workforce of the sugar company railway this project has preserved the intangible traditions of a small island railroad operation.

Second, after the demise of the sugar industry in 2005 the Saint Christopher Heritage Trust lobbied for the preservation of the national sugar factory in the capital city of Basseterre. Since there did not appear to have been any plan for preservation after the end of the industry by the time this lobbying took place the sugar factory was in the process of being dismantled. However, the trust did manage to identify some equipment to be preserved, photographs were taken and ownership was transferred to the trust. In addition, volunteers from the St Kitts Scenic Railway have now moved some additional equipment identified for exhibition in conjunction with the tourist railway to a safe place, pending plans for future use.

Third, for a number of years, even preceding the closure of the sugar industry there, the Minister of Agriculture has been a proponent of the establishment of a National Agricultural and Sugar Museum at the government-owned Belmont Estate. This was envisioned as a 'working museum', growing and interpreting the former crops of the estate, including sugar, telling the story of the people who tended these crops. While a number of studies have been done in St Kitts on the potential use of heritage resources, such as Belmont Estate, in interpreting the sugar heritage, there is no evidence of any momentum to actually develop Belmont into the proposed national museum interpreting agriculture and sugar. In any case, a public-private partnership would be needed in order to mobilize funding; perhaps capitalizing on the EU funding for diversification beyond sugar if this is still available when the project gains momentum. For St Kitts the suitable development of the Belmont Estate could be another key component in developing the island as a destination for heritage tourism related to the rich sugar heritage there.

Fourth, various private entrepreneurs on the island are doing what they can to interpret and bring the heritage of the former sugar industry alive. For example, at Romney Manor owner Maurice Widdowson is proactively redeveloping and restoring the adjoining Wingfield Estate to interpret the history of the site as a sugar plantation. Here various projects have been undertaken to involve volunteer tourists in archaeological digs, installing interpretive signage relating to the industrial heritage ruins of the former sugar-processing process on the site and repurposing some of the existing foundations by incorporating them in the construction of simple buildings that serve practical purposes for contemporary tourism. The evolution of sugar from industry to heritage is thus reflected in the Wingfield Estate, which, as it develops, has the potential to contribute to an increase in the heritage tourist experiences related to sugar heritage available to visitors to the island.

The Trinidad site of the developing Sugar Heritage Village and Museum and the St Kitts site proposed as the Belmont Estate National Agricultural Museum both have the potential to be one of a key number of sugar heritage sites around the Caribbean, joining others currently under development, which can contribute to preserving local and regional sugar heritages and identities, while at the same time contributing to developing sugar-related heritage tourism in the region.

Conclusion

While the story of sugar is intertwined with the history of the modern world, there is no pattern to either its preservation or interpretation through the institution of the museum. Rather, it appears that only a few dedicated museums have appeared that focus on the story of sugar. Those that do exist seem to have their foundations in either collections, industry research, or are found adjacent to sugar-processing and/or refinery facilities. Few countries with either operating or defunct sugar operations seem to dedicate museums to the story of sugar. In a few of the world's major producing countries, as well as at locations formerly involved in the sugar trade, there are, however, some dedicated sugar museums, either established at a technical level (as with the Sugar Museum in Germany and the Australian Sugar Museum in Australia) or as industrial attractions in association with current or former production facilities (as with the Frank Huston Sugar Museum adjacent to the Portvale Sugar Factory in Barbados).

For the curious visitor the experience of the story of sugar is more likely to be found in association with the land, through sightseeing in locations where sugarcane was and or is still grown. At these places there may also be transportation attractions, as a number of the former sugarcane train operations have been turned into tourist train attractions, as discussed earlier in the book in cases from Taiwan, Australia and St Kitts. It is, however, encouraging that there has been some recent attention to the possible development of sugar museums and or attractions in the Caribbean at locations where sugar industries have been terminated, specifically in St Kitts and Trinidad.

Museums could therefore play a critical role in terms of the preservation and interpretation of sugar heritage. The status of the museum as an institution in perpetuity could ensure the preservation of both the tangible and intangible culture and heritage of sugar. National museums, in particular in countries that still produce sugar and in those that are in transition from sugar to service based economies, could be pivotal in that process. Policies and procedures should be in place when sugar industries and facilities are being devolved, to ensure that the assets that were once valued for their production value are respected and preserved as heritage. Communities should be consulted in the process of preserving and or interpreting the rich, varied and at times contested heritage of sugar. This type of consultation and community involvement in the creation of sugar heritage museums does not seem to be happening on a widespread basis, perhaps with the exception of the sugar museum in Maui, Hawai'i and their plantation camp directory, and the community driven Sugar Heritage Village and Museum project in Trinidad.

A limitation of this chapter has been the focus on museums as places where the history of sugar is encapsulated for future generations. Looking at the broader attractions market, there are, in addition to traditional museums related to sugar, the plantation house attractions around the world that may include aspects related to sugar, such as Sunbury House in St Phillip, Barbados (discussed in Chapter 7), which, while mainly focusing on interpreting the plantation house with its fine furnishings representing a bygone age, exhibits outdoors some of the machinery formerly used for cultivating sugar on its grounds. This site's former history as a sugar plantation with enslaved workers is however not interpreted within the tours of the house.

Another issue for future research as part of the theories of postcolonialism applied to tourism (Simon, 2007) is that the museum is fundamentally a Western institution, created and nurtured by the very Western nations who were the colonizers at many of the locations of intense sugar production. While global museums have changed and are now inclusive and more responsive to their communities, it may be time for communities around the world who were shaped by sugar to consider forms of commemorating and learning from the past history of sugar other than the traditional collection based museum. Interpretive centres could provide a place for reflecting upon the past injustices permeated by the colonial sugar monopolies and industries. Facilities such as the powerful Kura Hulanda Museum at Curacao (Thompson, 2010), which do not draw upon original objects but instead employ replicas and interpretive means and provide spaces for reflection and advocacy, remind us that the same kind of greed that drove the sugar plantation owners to rely on enslaved labour is still present, with enslaved populations still existing in the contemporary world.

References

Abbott, E. (2008) *Sugar A Bittersweet History*. Toronto: Penguin Canada.

Alexander, E.P. (1979) *Museums in Motion: An Introduction to the History and Functions of Museums*. Nashville: American Association for State and Local History.

Barnet, M. and Lindstrom, N. (1980) The culture that sugar created. *Latin American Literary Review* 8 (16), 38–46.

Cornwell, G.H. and Stoddard, E.W. (2001) Reading sugar mill ruins: 'The island nobody spoiled' and other fantasies of colonial desire. *South Atlantic Review* 66 (2), 133–157.

Daniels, V. and Lohneis, G. (1997) Deterioration of sugar artifacts. *Studies in Conservation* 42 (1), 17–26.

Dookie, N. (2011) *Sugar Heritage Village and Museum Launched*, accessed 1 December 2011. http://www.wintvworld.com/e-news/?p=5230.

Edwards, J.A. and Llurdés i Coit, J.C. (1996) Mines and quarries: Industrial heritage tourism. *Annals of Tourism Research* 23, 341–363.

Gilmore, A. and Rentschler, R. (2002) Changes in museum management: A custodial or marketing emphasis. *Journal of Management Development* 21 (10), 745–760.

International Council of Museums (n.d.) Museum definition, accessed 15 December 2011. http://icom.museum/who-we-are/the-vision/museum-definition.html.

Macdonald, S. (2006) *A Companion to Museum Studies*. Oxford: Blackwell Publishing.

McKercher, B. and du Cros, H. (2002) *Cultural Tourism: The Partnership between Tourism and Cultural Heritage Management*. New York: The Haworth Hospitality Press.

Ministry of Tourism, Trinidad and Tobago. (2011) *Sugar Heritage Village and Museum Brochure*. Port of Spain.

Moore, K. (1994) *Museum Management*. London: Routledge.

Peters, P. (2003) *Cutting Losses: Cuba Downsizes Its Sugar Industry*. Lexington Institute, accessed 1 December 2011. http://lexington.server278.com/docs/cuba1.pdf.

Pollitt, B.H. (1997) The Cuban sugar economy: Collapse, reform and prospects for recovery. *Journal of Latin American Studies* 29 (1), 171–210.

Pollitt, B.H. (2004) The rise and fall of the Cuban sugar economy. *Journal of Latin American Studies* 36 (2), 319–348.

Ramnarine, K. (2010) Preserving sugar's history. *Trinidad Express*, accessed 1 December 2011. http://www.trinidadexpress.com/news/Preserving_sugar_s_history-104222954.html

Simon, R-H. (2007) The contested spaces of Cuban development: Post-socialism, post-colonialism and the geography of transition. *Geoforum* 38 (3), 445–455.

Swarbrooke, J. (2002) *The Development and Management of Visitor Attractions* (2nd edn). Oxford: Butterworth-Heinemann.

Thompson, A.O. (2010) *Confronting Slavery: Breaking through the Corridors of Silence*. Barbados: Thompson Business Services Inc.

Timothy, D.J. and Boyd, S.W. (2003) *Heritage Tourism*. Harlow: Pearson Education Limited.

Part 5
Conclusion

13 Issues and Trends in Sugar Heritage Tourism

Lee Jolliffe

The previous 12 chapters have reviewed the transition of sugar from industry and history to heritage and tourism at key locations around the world, both those still producing sugar and those transitioning from sugar to tourism. The organization of the book has highlighted themes in the study of the relationship of sugar heritage to tourism – preservation and interpretation of this heritage, transformation into destination tourism products and experiences, and the creation through tourism of opportunities for dialogue about the past relationship of colonizers and colonies, descendants and diasporas, industry and local populations. It is evident from the narrative to date how important sugar is to people and communities and nations.

From this foundation this chapter proceeds to highlight current issues and trends in the evolving relationship between sugar as heritage and its use for tourism. First, the issues of politics, globalization and tourism development in relation to the sugar-related aspects of the contemporary tourism industries are discussed from a critical point of view. Second, an international synopsis of the current state of sugar-related tourism in different regions of the world with a rich sugar heritage is presented. Third, in conclusion, key trends in sugar-related heritage tourism are acknowledged.

The Issues: Politics, Globalization and Tourism Development

The shifting contexts of heritage-related tourism are embodied in politics, participation and presentation (Smith & Robinson, 2006). Participation at a number of levels is important in terms of the emergence of sugar-related tourism, including the involvement of local populations in the determination of related heritage policies, which can be sensitive because of the contested heritage associated with sugar. In relation to presentation, politics can thus be involved in approaches to the interpretation of the 'dark history' aspects of the past production of sugar, using enslaved labour and the plantation model.

In terms of heritage tourism, it is acknowledged that in some cases the past has been ignored or erased (Timothy & Boyd, 2003), as is noted in this volume with the interpretation of the plantation houses of the elite and not the housing of the enslaved workers. This amnesia about the past may be either a part of developing new national identities or an effort to attract the former colonizers as visitors. This is reflected by plantation house attractions in the Caribbean; for example, at Mourne Coubaril Estate in St Lucia and Sunbury Plantation House in Barbados (for more details see Chapter 7). As earlier noted, there has been a trend in the Caribbean to enshrine the past of the elite plantation owners in such sites (Found, 2004). In another case, the past realities related to slavery have been embraced and presented in a space created for dialogue for both the descendants of the enslaved workers, the former colonizers and other interested visitors, at The Kura Hulanda Museum in Curacao. In yet another case in the UK, the International Slavery Museum in Liverpool, opened on the bicentenary of the abolition of the British Slave Trade, is creating a continuing dialogue about not only the enduring meanings of the transatlantic slave trade and the accomplishments of the diaspora, but about contemporary slavery. In all of these instances heritage may potentially have been reshaped for political purposes, affected by both national and personal agendas.

The politics of interpreting the story of the transatlantic slave trade and its connection to the global sugar trade are reflected in the creation of dedicated slavery museums as noted above, and also exhibitions about slavery and slave routes and trails, in part as postcolonial approaches to tourism. Here culture can potentially be altered, as it is presented or represented for new audiences. As an international agency UNESCO, with the input of member states, has played a key role as an advocate for a balanced view (see Chapter 5) in bringing together those with a vested interest in the story; however, on a national basis one could question the objectivity of the descendants of the colonizers developing slavery museums, or the interpretation of former sugar plantation sites without the views of those descended from the former enslaved labour force (see Chapter 7). National governments of those countries formerly involved in the transatlantic slave trade have, however, also been involved in commemorating the abolition of slavery, for example in the National Slavery Monument Oosterpark Amsterdam, dedicated in 2002, which commemorates the abolition of slavery in the Netherlands and its colonies in 1863.

National and local museums and attractions of various types may have interests, related to their mandates and collections, in interpreting various aspects of the slavery and sugar nexus. For example, in the UK Kew Gardens interprets the story of sugar and slavery from a botanical aspect, providing an opportunity for visitors to interact with the sugar-related slavery story from another perspective. In Manchester, Bristol and Liverpool – UK cities that profited from the transatlantic slave trade – slavery heritage walking trails have been established, highlighting the link between individual places in these cities to slavery, educating and creating situations for dialogue on the relationship of slavery to sugar industries. As a national museum, the International Slavery Museum in Liverpool also interprets the successes of the black diaspora and educates about current forms of slavery. Other museums in the UK interpret the story of sugar from a migration focus, for example the Museum of the Docklands in London with its exhibition commemorating the transatlantic slave trade.

Globalization has impacted the rapid expansion of mass tourism, reversing the former colonial travel patterns, turning former colonies into tourism destinations (Carrigan, 2010). As rich nations visit poorer nations the consumptive practices of both tourism and tourists propel both environmental and cultural transformations of the new destinations. Tourism developments and visitation, if not sustainably planned and implemented, can have negative environmental impacts on sensitive environments.

The extent and economics of the global sugar trade, even in contemporary times, impacts the interpretation of sugar. Museums of sugar can interpret current industrial production and highlight the economic significance of the commodity, as well as potentially reflect upon the participation of individual farms and farmers on a small scale. Globalization has affected the viability of the production of sugar; for example, in the Caribbean where it costs more than the market price received to produce sugar, agricultural consultants recommended that some governments should consider moving on to more lucrative industries, such as tourism (Ahmed, 2001). Forced to examine the viability of their sugar industries in the light of declining productivity and negative trade policies, many countries (for example St Kitts and Trinidad and Tobago) did indeed abandon sugar in favour of tourism.

Countering the negative impacts of globalization on the sugar industry, as production relocates to the most competitive production locations both the fairtrade sugar and the fairtrade tourism movements can potentially be linked to developing countries where sugar production is in decline, thus creating fairtrade sugar heritage tourism products and experiences. The concept of fairtrade, which relates to improved working conditions for local workers with a better return on sales to the benefit of local communities, has most often been linked to tourism through the sale of souvenirs, such as coffee and crafts, but is also used as a marketing tool (Evans & Cleverdon, 2000). These are products that can possibly be justly developed for the benefit of local economies and the sustainability of local cultures. For example, in Nova Scotia, Canada, the Just Us! Coffee Roasters Cooperative buys organic sugar from a small cooperative in Central Paraguay, a possible destination for volunteer tourism, which the Canadian cooperative has previously undertaken with coffee roasters in Latin America (Chesworth, 2010). The concept of fairtrade as applied to sugar as a commodity and to sugar-related tourism products therefore does have advantages for the development of sugar tourism, in particular in terms of benefits to local communities and market recognition (Harris, 2003).

What other issues occur for cultures through the interpretation of sugar history for sugar-related tourism development? The cultural transformation that accompanies mass tourism can include cultural commodification, as the tourism industry draws from and packages only those elements of place that are directed at particular market segments (Williams, 1998). The effects of cultural changes influenced by tourism are therefore felt in the newly decolonized and now independent developing countries still grappling with the effects of Western colonization (Smith, 2003). It is a question of how the 'story of sugar' can be told without enshrining colonial desire and Eurocentric viewpoints (Cornwell & Stoddard, 2001).

Tourism is a structure of consumption with the inherent possibility that authenticity may be threatened; for example, as cultural artefacts and performances are commoditized and organized into tourism products that can be conveniently purchased by tourists. This tendency is reflected in the Caribbean with Carnival, a festival with roots in the region's sugar plantation heritage. Originally commoditized based on the Trinidad and Tobago Carnival, the concept has now been replicated across the region and also by the diaspora living in the 'North' (Nurse, 2008).

Issues of commodification and loss of authenticity can be potentially avoided by the involvement of local residents in learning about and recognizing the sugar heritage of the past as living legacies, developing alternative tourism products. This may be accomplished through community based tourism, where the communities and not the international tourism industry determine the cultural aspects to be commoditized and identify the messages to be delivered. For example, in Sri Lanka a sugar factory and its associated sugarcane fields have been recognized as a resource for developing community based tourism in a rural area (Silva & Wilmalaratana, 2009).

Community participation can also be important for recognizing the legacies of former sugar-producing companies (both positive and negative) and lobbying for the employment of their remaining resources (land, funds, etc.) for the benefit of visitors, both locals and tourists. This possibility was reflected earlier in the book in the case of sugar refinery properties in both Taiwan (see Chapter 8) and New Zealand (see Chapter 11). Care must certainly thus be taken so that the commodification of sugar heritage related to all aspects of sugar cultivation, production and processing, so much a part of the national identity of many countries, does not threaten contemporary cultures.

There are, however, potential conflicts between sugar heritage and tourism development; for example, attracting the colonizers back to a post-emancipation paradise may mean downplaying the contested aspects of the story of heritage. Encouraging tourism for economic development, including slavery heritage tourism, also, according to some academics (Buzinde & Santos, 2009), puts the employees back into a so-called 'plantation system' relationship, serving the former colonizers. Using sugar heritage for touristic purposes may therefore encourage a nostalgic view and romanticization of the realities of the past heritage (such as at plantation houses that portray the life of the former owners); heritage policies have the potential to either encourage such trends or to challenge them. This is where new heritage tourism products developed in a postcolonial context may have the opportunity to break away from traditional colonial interpretations of sugar heritage; for example, as with the Freedom Footprints tour in Barbados, developed by the Barbados Museum at the request of the Ministry of Tourism, and the International Slavery Museum, developed as part of the national museum system in the UK.

Sugar-Related Tourism: An International Synopsis

Based on the chapter case studies, this section examines sugar in relation to tourism in different regions of the world (Europe, Caribbean, South America, Asia and Australasia). Examining sugar heritage regionally is an important access point for a deeper understanding of the global transitions of sugar towards tourism.

In Europe the 'story of sugar' is told through museums portraying various aspects of the story, in particular Britain's colonial role in the transatlantic slave trade in relation to sugar, as well as the botanical and culinary aspects. Sugar is also instrumental in the creation of sweet souvenirs, such as the Devon fudge profiled in Chapter 9.

In the Caribbean both tangible and intangible aspects of sugar form primary resources for tourism in this region. Ruins of the sugar mills, formerly key to the plantation operations, remain as tangible cultural icons and now as symbols of nationalism (Cornwell & Stoddard, 2001), especially in the following examples: Barbados (Morgan Lewis Sugar Mill), St Kitts (Milliken Sugar Mill), Tobago (Arnot Vale Water Wheel) and Antigua (Betty's Hope Sugar Mill). Besides the remains of sugar mills, the vestiges of former sugar industries are seen in the landscapes, plantations and some still operating sugar industries (see Chapters 5, 6, 7, 11). Sugar is embedded into the intangible culture of the region, as reflected by cuisine, song, dance, literature and festivals such as Carnival.

As the heritage assets of the 'story of sugar' are repurposed for tourism, the plantations, landscapes and sugarcane railroads of the Caribbean are commodified, which may threaten authenticity yet makes sugar heritage accessible for various constituencies, including local populations and visitors. Some sites, including UNESCO World Heritage Sites in the region (see Chapter 5), do interpret aspects of the present and former sugar industries, including educating on the transatlantic slave trade and enslavement in relation to sugar as industry and culture maker.

In terms of South America, while Brazil is highlighted in Chapter 4, sugar-related legacies also contribute to tourism in other countries in the region; for example, rural tourism in Columbia's Valle del Cauca acknowledges 'A Lineage of Sugar' as reflected in the haciendas built with the wealth of the historic sugar industry there. As sugarcane is still processed in Colombia for both sugar and fuel (ethanol) some of these historic farms are diversifying, turning to agro-tourism by using their historic haciendas as facilities for meetings and events (Erickson, 2006). A culinary aspect of the 'story of sugar' in Brazil (see Chapter 4) is that of the adoption of the sugar based alcoholic drink, Cachaça, which has been assembled into a tourism product in the form of circuits, tours, visits to production facilities and culinary events, paralleling the development of the sugar derived alcoholic drink rum as a tourism product in the Caribbean.

In Asia sugar is also important to the heritage, culture and current industry of the countries there. As demonstrated in Chapter 2, in India, a country with a rich sugar heritage, related tourism is not currently highlighted but does have possibilities, in particular for the development of rural tourism. In Taiwan (see Chapter 8), where the history of sugar is closely tied to the former Japanese occupation and subsequent industrialization of the country, sugar is also drawn into rural tourism, as the assets of the former nationalized sugar industry are transitioned into leisure and tourism facilities. In Sri Lanka, sugar factories and landscapes have also been recognized as a resource for developing tourism. Rural tourism and community based tourism may thus hold the potential for all of the countries in Asia to develop forms of sugar-related tourism that reflect their history and heritage with this sweet commodity. Mauritius is another Asian country that has transitioned from sugar towards tourism as a mainstay of their economy.

In the Australasia region sugar is grown in Australia and refined in both Australia and New Zealand. In Australia, where sugar is still very much in production, there may be a missed opportunity for sugar-related tourism, as discussed in Chapter 3. However, operating sugar factories and refineries, sugar landscapes and former sugarcane trains operating as tourist trains do contribute to the tourism experience (see Chapters 3 and 10). Sugar is also embedded in the national culture of Australia through literature and drama, as reviewed in Chapter 10.

Paralleling the example of the repurposing of a sugar refinery property in Auckland, New Zealand (see Chapter 11) is a similar development in Sydney, Australia, where the local council has erected interpretive signage for the former Australian Sugar Company's historic mill buildings that opened as Canterbury Sugar Works in 1842.

Conclusion

Overall trends and directions in sugar-related heritage tourism represent a gradual heightening of awareness and recognition of sugar heritage resources at international and national levels. This has increased opportunities for dialogue on all aspects of sugar heritage, including the sugar and slavery nexus. While globalization is a threat to the authenticity of cultures shaped by sugar it can also create opportunities. Through international travel there is the chance for people of all cultures to gain insight into the nature and import of sugar heritage and culture on a global basis. In particular, the fairtrade sugar and fairtrade tourism movements have the potential to influence the balanced development of sugar-related tourism. The trend towards experiential and creative tourism can create new and sympathetic markets for sugar-related heritage tourism. A broadening of the interpretation of sugar heritage to include contested heritage aspects leading to the development of tourism products and experiences gives potential participants insights into aspects of sugar heritage, such as industrial processes, labour (enslaved and free) and cuisine. Opportunities are created for sugar companies to repurpose, reposition and transition their assets from industry to heritage. Inherent in all of these trends is the potential for an increased public response to and participation in tourism related to global sugar heritage.

It is therefore hoped that this chapter has helped to position both sugar-related tourism and associated cultural change within our current global society. Some of the trends identified highlight the challenges of interpreting sugar as a commodity, including its history and heritage, as well as showing viable alternatives for reflections on the historical legacies and current realities of the global sugar industry. Past histories and current circumstances may determine how sugar heritage is interpreted. It is possible to view sugar heritage as a continuum, moving from industry to heritage to tourism under the influence of politics, globalization and contemporary tourism development. As a tourist, it is therefore still possible to visit traditional sugar attractions that portray all aspects of the complex story of sugar, from operating sugar factories and refineries, to the remains of colonial sugar plantations, to museum exhibitions that from curatorial viewpoints delve into the complex narratives of migration, enslavement, abolition and industry, which are the foundation of the 'story of sugar'. However, in postcolonial tourism settings new products are breaking ground by offering both locals and visitors insight into the historical contexts of sugar from new points of view; for example, interpreting emancipation and freedom instead of enslavement in the case of the transatlantic slave trade and its supporting role in the sugar monoculture economies of the Caribbean, and extending the sugar and slavery nexus into dialogues about contemporary slavery in Europe. The story of sugar in relation to tourism is ongoing, and even as this book goes to press the relationship between these two interdependent and connected global industries is evolving in a rapidly changing world.

References

Ahmed, B. (2001) The impact of globalization on the Caribbean banana and sugar industries. In Courtman, S. (ed.) *The Society for Caribbean Studies Annual Conference Papers*, accessed 1 December 2011. http://www.caribbeanstudies.org.uk/papers/vol2.htm. Society for Caribbean Studies.

Buzinde, C.N. and Santos, C.A. (2009) Interpreting slavery tourism. *Annals of Tourism Research* 36 (3), 439–458.

Carrigan, A. (2010) *Postcolonial Tourism: Literature, Culture and Environment*. New York: Routledge.

Chesworth, N. (2010) Just us! Coffee roasters. In L. Jolliffe (ed.) *Coffee Culture, Destinations and Tourism* (pp. 171–180). Bristol: Channel View Publications.

Cornwell, G.H. and Stoddard, E.W. (2001) Reading sugar mill ruins: 'The island nobody spoiled' and other fantasies of colonial desire. *South Atlantic Review* 66 (2), 133–157.

Erickson, B. (2006) Colombian sugar cane growers gearing up to meet world demand for food and fuel. *Top Farmer Crop Workshop Newsletter* (September), 1–3, accessed 18 July 2012. http://www.agecon.purdue.edu/topfarmer/newsletter/TFCW9_2006.pdf.

Evans, G. and Cleverdon, R. (2000) Fair trade in tourism – community development or marketing tool? In G. Richards and D.R. Hall (eds) *Tourism and Sustainable Community Development*. London: Routledge.

Found, W. (2004) Historic sites, material culture and tourism in the Caribbean islands. In D.T. Duval (ed.) *Tourism in the Caribbean Trends, Developments, Prospects* (pp. 136–151). London: Routledge.

Harris, H. (2003) *Fair Trade in Tourism: Theory and Praxis*. Canterbury, UK: Canterbury Christ Church College.

Nurse, K. (2008) *Development of a Strategic Business Management Model for the Sustainable Development of Heritage Tourism Products in the Caribbean*. Barbados: The Caribbean Tourism Organization.

Silva, D.A.C. and Wilmalaratana, W. (2009) *Community Based Sustainable Tourism Development in Sri Lanka: Special Reference to Moneragala District*, accessed 19 July 2012. http://www.haroldgoodwin.info/PPT/PPTMonaragala.pdf.

Smith, M. (2003) *Issues in Cultural Tourism Studies*. London: Routledge.

Smith, M.K. and Robinson, M. (2006) *Cutlural Tourism in a Changing World: Politics, Participation and (Re)presentation*. Clevedon: Channel View Publications.

Timothy, D.J. and Boyd, S.W. (2003) *Heritage Tourism*. Harlow: Pearson Education Limited.

Williams, S. (1998) *Tourism Geography*. London: Routledge.

Index